THE WINES OF OCTOBER

An Italian-American Tale

By

Dominic Perenzin

authorHOUSE

1663 LIBERTY DRIVE, SUITE 200
BLOOMINGTON, INDIANA 47403
(800) 839-8640
www.authorhouse.com

Contents

Interlude One
Refreshments

Part Four
Thank You Voltaire

Interlude Two
Days Of Lament

Part Five
Breathless In The Sixties

Part Six
Things That Happen In Hotel Rooms

Part Seven
Days Of El Dorado

Part Eight
Musings

Part Nine
Pink Flamingos

Part Ten
The Origin of the Species

To all my children with the hope these memoirs will help them to better understand their own lives.

Acknowledgements

I am especially grateful to my wife Alicia for the many hours devoted to typing the manuscripts of this book and for her valuable and insightful suggestions as to its contents, without her this book would not have been; to my sister Mary and posthumously to brother Leon for their aid in reconstructing events of the distant past.

Forward

September 2, 1957. I stood next to my father's coffin unable to see him for the last time as the coffin had been closed with finality. Sadness and disappointment was joined by self-searching questions as I looked down at the burnished dark-brown encasement. Who was this man I called my father, did I really know much about him? What was his world like before I was born, what were his failures, regrets, his moments of joy. Who were the interesting people he met and those who influenced his life.

Remaining transfixed by these thoughts, I made a vow that if I ever had children of my own they would not be asking these questions about me. This book is the fulfillment of that vow.

In the process of writing these memoirs many things I once took for granted assumed a special significance, memory itself for example. Not only is it crucial in the utilitarian sense that in its absence survival would be precarious at best, but also because it imparts to our lives a sense of continuity, of unity and of identity.

What a marvelous thing I find memory to be as it cherishes the faces of dear ones who are no longer and the sounds of silenced voices, as it acts as a repository of houses, rooms and other objects that no longer exist. As years accumulate these fixed-in-time images assume a larger reality than the ever-changing external world itself, for they appear to be less demanding, more dependable, congenial and lasting companions.

In writing these memoirs I have given renewed life, *albeit* literary, to some of the people who crossed my path during my life and who are no more. To them I will always feel a genuine sense of gratitude for having been a part of my life.

Born of Italian immigrants to the United States who arrived during the first decade of the twentieth century, I was brought up in a micro Little Italy where I was surrounded by things Italian; family, neighbors, customs, commerce, food, music and worldviews. The effects of my genetic inheritance reinforced as it was by these environmental factors would in one way or another accompany me throughout my life, occasionally receding from conscious awareness, at times intentionally repressed, but always at least subliminally present.

The early immigrant Italian communities were evidence that being a part of the American melting pot was not a walk down a primrose path. Life was not as easy as the immigrants believed it would be as they huddled in the bowels of ships crossing the North Atlantic at times undergoing the humiliation of having banana peels thrown at them by upper-level passengers. There's the anecdote of the Italian immigrant who had bought into the story that the streets in America were paved with gold. After a short time here he wrote to his brother back home that, "the only thing you get in the United States if you do not work yourself to the bone is hungry." Inability to speak English, a wish to maintain family traditions (as a bulwark against the encroachment of the strange ways of the new life), a felt need for protection against anti-Italian prejudice, and solace and strength from being near *paesani* combined to form the *raison d'etre* for the rise of these ethnic communities. First generation Italians-Americans were to become social and character incubators that served as genetic pools from which future generations would emerge.

It is normal to assume that over time and a number of generations the melting pot process will take hold. Italian-Americans marry non-Italians, have children who then proceed to marry non-Italians and so forth. The children of these marriages are then raised in an American culture where the central role of the family is demoted and the potent leveling effects of the mass media are pervasive. Allowed to run its course this process of ethnic dilution would facilitate the melting pot homogenization, in some cases leaving behind only surnames as remnants of what was.

However, on a broad scale this scenario has not played out unimpededly thanks to several national Italian-American associations and a large number of local clubs and organizations that endeavor to preserve the Italian heritage in a variety of ways. On a personal level, the story of my life in a large sense has involved encounters with reminders of who I am and of the richness of my inherited cultural wellspring.

The deficiency in communicating in English was the threshold problem of the immigrants and their first generation offspring. But this and other early stultifying situations were insufficient to hold back the creative character and spirit of the Italian genius, for from the bloodlines of those early immigrants – nurtured in the Little Italys of America – emerged men and women who would contribute to and enhance all areas of human activity in the life of America, and in some cases were destined to become towering figures on the Nation's landscape.

Whenever I look back at the event of my birth, I never fail to be amazed at what amounts to an incredible fact. To begin with, on a macro level consider that the state of matter in the Universe appears, as far as is known, to be one of randomness with atoms and their particles strewn around in a formless mishmash. Contrast this situation with that of human beings who are completely ordered and structured and in so being violate the rules of probability.

If the above were not enough, consider that the probability of me having been born at all and to immigrant Italian parents was statistically amazing considering it occurred against colossal odds of genetics as to what else might have been. For anyone to be born requires that over millions of years along both the maternal and paternal ancestral lines certain persons have had to have mated with certain specific others and that they have had children one of whom mated with a certain other person and so on over the centuries. One single exception in the long, delicate historical chain would have cancelled out my existence.

On January 17, 1930 against these genetic odds of Himalayan proportions an Italian-American was in fact born. The story of what evolved from the event of that date is the subject of this book.

PART ONE

IN THE BEGINNING

AN ITALIAN-AMERICAN BIRTH

It is not to diffuse you that you were born of your
father and mother, it was to identify you. Something
long preparing and formless is arrived and formed in
you.

(Walt Whitman's Leaves of Grass)

The Event

The sky was mostly misty on this January morning, not cold enough to
snow only an occasional thin drizzle. Antonia Perenzin lay in bed in her
second floor apartment at 123 Rockland Street, Fitchburg, Massachusetts. The
painful contractions were coming at noticeably shorter intervals. During the
moments of ease she glanced at the raindrops on the bedroom window and
noticed how slowly some of them slid down the pane. She was reminded of
how slowly the nine difficult months had passed, an eternity it seemed before
she would have her American born child, girl or boy, it didn't matter. What
did matter was that it would be an American. At first she was concerned that
maybe it was crazy to have even considered having a baby at 42 years old, but
she wanted it and she knew Antonio wanted it more than anything else in the
world. She turned her head to the picture of St. Anthony on the wall and felt
comforted.

Her thoughts were interrupted by Mrs. Cravale, her neighbor and mid-
wife, who entered the bedroom carrying more towels. She assured Antonia the
doctor would soon be there and that Antonio had gone down to the street to

3

wait for him. In the front of the house the father-to-be, oblivious to the light drizzle, walked impatiently back and forth on the sidewalk anxiously looking down both ends of Rockland Street for a sign of doctor Morgan. "Why is he so slow, dam doctor, if he gets here too late I'll break his neck," was Antonio's thinking when interrupted by a voice from across the street, the voice of Mrs. Chelemi inquiring about how Antonia was doing and adding that if she could be of help to let her know. Antonio waved his hand in appreciation but said nothing, for he really didn't want to talk to anyone at a time like this. It seemed like a life-time before he saw an old black Ford swing on to Rockland Street and make its way towards the house with corpulent Doctor Morgan at the wheel.

Antonio and Antonia Perenzin shared the same dream – an American child. Yes, there was Leno and there was Mary, but they were born in Italy and were still Italian citizens. This couple was now living in the land of their dreams. How many times had they laid in bed in Italy hundreds of miles apart thinking parallel thoughts of that far-off land where everyone had a chance to work, raise a family and make a decent living. Now after some fifteen years of being in the U.S.A. how better to give the world visible evidence that they were truly part of this wonderful country and that they really belonged here than by holding up their American child for everyone to see.

It was against this parental background that on January 17, 1930 I made my appearance on the second floor of my parents' Rockland Street apartment, an appearance I almost missed. The story I was told about what happened went something like this:

Doctor Morgan: Look, Mrs. Perenzin it's a boy.

Mrs. Cravale: Doctor look the baby's turning blue.

Doctor Morgan: He's not breathing, I've hit him several times, it's not working. [my mother gave signs of passing out and the doctor placed me on a chair and turned his attention to her]

Mrs. Cravale: *Dotore, dotore, guarda, guarda, il bambino e vivo,* as she picked me up and pointed to my chest and to a small lump quivering its way up the chest towards my neck.

The doctor took me from her slapped me a good one across my bottom and out came a blob of mucous followed by a cry of life, a cry which soon brought my father knocking at the door of the bedroom asking what had happened. The doctor opened the door and holding my father back said, "It's a boy." Doctor Morgan was an elderly, overweight German whose English was understandable through his thick German accent only by paying careful attention and with a bit of guesswork. Not that the accent made much difference to my father since he knew little English.

Confused my father repeated, *"Che ha detto? Che ha detto?"*

Mrs. Cravale carrying the infant went to the door and said *"Antonio, questo é tuo figlio."* My father remained stiff as if momentarily unsure of what to do, then slowly reached his hand out to touch the bundled up infant but perhaps afraid he might hurt it, pulled back. His eyes turned to his resting wife as he stepped into the room. Standing next to her bed, he placed his hand over hers, and asked how she felt. Antonia smiled through her exhaustion and nodded an "I'm alright."

"Grazie, a fatto bene e un figlio" whispered Antonio who then turned around and with pursed lips, as if holding something back, walked into the kitchen. All his earlier indecisiveness was gone as he went directly to the icebox, pulled out a pitcher of red wine, filled a glass to the brim, sat down at the kitchen table and took a long deep swig.

Meanwhile, in the bedroom doctor Morgan, placing his instruments back into his black bag, gave my mother instructions on what to do and what not to do for a few days. Then he walked over to Mrs. Cravale and laying his hand on her shoulder smiled appreciatively and said, "good job." They walked into the kitchen and to the stairs leading to the street when the doctor stopped, turned to look at my father and told Mrs. Cravale to tell him in Italian that he had a good looking baby boy, very healthy. My father nodded in appreciation and raised the pitcher of wine and a glass and offered the good doctor a drink. The doctor smiled and told Mrs. Cravale, "Tell him Italians drink too much wine but that on this occasion it's understandable."

"Tell him Germans drink too much beer that's why they have such big bellies and we Italians don't," was my father's comment accompanied by that familiar broad smile. Doctor Morgan forced a half grin, turned around and walked down the stairs mumbling something in German which went un-translated.

The Location

Fitchburg in 1930 was a different place from what it was at the beginning of its early settlement. Yet in some important respects it was a natural result of the seeds planted at its birth back in the early 1700s. Like some of the great and not so great cities of the world, the town's first settlers were located along a river, in Fitchburg's case the Nashua River which is where the town's first businesses were soon to be located. The Kimbal brothers back in 1750 constructed a water-driven mill along the Nashua and there began grinding corn which they then supplied to the townspeople and neighboring farmers. Now in 1930 though the town had spread far beyond the river, the major industries were still to be found along its banks: numerous paper mills, Independent Lock Company, the Margolis Shoe Factory, Simons Saw and Steel Mill, Fitchburg Yarn Company, General Electric Turbine Division, among others.

Until the turn of the 20th Century the demographic composition of Fitchburg remained largely unchanged. English/protestant names like Whitney, Burbank, Kimball, Snow, Foster, and Young were telltale of the town's ethnic composition. These were the people who set up the businesses and factories in the town and who would become its social and financial elite. They are those whose names identified many important places such as the Burbank Hospital and Crocker Field, and whose names are still to be found on the gravestones and tombs in the protestant cemetery, in some instances bearing dates going back over two centuries.

With the advent of the Industrial Revolution, Fitchburg, like other areas of the country, found itself with a serious shortage of workers who were needed not only to labor in the new factories but also to build the factories themselves, to lay the railroad lines and to build the streets for the growing number of automobiles. And thus began the great era of immigration into the United States.

The raggedy immigrants poured into the U.S.A. from all over Europe – for it was basically a European-sourced immigration – Italy was one of the main fountain heads. The Italians, mostly from rural areas, came carrying their worldly possessions in boxes and jerry built suitcases, with hope in their hearts and a fathomless reserve of energy ready and anxious to be expended on creating a new life in this promising land. It was these immigrants who for the next fifty years contributed so much to the dynamics which resulted in America becoming the world's leading economic power. In the process, they infused a new kind of fierce loyalty to family and employers into the country's bloodstream. Many died or suffered draconian working conditions in the country's factories, quarries, mines and on railway construction. These were the true unheralded heroes of what was to become the American miracle.

The Cast

What can be said about a main character who, unlike the rest of the cast, had no history, no prior existence before the drama began. If he had had a prior life it was unknown. With nothing else to go on let us look for clues of who he might be or become by considering the only thing he had which was his own, his name.

The birth certificate would read "Domenico Antonio Perenzin", a first name which over time became Anglicized to "Dominic." Why this name. No great exercise in coming up with it, no scanning of long lists of possible choices. My grandfather was Domenico and I was to be his namesake.

The name is a variation of the Latin word for "Lord" (*dominicus*). Two explanations have been given for the derivation, one is that it is intended to mean "Belonging to the Lord" and the other is that it signifies "Born on the Lord's Day" i.e. Sunday. What is clear is the fact that the appellation Domenico has a spiritual connotation.

Perhaps as evidence of the spiritual aura surrounding the name is the fact that two Dominics reached sainthood, Dominic of Cuirass a a penitent who was given to inflicting mortification on himself, and Santo Domingo de Guzman, the founder of the Order of the Dominicans.

According to my zodiac profile I was a Capricorn. People born under this sign are ambitious and disciplined, determined to achieve their goals, practical and realistic, and cautious to not get in over their heads. Capricorn is ruled by the Planet Saturn. According to Roman Mythology Saturn was the father of many of the gods, including Zeus. Again the spiritual overtone.

According to the Chinese Zodiac the birth date of January 17 corresponds to the snake. People born in the Year of the Snake have highly developed sensitivities. They are brilliant at lying in wait and when the right moment arrives they tightly focus their accumulated energies and make their decisive move. People are warned never to make an enemy of a snake.

Under the system of Pathogoren Numerology Dominics have personalities drawn to social reforms and to the plight of the underdog. The name is also said to be associated with the color yellow. In ancient times colors were related to the days of the week with yellow corresponding to Sunday in honor of God's Light. Again the religious connotation.

In the book "The Hidden Truth of Your Name – a Nomenology Project," it is said that Dominics have their feet firmly on the ground, are much connected to life's physical comforts for whom family is of paramount importance. It is also said that if you want a Dominic to sign a contract or to agree to a business deal simply send a beautiful messenger and he will sign anything.

And so it was that the newborn Dominic had several character paradigms from which he presumably could evolve. Would he, true to his Capricorn sign, be a relentless pursuer of goals or would he assume the quiet perceptive canniness of the snake? Would he crave earthly pleasures and comforts or set his gaze towards heaven? Would he go into a melt-down in the presence of beautiful messengers?

The Doctor

For my first 12 years or so doctor Morgan was our family doctor. He treated my chicken pox, measles, stomach aches (once for eating a whole coconut) and he relieved me of my tonsils which he graciously agreed to do in my bedroom. I never got to see his office since in those days, as odd as it may sound in this age, doctors made house calls even when the call involved removing tonsils.

Doctor Morgan arrived in Fitchburg during the first years of the 20th century, around 1903. No one could understand why a German doctor would leave Germany to go to a small town like Fitchburg. Whatever the reason it didn't take long for him to develop a good medical practice. By 1935 doctor Morgan had endured two major tragedies which left him psychologically devastated, and greatly accelerated his biological clock.

In 1917 the United States entered World War I against Germany. It was anecdotally reported the doctor's house occasionally became the target of rock-throwing by angry Fitchburgers. He endured all kinds of harassment and threats against him and his family. There was one particularly ugly incident that was rumored. A call came to the doctor asking him to please rush to a certain house where a young boy was gravely ill. He went and upon arrival knocked at the door, as it opened he was greeted by a shower of yellow urine. The house belonged to the family of an American soldier who had been killed by Germans a few weeks before and whose mother had received one of those most dreaded telegrams from the War Department notifying the death of sons, brothers and husbands.

The second tragedy had to do with the untimely train-crash death of his nephew Heinz Rackman, a German medical doctor who had been brought to Fitchburg by doctor Morgan. Rackman was returning from a trip urged upon him by doctor Morgan when the accident occurred. A part of Doctor Morgan also perished in that train crash. His career began to spiral downwards and it was said he returned to Germany, a Germany suffering its own devastation and rushing headlong into World War II.

Mid-Wife

Teresa Cravale was a very special person and much appreciated in the neighborhood. She lived with her husband and children in the apartment building next door to us. While I don't recall from what part of Italy she came, I do remember she stood out among the other woman in the neighborhood. She seemed more educated, better dressed and more soft-spoken. Where she obtained her knowledge about the treatment of a variety of illnesses was never made clear but she was often called upon by the neighbors whenever a family member got ill. For her services she charged and would accept no fee of any kind. People treated by her would show their appreciation by sending simple gifts to her home - a bottle of wine, grapes, tomatoes and her favorite, navel oranges.

What was odd about all of this was that the Cravale family appeared to be well off financially as Mr. Cravale either owned or ran a small variety store. The children were always relatively well groomed and impeccably dressed. Given her status appearance she could reasonably be expected to remain aloof from her poorer neighbors or, perhaps, to not be living on Rockland Street at all. Fortunately for me, her presence and attentiveness on the morning of my birth made a vital difference.

The Progenitors

Antonio Perenzin, the son of Domenico Perenzin and Bernadetta DeNoni, born January 22, 1887 in Conegliano, Italy, one of seven brothers and two sisters. Grandfather Domenico was a patriarch of sorts in Conegliano – fairly well off financially and the owner of a thriving dairy/cheese business. But life was made far from easy for the Perenzin boys for Domenico made sure they all worked hard so that from their sweat and tired bodies they would appreciate the true value of their possessions. All worked in the family's dairy business. Domenico was well known and highly respected in and around Conegliano, a tough and enterprising businessman with a warm heart for friends in need and a soft touch for uncollaterized loans, some of which were never repaid.

Antonio Perenzin's favorite task in the dairy business was to go out with the horse-drawn buggy to pick up milk from the surrounding farms. He loved being out in the early morning freshness, seeing the first rays of the sun as they slowly suffused the verdant countryside, filling his lungs with the freshness of the young morning as it reached across the valley. It was strenuous work to load the hefty milk containers on to cart but it was a price he willingly paid. In later years he attributed his sizeable biceps to this heavy lifting.

It was on one of his stops that signore Pisciotta told Antonio he was very happy because his son Pietro had returned from America to visit a while. Antonio knew the son for they had been buddies a few years earlier. During the next month Antonio and Pietro spent time together on weekends. Pietro's stories about America began to work their way into Antonio's mind. At night before falling asleep he recalled Pietro's tales about that far away America, the many opportunities awaiting all who went there, how easy it was to get a job. It wasn't even necessary to speak or understand much English, for everyone spoke Italian. It wasn't long before Antonio began musing over the idea of going to America to start a life of his own.

Some 150 miles to the west of Conegliano a young, slim and pretty Antonia Zanin opened a letter she had just received from her brother Battista, posted in a place called Fitchburg in America. "Come," he urged her, "you will love it here." I can find you work easily. There are many Italians here. Antonia kept the letter which every so often she would re-read. Would she dare go? What would her parents say; they needed her on the farm. But she was bored with her life – the same routine day after monotonous day. What future lay ahead for her here in this town of Stroparri except to marry some dull farmer boy, have kids, work her hands to the bone. No, no, she was quite convinced that was not what she wanted. There had to be a better future for her somewhere and America seemed like the place she could make it happen. She would tell her mother first to see how she reacted to the idea of her going to America. Then she would tell her father.

On separate dates in 1910, Antonio Perenzin and Antonia Zanin arrived at Ellis Island, New York, as new immigrants to America, took trains north to Boston where they boarded Boston and Maine trains that carried them west to the small town of Fitchburg. Antonia went to live with her now married brother Battista and soon got a job as carder at the Fitchburg Yarn Company. Antonio boarded with the family of one of the passengers he had met in the train from Boston to Fitchburg.

Obviously, Antonio Perenzin and Antonia Zanin did eventually meet. How that happened was told to me years later. Gregarious Antonio had been in the United States only a month and he already knew a lot of the Italians in the neighborhood yet there was something missing. One Saturday afternoon he was having a beer at the Hillside Café (owed by the Alteri family) and chatting with his friend Paul Lasarra when he mentioned the fact he had not yet met any young Italian girl who interested him. His friend said he was married and didn't know much about the girl scene. "Wait a minute," he recalled, "do you know Battista Zanin that big six – foot foot giant who lived at the bottom of Beech Street. Well his young sister arrived a couple of weeks ago and is living in his house. You should meet her." Antonio agreed to go with him to the Zanin house the next day, Sunday, since there was always a lot of people there during the afternoons, a sort of informal social meeting place for Italians living in the area.

They knocked at the door of the Zanin apartment from which the sound of people talking and laughing could be heard. Mrs. Zanin invited them in and suggested they just go around and introduce themselves to anyone they may not know as she handed each of us a glass of wine.

What happened next was told to me by my mother. She said it was another one of those Sunday afternoons when all kinds of people came to my brother's house. I didn't like being there for I knew that after a while the men would usually have too much to drink and get fresh. Back in Italy the men were more respectful. I didn't know many of the people there that Sunday and none seemed particularly interesting except for this one man who came with Paul Lasarra. There was something about him that seemed different and interesting. Tall he was not, yet because of the way he stood straight with his head high and the way he carried himself he gave the impression of being taller than he was. He walked around the room as if he owned the place. I had never seen a man like that with so much presence, almost cocky.

After a while, I caught him looking at me which I found embarrassing causing me to quickly look away. I asked the lady sitting next to me on the sofa if she knew who that man was. She further embarrassed me by pointing to him and saying in a not low tone, "He's new around here, arrived a few weeks ago, handsome devil isn't he? They say he's strong as an ox too." I semi-smiled. She was right, he was good looking. He seemed so sure of himself. Then it happened. He was standing across the room when our eyes happened to meet again. As usual I felt ill-at-ease and turned away but this time it would be different. He put his glass of wine on a table and started making his way to where I was sitting. Oh my God I thought as I saw him walking in my direction, not knowing whether to get up and run away, start praying or just ignore him. I tried to look elsewhere but keeping the approaching figure in the corner of my eye hoping this pretended disinterest would induce him to not continue. But my hope was dashed for he was now standing in front of me and looking straight into my eyes and with extended hand said "I am Antonio Perenzin from Veneto."

On April 22, 1911, Justice of Peace John Chalmers looked up from his Bible at the two young Italians standing before him.

"Antonio Perenzin do you take this woman Antonia Zanin as your lawful wife to love in health and in sickness…"

Mr. Chalemmi translated, "Antonio said yes"

"Antonia Zanin do you take this man Antonio Perenzin to be your lawful husband, to live and to hold in sickness and in health?" "Si"

Antonio was 24 years old and Antonia 20. The marriage lasted until until God parted them in 1957. In between those dates of 1911-1957 lay a large segment of the saga of the Fitchburg Perenzins and the scenario in which the first twenty years of my life were to be played out.

PARALLEL WORLDS

As epic an occasion as was my birth for my parents, the rest of the world hardly noticed and never missed a step. I didn't mind though for I was soon to be fully occupied with exploring my own world, getting familiar with the attributes and functions of my body such as sitting up, crawling, walking, touching and tasting. Between the date of my birth and my first memories important events were occurring in the parallel external world.

These were the first years of the Great Depression. While I was learning to sit up on my own and occasionally tumbling over, New York's Bank of the United States tumbled over in failure and a million people lost their entire savings. Widows went to the bank to demand their money; it was reported that they screamed and pleaded through the night for their life's savings but that no one came out to even acknowledge their presence. Emotionally drained, they returned home and remained reclused like the living dead.

While my parents were proudly applauding the first words uttered by me, in Stockholm Sweden Jane Adams was warmly applauded as she received the Nobel Peace Prize, the first American woman to receive this honor. Having been actively engaged in the peace movement since 1914 and during the War she was attacked as unpatriotic and demonized as an advocate of socialism and communism. She was equally well known and admired for her founding and work with the Hall-House, a Chicago settlement house and educational center that attracted large numbers of poor immigrants.

Perhaps as a remnant of a primitive past, I entered the stage in which I figured the best way to get to know what something was to put it in my mouth for a taste test. In Lemon Grove, California a different type of test occurred on January 5, 1931, one involving the practice of segregation, not for blacks but for Mexican immigrants. Mexican children were separated from white children and forced to attend classes in a renovated barn. On that date the Mexican parents refused to send their children to school. In response the local school board claimed it was better to separate children by academic level, camouflaging possible racist motives. The Mexican parents steadfastly continued to boycott the school.

The issue was brought before the courts and a decision obtained holding that racial segregation among children was illegal. Interestingly, the rest of the country was laggard in following the lead of the California decision for it was not until 23 years later that the U.S. Supreme Court put an end to segregation in Brown vs. Board of Education.

Then came my first efforts to walk on my own, at first faltering and unsure but gradually with greater confidence. At the same time 5,000 unemployed men marched on the Ford Motor Company in Dearborn demanding they be given work. Across the globe India's Gandhi led a walk to the sea to protest England's decision to tax the sale of salt. He got such massive support for this show of civil disobedience that the British Government realized it could no longer ignore India's cries for independence. In Chicago the Democratic National Convention nominated Franklin Delano Roosevelt as its candidate. Not only was he elected president in 1932 but was later re-elected for three consecutive terms during the most turbulent years in American history. This he did while unable to walk on his own.

While the earliest events in my personal life that I can remember were occurring, the Japanese Army took decisive control over all of China's Manchuria Province; Charles Lindberg's child was kidnapped; Adolph Hitler became Chancellor of Germany; John Dewey pressed his Progressive Education theory to replace the rote memorization, and the Social Security System was inaugurated.

The reverberations from some of these events would extend far into the future where I would personally encounter their effects.

FIRST MEMORIES

I heard the footsteps of someone climbing the stairs to our apartment and then my father's voice shouting, "Tonya (my father's nickname for my mother) your husband is back." He had just arrived from a trip to Italy. Though his return is fixed in my memory I don't recall him ever leaving or being away. There were hugs and kisses for everyone. Mary came out of the living room when she heard the commotion and in her characteristic get-down-to-business-and-let's-skip-all-this-talking-stuff attitude asked dad whether he had brought any gifts.

Mother instinctively turned to do what she always did when someone visited us or, in the case of my father, when he came home – she brewed a fresh pot of coffee. "I've got something for everyone, nothing extravagant you understand but something to show I didn't forget any of you," beamed my father. I don't recall what he brought for the other family members though they got theirs before I got mine. "Now for you little Domenico, something you can use with pride, look at this," as my father held out a blue and white garment in one hand and a cap in the other.

"What is it pa?" I asked.

"Why it's the same suit the Italian sailors wear," he answered. "Look here on the front of the cap, see where it says MARINA D'ITALIA." I took the uniform and rushed into the bedroom to try it on. As I was about to discover my father's good intention and warmth of heart far exceeded his sense of size, for almost two Domenicos could easily fit into the garment. I rushed into the kitchen wearing the gift only to be met by Mary's loud giggles and my father's look of surprise. Noticing my embarrassment my mother quickly came to my rescue saying it would be easy to make a few adjustments so that it would fit perfectly and that I would look just fine. This she did. On many occasions I would put on the suit and march around the house, stopping to admire myself in a mirror. I felt like parading down Main Street so that everyone could see me and salute me in my bright new navy uniform. Over the next few days I proudly showed the suit to my neighborhood friends. But a few years later this sailor suit would bring me my first public embarrassment as I wore it to school for a celebration honoring an American. national holiday to the snickering and snide remarks of some of the teachers. After that humiliating experience I never again wore my Italian sailor suit. The incision on my young impressionable mind was deep and the psychological scars from the wound would take long to heal.

****

To my parent's chagrin my brother Leno fell in love not with a pretty blue-eyed Alice Landry, a French-Canadian girl, who lived two houses away from our Rockland Street apartment. There wasn't much communication between the Landry family and ours or for that matter between the Landry's and other families on Rockland Street for the simple reason that the elder Landrys spoke only French and Rockland Street was predominantly Italian turf. Alice's parents gave their consent to Alice's marriage to Leno, though I've often wondered if they really understood what Leno was saying when he asked for her hand.

My mind is blank when it comes to seeing Leno and Alice together or of Alice visiting our apartment except for one mischievous occasion. I was playing in the street with neighborhood friends when Leno, who was sitting with Alice on the front porch of the Landry house, called me over "Here's a dime get me some cherries from Mrs. Frey."

Mrs. Frey had a house on Beech Street with a huge elongated backyard extending down to the corner of Rockland and Federal Streets. The yard was packed with all kinds of fruit trees, apple, pear, peach and cherry. The wooden fence around the yard stood some six feet tall sending a clear message that people were *non grata* and should stay out. To put real teeth into this warning Mrs. Frey had two German shepherds whose sole mission in life was to make sure the fruit remained on the trees until Mrs. Frey willed otherwise. We kids bought cherries from Mrs. Frey which she sold in plain brown sandwich bags at the colossal price of 10 cents a bag. What does one do when hungry for cherries but can't come up with the requisite dime? Youngsters have their imaginative ways of finding solutions to such knotty problems, for instance, one could climb the fence at the bottom of the yard on the Rockland Street side, grab a few cherries then dash back over the fence before the duo-dogs of terror got a whiff of what was happening. Admittedly a risky maneuver but no more direct solution.

With Leno's dime in my pocket I headed up Federal Street toward Mrs. Frey's house with a friend. On the way we got a sudden urge for ice cream. Now 10 cents would buy one pint of ice cream which Mr. Cuciara (owner of Cuciara's variety store) would be happy to cut in half, one half for me and one for my friend, just as he did when kids were on their way to the movies and had only 5¢ left after paying for the movie ticket. But what would we tell Leno? We could say we were held up by robbers. No, he won't swallow that. We lost it, how about that? No, he might get mad. Well there's only one thing left, lets apply the direct solution and climb the fence and engage in a bit of self-service.

I climbed one of the trees and threw the cherries down to my friend who started filling his pockets and, every once in a while, his mouth. Suddenly a yell from my friend, "The dogs are coming!" He was right, there they were running full speed from the house towards us with Mrs. Frey yelling from an open window and urging them to get us and telling us to "Get out you hoodlums, out, out!!!" I jumped to the ground and followed my buddy over the fence to the other side. We looked between the slats in the fence for the dogs and saw they were not in fact heading towards us but had veered off in pursuit of something else, probably a cat. Thank God we were safe but I had an undesired momento of the adventure, torn pants. My friend also had his momento, many crushed cherries in his pants pockets. We managed to salvage a few whole cherries and delivered a pitiful handful to Leno and Alice accompanied with the explanation that my friend had tripped and fell on the pocket in which he had the bag of cherries. Leno's face showed doubt while Alice looked away with a knowing grin on hers.

Off we went to Cuciara's store, picked out our pint of mixed chocolate and vanilla ice cream and had it cut into halves; I reached in my pocket for the dime and came up empty. It was nowhere to be found. "Well boys where's the dime?"

"We lost it Mr. Cuciara, please believe us." He looked tongue-in-check angrily at us for a while as a smile worked its slow way to his lips.

"OK, I'll put it on Tony Perenzin's bill."

"Thanks Mr. Cuciara," and off we went to the park across the street where we sat on the grass and complemented ourselves on outwitting Mrs. Frey. My friend reached in his pocket and pulled out the crushed remains of a few cherries part of which he placed on my ice cream and part on his. Two soul buddies sharing the fruits of their resourcefulness.

****

Next door to our Rockland Street apartment was a tenement house, on the first floor of which lived the prettiest little red head of a girl a boy could ever expect to see, Rosie De Lai. She walked around as if she were very aware of her prettiness. One day my buddies and I were playing stickball in the street. Rosie was sitting on the top of the railing of her front porch watching us. One of us was eating an apple and Rosie would occasionally fix her sights on him and said he had a nice apple. "You want a bite," he offered.

"OK," she answered. He went half way to her and threw the half eaten apple to her which she caught and wasted no time in devouring. That's when we got the idea. Do you think she will lift up her dress and show us her panties for a whole apple? Bet she would. We got an apple and convinced Rosie to squeeze under the front porch with us. No hesitation at all as she lifted her dress and grabbed the apple. One of us asked her if she would lower those panties a quick second for another apple. She said alright but had to go home first. We waited for her. Five minutes later she came back "Where is the apple," she asked. We showed it to her. She raised her dress, then lowered her panties.

"OK, give me the apple," she said. "Ah, ah," we said because beneath the lowered panties she was wearing another pair. At the moment Mrs. De Lai was on the porch and hearing the noise from below stepped down to see what was happening. We were trapped – only one way out and there blocking it was Mrs. DeLai shaking her fist at us and yelling at Rosie.

We pushed Rosie towards the opening where her mother took over by grabbing one of her ears and leading her into the house. With the coast now clear we climbed out and ran down Rockland Street not intending to go to any particular place but simply to put as much distance as possible between us and Rosie's house. Out of breath we stopped at the bottom of Federal Street and sat down to consider our situation. Our parents were sure to be told about what had happened under Rosie's porch. It was suggested we agree on saying it was all Rosie's fault, a trick to get an apple from us (a replay with a spin on the Garden of Eden tale?). We separated and went home to face whatever awaited us.

I entered the kitchen and immediately asked my mother if there was anything I could do for her, any errands, anything to clean, how about sweeping the stairs. With a furrowed brow made in an effort to understand what she had just heard, she said "no, not right now." It turned out Rosie's mother had not yet complained about the Little League orgy to my mother. Later when she did, the only feedback I got from mother was a "good boys don't do those things." I never found out whether my father had been told, he never said a word to me about it nor did I inquire.

From this early childhood experience I should have learned three important survival facts of life; never engage in a high risk venture without first having figured out a way to exit, just in case; always exercise care in the use of words when explaining what I wanted, and women are wiser than men because they know less and understand more.

Years later during my early teens my libido curiosity was up-graded beyond the undergarments phase. It started on an early September day during morning recess at the Clarendon Street Elementary School. A group of us were talking about sex when the question came up as to whether any of us had ever seen or touched a real rubber. Negative said the pursed lips of the heads nodding horizontally, though there were noticeable tempting moments of hesitation in some eyes.

Over the next few days four of us came up with the idea of buying a rubber to see what it was all about and to be ready just in case it should be needed. The first question that popped up was where to buy it. We knew they were sold in drug stores but we also knew we were not about to buy one at our local drugstore out of fear we might be recognized by someone. So it was decided we would go to one located downtown.

Next, how to get there. We could take a bus but that would cost money, a commodity definitely in short supply. Altogether the four of us could come up with 75¢ which we would probably need in order to pay for the rubber. Walking both ways was the only solution. Who would go? Since walking didn't cost anything we all decided to go.

And so it was that on a Saturday morning we entered Primeau Pharmacy on Main Street in downtown Fitchburg. We looked around for rubbers but with disappointment found no container with that name on it, so we went to the soda counter and asked a young soda-jerk where we could find them. Though he wasn't sure he believed the pharmacist kept them behind the counter and that we should ask him adding that he thought they had a scientific name something like "coldrums" or "cordrums." As we approached the counter where the avuncular looking pharmacist was standing, we noticed a woman employee had gone to talk to him so we turned around and pretended to be looking at boxes of cotton balls. By the way, which one of us would do the buying? Who would do the talking? Agreed, we would all do so at the same time a sort of libido choir. That way no one in particular would be embarrassed.

When we saw he was alone we approached the pharmacist. "What, can I do for you youngsters?" We were dumbly taken by surprise by how fast this crucial moment had arrived.

"We want to buy a caldrum," said the singular voice of Jasper as the rest of us chickened out and began to fidget about.

"A what?" asked the pharmacist with a puzzled frown on his forehead.

"A caldrum or something like that," repeated Jasper.

"Don't know what you want," said the pharmacist, "never heard of it."

"A rubber," blurted out another one of us.

Smiling now the guy behind the counter said in a voice we were sure could be heard all the way up Main Street, "Oh, I see what you want are condoms."

"Yeah, yeah," came our collective response. Then a tense silence as he looked us over doing his very utmost to refrain from laughing. Then came the unanticipated question, "What kind do you want?" What kind did we want? We didn't know there were different kinds. We huddled, put our joint heads together, but found no specific answer.

"The regular kind that guys use," was our response, "what other kinds are there?"

"Well, for example, we have condoms made in this country and some from France." By this time the soda jerk who could overhear most of the conversation was bursting with laughter. "OK, enough of this fellows," said the pharmacist now assuming a more professional attitude, "let's be serious, which of you is 21 years old?" No response. "Just what I thought, so I suggest you forget about buying. The law won't allow it. Come back when you are 21."

"You don't understand," said Jasper, "it is not for us but for a friend who is more than 21 years old who is in the hospital and can't come here himself."

"I'm surprised to hear that nurses are so accommodating," observed the pharmacist with a smirk and quickly added, "Tell your friend to come here when he feels better."

All that was left for us was to parade back home empty-handed like defeated warriors who had lost the Battle of Eros Pass. We didn't even know what the word "accommodating" meant. To soothe our wounded aspirations we stopped off at Cuchiara's where we had one large vanilla ice cream soda with four straws.

****

I had never before seen the man who came to our Rockland Street apartment; he looked so important with his dark suit, necktie and always carrying a lot of papers. One day after talking to my mother and father and showing them important looking papers, the man in the dark suit said that they could see it right now. My parents nodded in agreement and off we went up Federal Street to Beech Street.

"Where are we going ma?" I kept asking, trying to break into my parents' conversation.

"Domenico, we are going to see our new home, a nice big house." As we reached the top of Federal Street my mother stopped and pointing to a brown shingled house on the corner lot said that was the house.

"That's really ours?" I asked excitedly.

"We shall see," answered my father as we climbed the steps up to the front porch. The man in the dark suit knocked at the door several times until finally a woman all sweaty and disheveled opened the door and gave us a quizzical look, as if to ask what we all wanted. Mr. Dark-Suit said something to her and stepped into the house leaving us alone on the porch. We looked around at the neighborhood and liked what we saw. Neat little houses with gardens. So

21

much space between the houses too. We could hear talking from some of the houses – the language was familiar, it was Italian. My mother whispered to me that Beech Street was where the upper-class lived.

The front door opened and Mr. Dark-Suit motioned us in. Facing us was a staircase, "Wow," was my reaction, the house had a second floor which would also be ours. The lady who first answered the door was in the kitchen pulling clothes out of the washing machine which was standing next to the sink. She put the water-logged clothes into hand-operated wringers attached to the machine with which she squeezed out most of the water into the sink. She never said a word to us, only occasionally stealing a glance at what we were doing. She was never introduced to us. We later learned she and her husband owned the house.

We saw the whole house, my mother looked absolutely radiant in her smile as she went from room to room and out into the backyard at times looking sheepishly at the lady of the house. Two weeks later I would be seen carrying two portraits up Federal Street, my contribution to our move into 118 Beech Street. Once settled into our new home, I recall my mother asking my father whether maybe they had made a mistake in buying the house. It was 1935 and a crushing depression gripped the U.S. People were literally starving. The prior owners of the house, Mr. & Mrs. Kennedy, were unable to make regular payments on their mortgage so the bank foreclosed.

It took Mr. Kennedy some time to overcome the grief at having lost his house. Occasionally, when drunk he would at all hours of the night come to our front door and knock heavily saying: "This is my house, let me in, all of you get out." The first time this happened my father went to talk to him with no success. After that we simply waited until he got tired and left. I felt bad for the Kennedys, they seemed to be good people caught up in a situation not of their making and before which they were helpless, the stuff out of which tragedy is made. Were we in some way responsible for having them thrown out? The question came up several times and my father's answer satisfied all of us. If we didn't buy the house someone else would have bought it. The explanation sounded like we hadn't done anything wrong, yet, there was the emotional side of the story represented by the lingering image of sad, defeated and drunken Mr. Kennedy crying at our door. Even after he stopped coming to our house, I had the feeling I could hear someone at the door. For the first few weeks or so, I never went downstairs to the bathroom at night since to get there I had to pass by the front door.

This house-purchase episode was my inauguration into the troubling area of ethics and social justice. Though it caused me no loss of sleep I was made aware of the existence of problems caused by the encounters of conflicting ethical-legal-economic interests.

My father died in 1957 while still living in the house at 118 Beech Street, as did my mother in 1985. At this time some 68 years later my sister Mary lives in that very same brown house at 118 Beech Street.

SCHOOL DAYS

*What I Didn't Learn Could
Have Gotten me into Harvard*

DiD we have Kindergarden?

Strange how little it seems I learned during the elementary school years or, as we called it, grammar school. I remember my teachers but not what they taught, at least I can't point to any specific thing I learned. But again, who does remember after so many years. I must have learned English though because when I entered the first grade it was practically a foreign language to me, Italian being my first language. There was no kindergarten let alone pre-kinder in my world. Kids went from mother's apron strings to first grade with no warm-up, unless, that is, a kid's parents were so rich that the mother did not wear an apron and could afford to send their kids to pre-school. In our neighborhood there wasn't anyone that rich.

My elementary school was the Clarendon Street School. Since there were no big yellow school buses back then, I walked to school and back, some three miles each way which I did on sunny days, in the rain, and in the bone-chilling cold of winter. The school was made up of two brick buildings located on a strip of land elevated above the street level and connected to the street by stairs of some twenty steps. Because of this height advantage the school towered over the surrounding area. The two buildings were located back-to-front so that when one exited from Building # 1, one could walk across thirty feet of pavement straight ahead into the Building # 2. Building # 1 was where the first and second grades were located. All students in that building shared a single wish, namely, to get out of Building #1 and into Building # 2 which

24

would be the first promotion in a student's young academic career, in our minds meritorious of a formal graduation ceremony. But again perhaps not since the only requirements for graduating from one building to the other were that the student have spent two years in Building # 1, show signs of breathing, and be able to walk the thirty feet separating the buildings.

I can remember two salient events that were replayed day after day in first grade, the teacher telling us we could now take a nap by resting our heads on our arms folded on our desks, and the teacher telling me to take Edward Zitti home because he had pissed in his pants. On the way to his house I made sure he walked out of the range of my sniffing zone. I must have exhibited some talent for this kind of smelly task because later I also occasionally had to walk Nancy Mandroy home when she wet herself. I didn't mind as much because her father was doctor Mandroy and that meant I could show off by walking with her, even though she didn't smell all that great either. Everyone held her in awe for having such an important father, ours were mostly common factory workers. Question! Why didn't doctor Mandroy treat his daughter so that she could learn to hold her water? The probable answer came at the beginning of second grade when it was reported Doctor Mandroy had suddenly disappeared with his family in the wake of the discovery that he was under investigation for practicing medicine without a license. This plus the fact Edward Zitti never made it to the second grade dealt a death blow to my budding specialization.

Once in Building # 2 things went a little better for me as evidenced by a couple of events that did short-term wonders for my self-esteem. The first occurred in the fourth grade. Our teacher, Miss Upton, asked a math question to which the class shouted out the correct answer which was 24. Everyone was right except me; I said 20. The teacher asked who said 20. I raised my hand. She told me to stand up. My head began to spin as I thought I was about to be publicly pilloried but instead she addressed the class and told the kids to look at this young man and learn from him, for he will be a man everyone will trust and respect for his honesty and willingness to admit his mistakes. "Dominic more power to you." I can't recall ever having been made to feel so good about myself after making a mistake, and although I didn't fully understand what she meant by "more power" to me it sounded real good to have more power for after all that's what made Superman famous. Those four words meant more to me than anything else that was ever said in that class.

I was now in the fifth grade and was selected to perform a part in a school play, one that would be presented before the whole student body, cum teachers and all. I played the main character in the play, the part of a student sitting at the kitchen table doing his work assignments when the Evil One came to tempt him to abandon his homework. Why the school picked this play was inexplicable since we never got homework. As a matter of fact I wouldn't be surprised if some of the students didn't know what the word meant. Mr. Evil even offered me a dime which, of course, I refused to take. I remember the applause when the play was over – I felt real important. On my way back to my class I ran into the drama teacher and handed her the dime that was used in the play. She said, "Keep it Dominic you did a fine job."

From that moment on and for several weeks I was convinced acting would be my career and that one-day I would be on the Silver Screen and all the Fitchburgers would go to see their hometown boy at the Strand Theater. I was sure I would be able to play Red Butler in Gone with the Wind better than Clark Gable did. I often walked around the house pretending I was Humphry Bogard or Edward G. Robinson. I even went as far as to try to form a theater group but couldn't find any boys who wanted to do that "sissy" stuff. Girls were willing but no way was I going to be the only boy in the group. It never occurred to me that some of the girls could play the part of boys, a sort of mirror image of what was done at Shakespeare's Globe Theater where men played the parts of women. But then why should it since at that time I hadn't heard of Shakespeare let alone about his theater group.

My memory is excellent when it comes to remembering my elementary school teachers which I cannot say about those I had in high school.

First Grade:	Miss Bryan: all she did after explaining the use of a pencil was to tell us we could nap while she read a book or shot the breeze with the second grade teacher.
Second Grade:	The pretty Miss O'Connor (cousin of Mr. Kennedy who had lost the house we moved into on Beech Street): looked like movie star Gene Tierney. Don't recall learning anything but do suspect I fell in love with her.
Third & Fourth Grade:	Mrs. Upton: She must have had bad or no teeth she could claim to be her own, for the sandwiches she brought from home were cut into tiny squares as were her apples.
Fifth Grade:	Miss McNutty: was either lazy or had bad health for it seemed her substitutes were in class as often as she was. She lived in a white house surrounded by a real white picket fence (she honest-to-goodness did) at the bottom of Beech Street, so in a way I guess she was a neighbor.
Sixth Grade:	Miss Keats: we labeled her "stretch" because she was so tall she should have been playing professional basketball. Her

favorite subject was English and she drilled and drilled us on proper grammar.

Seventh Grade: Miss Mary Larkham, also the Principal of the school: without exaggerating she must have weighed at least 250 pounds. She was the school's disciplinarian whose favorite form of persuasion was a yard-stick with which she whacked outstretched the hands of wayward students.

Miss Larkham had her favorite students, a group of five of us. Her feelings and esteem for us had nothing to do with we being particularly good academically but rather on the fact that on every other Friday we were driven in her gigantic car to her large house to mow her golf course size lawn.

A freebie from us guys to the Principal of Clarendon Street School. Well, not exactly a freebie since she did give us a glass of lemonade. But hey, we were not about to complain for it did get us out of school for a few hours.

Many of the students but none of our teachers were of Italian descent. We had limited knowledge of English a fact reflected in the gap between our grades compared to those received by kids whose parents spoke English. This language dichotomy probably made us feel inferior which we attempted to cover up by saying we Italian kids could beat the hell out of them if we wanted to.

If I had to single out a prominent event during my early school years that stood at a par with my brief acting performance as the most memorable, I must bow my head in embarrassment and say the event was connected with sports. This I say since I have long felt sports have wrong-headedly been given far too much importance and attention in the American educational system. Athletes have become the new stars in the firmament of heroes and role models.

It happened when I was in the seventh and last grade and a member of the Clarendon Street School baseball team. Easily distinguishable from the stars during the season, I got no hits and made no attention-grabbing defensive plays. We had arrived at the last game of the season and, of course, my final game proudly wearing the blue and white uniform of the school I had attended for seven years. Our opponent was the number one team in the league, Laurel Hill School. We were in second place just ½ game behind them. It was a low scoring game as we entered the sixth and last inning. We were ahead 2 to 1 but they had a man on third and another at second with two out.

During the season I had played just about every position on the team, probably because our coach was trying to find one position I could do the less harm in. On this last day our coach had me out in left field which I didn't particularly relish since I had trouble judging where fly balls would come down to earth. My greatest fear came to life, the Laurel Street batter hit a ball high in the air to left field. As I watched the ball my whole baseball life flashed past my mind. Hell why did we have to have our school janitor as a coach, someone else would surely have done a better job in preparing me for moments and plays like this. My teammates were yelling for me to catch the ball and in the process my emotional state switched from nervousness to near panic. I was about to make a last desperate lunge with both arms extended when I tripped on something, my body fell forward and the ball landed in my glove as I landed on the ground. There was the ball in the webbing of my glove. I sat up holding the glove over my head signaling the fact I had caught the ball. My teammates ran out to me yelling, "We won, we won." I got mobbed, I was the hero of the game. I sat there excited beyond belief and holding tight to the ball lest I should drop it and forfeit my hero status. The next day teachers patted me on my back and showered me with words of congratulations. But this was late spring of my last school year with a meager few weeks left. My sports hey-day, my day in the sun and my ego-inflating hero status was, like the pleasant Spring weather, soon to fade away.

High school was a near non-occurrence for me. For the first time I found myself in a school with not only mostly new but also non-Italian faces. Getting an education was as far from my mind as possible, occupied as it was with interests sprouting from an earlier event involving music which is described in a later chapter. Here are some names and associations from my four years at Fitchburg High School.

- Mr. Palmer (teacher) – never wore the same tie twice.

- George Talbot (band director) – we called mousie because of his resemblance to a rodent.

- Football - tried out for the team but quit after one day.

- Cafeteria (lunch) – place to avoid.

- Homework (assignments) – rare occurrences.

- Chemistry (laboratory) – occasionally someone dropped a stink bomb, forcing evacuation of room.

- P.E. – first day teacher told boys to wear a jock strap to protect our "family jewels."

- Girls – the best looking were already taken by football players.

- Mr. Flynn – taught history, spoke so softly no one could hear him, not that anyone cared.

- Miss Mallahy – without doubt the prettiest of the women teachers but because she only taught courses in the college program I had to settle for admiring her from a distance.

Where were my parents through all of this muddling through on my part? Why didn't they take an interest in what I was doing or not doing in school? In retrospect, I believe they were basking in the fact I was in school for it was far from unusual in those days that kids quit school to enter the labor market. Neither one of my parents got much of an education in Italy. Then there was the factor of the social milieu of the times, hard-working immigrant families thankful to be in America, employed and earning money. They were a part of a friendly Italian community and perhaps there was an underlying fear their children might venture out into the other America and in the process abandon the old world customs with which they had been weaned. It never seriously occurred to many of us children of immigrants that for us there could be college beyond graduation. College was for those rich American kids. Destiny for us was to get a steady job in a factory. Given the times in which we were living in this seemed a noble enough goal.

THE ITALIANS Of BEECH STREET

I can't think of anything unpleasant about life in our Little Italy section of Beech Street between 1935-1941 other than the times I had to cut the grass or water the tomato plants. The early 30's were hard depression years, though it would have surprised me to hear that back then. I don't recall my parents talking about the lack of money or the need to get a job. This was probably due to the fact we, like all the Italian immigrant families on our section of Beech Street, were accustomed to economic deprivation and to living simply. Both men and women worked long hours for small wages, but this was balanced out by the fact families did not spend much. Worn-out shoes were not thrown away and new ones bought, they were taken to Johnny Parisi, the local cobbler, who furnished them with new heels or soles and rendered them better than new. Buying shoes or clothes because of style changes was unheard of.

No family in my immediate world had an automobile. People walked, rode bikes or took buses, with walking being the overwhelming favorite among the three. Entertainment consisted of the movies – 10 cents for a double feature. We kids made our own sling-shots and bows and arrows, put together our own skis from barrel staves fastened to our shoes by rubber bands cut from old automobile tires and nailed into the skis. Baseballs were used until the covers were worn off. Fringe benefits came twice or three times a week when I was allowed to buy ice cream from the good humor man who, during the summer, made a daily swing up Beech Street at the exact same time – 7 pm. The selection wasn't anything to brag about compared to today but we were happy to have the chance to select among pop-ups, ice cream cups, chocolate covered ice cream on a stick or the hot weather favorite, popsicles.

We learned to be resourceful in coming up with ways to entertain ourselves. Stick-ball on the street, swimming at Parkhill Pond, Cowboys and Indians up in the Quarry. Then there was the B.A.B. (Bare Ass Beach) up on the Quarry, a pool of crystal clear water of unknown origin that formed between towering rock formations. We guys swam naked. At times we knew there were girls hiding behind boulders at a safe distance who got a giggling kick out of watching us. They would hurriedly disperse whenever we pretended to run in their direction. We stopped going to the B.A.B. after we found a dead cat in the water.

We formed a club and actually built a club-house mid-way up a sturdy tree in the Palozzi yard on Beech Street Lane where we had meetings of a sort. Experiences in the club showed that two traits of Italian character remained alive and well among the offspring of the immigrants. The first was the historical fact Italians – unlike the other European countries – had never mastered the art of political stability and orderly self-rule. Every once in a while someone would bring up the subject of having club officers or leaders just as everyone else had in America. There was a general consensus that this should be done but being young we didn't know much about what officers a club should have. All we knew was that we had to have a President. It was agreed that Alfred be given the job of finding out what officers a club should have. He reported back that besides the President we needed a Vice President, a Secretary of State, Secretary of Treasury and a Defense Secretary. That's what the book he read said that the United States had. That's when arguments broke out. Jasper said he wanted to be the Secretary of the Treasury because he had always dreamed about finding treasures, as a matter of fact he had read more treasure books that anyone else. Everyone wanted to be the Secretary of the Treasury so we were stymied as to that position. Rudy said he didn't care what the others wanted and that since he was the toughest of all of us, he said he should be the Secretary of Defense, that way he could defend the club-house. He was booed down. There was agreement only on one point, a Vice President was a no-no because we had all been told by Sister Angela in our catechism classes that vices were what bad people had and that they were the ones who would burn in the fires of hell. In the end we threw out the whole idea of electing officers and no one was elected to anything.

The other Italian character trait is the ability to quickly grasp situations and devise clever solutions. The biggest crisis we faced was when one of the guys brought a girl to the club house. She said she wanted to join together with another girl. At first we thought the idea was gut-busting funny but as she persisted our mood changed to one of concern, after all we were guys and did things and said things like guys do. We told her this was an all boys club with no room for girls. The girl said if we didn't let her join she could get a bunch of girls to come here every time we had a meeting and yell and scream so that the neighbors would complain. We huddled for a conference. We came up with an idea. OK, we told the girl she could join, but would be treated like all of the members. She said that was fine because she was just as strong as any one of us and could do anything we did. That's just great we told her and she could begin by taking off all of her clothes and walk around naked for ½ hour as we all had to do. But I'm a girl she said. Yes, but didn't she want to be treated like all other members? She decided then and there that she wasn't interested in our lousy club any longer. If this had occurred at the time this is being written we probably would have been sued for violation of the girl's Civil Rights. No such risk back then. And so it was that the first attempt to impose women's rights on us guys failed when confronted by Italian ingenuity which we accomplished without actually saying "no." Somehow word of our strategy must have gotten out to the wider world because a similar strategy was used many years later to circumvent the Anti-Discrimination Laws.

****

One of the charming features of living in our neighborhood during this period was the steady and diverse parade of services that were delivered to our door giving life a certain pulse of dependability and regularity. And in a way a homage to the importance of home as a social unit.

The first to arrive at the break of dawn was the milkman Walter, a Finish dairy farmer (there were no Italians in that business). He picked up the clean empty bottles left outside our kitchen door and replaced them with quarts of fresh milk. On Saturdays he entered our kitchen, the door to which was never locked, and left eggs, cream and cheese on the table. Around 9 a.m. Tony Catalini the bakery man stopped his vehicle in the front of our house and rang a real ding dong bell. Soon the smell of freshly baked goods wafted through the air and made its way to the surrounding houses. Housewives materialized out of nowhere to make their morning choices and to chat a while with Tony. I headed directly to the delivery truck's pastry trays and with a little luck on my side mother would say, "Alright, but only one." My favorite were the cream filled horns.

Ten o'clock was the time the ice truck made its way up Beech Street, stopping every three or four houses to deliver blocks of the frozen stuff for the ice boxes – refrigerators had not yet become cheap enough for the pockets of any of us on Beech Street. Mateo the iceman wore a thick long leather apron-like garment and used a large pair of sharp tongs to lift sizeable ice blocks which he carried into kitchens and placed in trays located at the bottom of the iceboxes. He knew by heart the size and capacity of each ice box along his route. Before delivering an ice block to a particular house he would chisel and trim a block until it fit the space of a particular ice box as perfectly as the keystones the Romans dropped into their arches. On hot summer days Mateo was our Pied Piper. We would follow his truck along Beech Street and when he was in a kitchen making a delivery, we made our way on the ice truck to pick up the ice shavings for eating or sucking, if there were none we were not beyond using stones to break off pieces from the blocks and then running for our lives before we could be seen.

Mid-morning on Wednesdays Giorgio, the knives and scissors man, drove his bike-wagon along Beech Street. He claimed he could sharpen any cutting instrument ever made. While he sat at his wheel doing his work, he would often sing Italian songs long remembered from his native land. I used to enjoy watching and listening to him.

In the summer, late afternoons were watermelon time as a truck loaded with these summer refreshers came crawling along Beech Street. A good size watermelon, with a wedge cut out to expose the ruby redness of the interior, went for around 30 cents. The daylong caravan of mobile deliverers concluded with the come-and-get-it music emanating from the ice cream truck.

Gradually things began to change. Refrigerators came and the iceman was gone. The bread and pastry truck stopped delivering, and the knife and scissor sharpener opened a shoe repair shop downtown. The watermelon truck went the way of the bread and pastry truck. The milkman and the ice cream truck continued but they were alone now, remnants of a huggable time when the home was the center of family life and in homage to it goods and services were brought to its doorstep.

Without question one of the most pleasant features of life in our section of Beech Street was the close knittedness of the Italian families that lived there. We visited each other, greeted each other from front porches, helped each other in times of need, and generally shared good and bad times. On Sundays after mass my father religiously visited three or four of the neighbors on his way home and had a glass of wine at each stop. The men organized the Venetian Club which had its physical location in the Alfred Stropparo's spacious cellar adjoining a huge, elongated backyard equipped with tables, chairs and a bocce court. Husbands checking out the neighbors' gardens and exchanging husbandry ideas on how to improve the production of the tomato plants, members of a family walking to church with members of a neighbor's family. It was that kind of neighborhood.

What a wondrous time in life were our young years. A period of loose restraints, of testing limits such as those of one's strength, endurance, imagination and parents' patience. A time to dream of things to come, of big accomplishments. A bottomless reserve of energy ready and willing to flow in whatever direction chosen by one's fancy, unencumbered by serious responsibilities or duties. A lightness, an airiness, a voracious enjoyment of living free of the restraints and circumspections that come with the responsibilities of adulthood, free from the doubts and hesitations brought on by the rules of schooled education. A time to kick off shoes and enjoy the feeling of grass beneath one's feet, to jump, run or just lay back and look at clouds passing. To swim naked in crystal clear waters, to cook potatoes in the ashes of an outdoor fire, to lose one's self in the pretty face of a girl, to sled-race down snow covered streets, to enjoy jelly donuts bought with money from shoveling driveways.

Many years later as I recalled those times I realized the profound truth underlying the elegant Taoist aphorism that "The ordinary is the extraordinary."

This depiction of my life on our part of Beech Street paints a distorted tableau of what life was like in broader America during the 1930s. These were the Great Depression years with millions of workers unemployed, homes foreclosed, property values resting at historical lows, men selling apples on street corners, others wandering the highways and byways in search of employment, families torn apart, self-esteems irreparably damaged, hope and faith in the future shattered.

If young Dominic Perenzin had been asked about all of this while he was living through the decade, he would have replied that somewhere he had heard about these problems but that things were just fine at home and in his neighborhood. This reminds me of the conversation in John Steinbeck's classic, "The Grapes of Wrath" between Pa Joad, Preacher Casey and family members when a ragged man in a transient camp described the agony he had suffered in California where Pa and his family were headed:

Pa said, "Spose he's tellin' the truth – that fella?

The Preacher answered, "He's telling the truth awright. The truth for him. He wasn't makin' nothin' up?"

"How about us," Tom demanded, "is that the truth for us?"

"I don't know," said Casey.

No question but that the closeness of our Italian community was an important factor in mitigating the effects of the Depression for all of us. That was our collective truth.

THE MAGNIFICENT STRAND

On the outside underneath the marquee still shots of scenes from the feature film were on display each protected from heist-tempted hands by plate glass. In front of the entrance to the building was a small booth where for 10¢ one could buy a ticket from the huge ticket roll.

Enter the door and straight ahead was the concession stand offering popcorn and candy bars. No drinks. Turn to the right a seventy-five square foot area where wall-to-wall stairs led up to the second floor. Climb the stairs and there some ten feet away stood a four foot wall from where three aisles led into the auditorium, one at each end and one in the center.

Welcome to the Strand Theater located in downtown Cleghorn (our section of Fitchburg). A true landmark. This was the special place where people went to be transported to new worlds, where the burdens and cares of everyday living were *non grata*. Beautiful love stories with those fabulously good-looking movie stars. Where the bad guys always got their due and justice was dispensed on a regular basis. This is where Flash Gordon transported us to the imaginative worlds of outer-space. This is where the innocent adventures of affable Mickey Rooney and lovable Judy Garland made us laugh, then cry and then led us to a sigh-of-relief ending, again re-affirming that all was well with the world.

The real everyday world was getting uglier with the stubborn depression and later the advancing shadow of World War II. Americans felt a strong need to escape the trying hardships of their world and what better place to do this than in the darkness of a theater where the silver screen assured all that things were really better than they seemed to be. If life was not easy it certainly by comparison was easier than the one depicted in the movie "The Grapes of Wrath." The Japanese whipped our butts at Pearl Harbor but the movies showed up how we were going to pound the hell out of those sneaky bastards. What better way to magic-carpet away from the painful real world than to be mesmerized by the graceful beauty of Fred Astair and Ginger Rogers.

Those were the pre-television days. For us the everyday and only public source of entertainment was the radio, while the once-a-week entertainment was the movie theater. It was a magical event anxiously awaited all week long. For six days we listened to what the big box told us, using our imaginations to fill in the images to fit the storyline. With movies no more imagination needed for the pictures were there to be seen, nothing to do but to sit back and take it all in.

As if the simple fact of movies was not enough of an attraction the movie studios came up with yet another marketing technique to keep the kids anxiously awaiting the next movie date. The idea was the "serials," with fifteen separate episodes, shown one per week inspired no doubt by the serialized soap operas of the radio. Without fail all of the serials were based on adventure stories constructed so that at the end of each episode the hero or his girl friend faced certain death – they were about to fall into a snake pit, or they were in a room where all of the walls were converging on them. "Don't Miss Next Week's Episode to Find Out What Happens" was the urgent advice flashing across the screen.

Then there were those exceptional days when the featured movie was in Technicolor the latest cinematography technology featuring eye-bogglingly beautiful and spectacular musicals with fantastic costumes and scenery. "Gone With the Wind" was a blockbuster as was "The Wizard of Oz."

Another feature were the News Reels, boring for the kids but loved by the grown-ups. These ten-minute shorts showed the events of the week. This was the only time most of the audience would ever see important national and international political personalities, athletes and other famous people walking and talking as they really were and not as still pictures in newspapers or in Life or Look magazines Did we enjoy the movies? You bet we did. We kids booed and hissed the bad guys. We yelled out warnings to the good guys who apparently were oblivious to the black-hatted menace closing in on them. We applauded when the bad guy got what was coming to him and when the good guy got the girl. Should the poor desperate widow give her daughter to the ugly and greedy landlord with the tell-tale thin moustache in payment of her back rent? We yelled out the answer "No! don't do it."

The Strand Theater was owned by the twins Edward and Paul Coutier. They together with the wife of Edward did everything except operate the film projectors and they may have actually done that too. Mrs. Coutier sold the tickets, Edward attended the concession counter. Paul Coutier collected the tickets at the top of the stairs on the second floor. This he did seven days a week, at times with the risk of bodily injury as the crowd of eager kids stormed up the steps in a frenzy to get to the front row seats.

The Strand employed a ceremony which was quaint but dramatically effective. During the time no movie was being shown the white screen was hidden from view behind a wall-to-wall velvet curtain. As two o'clock for matinee shows and seven for the evening shows approached the kids would begin stamping their feet and the adults clapping their hands in cadence. This would bring on the Coutier brothers at the back of the theater, one on each side, who then proceeded to walk with slow deliberate steps down their respective aisle to the foot of the stage as the foot stamping feet and clapping gave away to wild cheering. The brothers would majestically climb the stairs to the stage, take hold of huge ornate cords and slowly pulling on them drew open the velvet curtains exposing the white movie screen. While this pageantry was happening the audience fell into an expectant silence. The lights gradually dimmed and the show began.

Today, the building in which the Strand was located is a now a bowling alley. I've been there only once on a bitter-sweet visit. As I sat watching the bowlers hurl balls down the alleys, I could picture the Coutier brothers walking down what were now lanes #1 and #10 to the stage of the Strand Theater. The sound of pins falling gave way to the sounds of eager young kids applauding the Coutier brothers' Aida-like walk to the stage. Where dumb pins were now being knocked down by subdued players, years ago dreams were being dreamt and spirits up-lifted by the fantasy world passing before wide-eyed, mesmerized audiences. What the years have wrought reminds me of the Shakespearian quotation that headed each episode of a comic strip series, "What Fools These Mortals Be."

FIRST JOBS

I must have been around 13 years old when I earned my first for-pay services. How I ended up pitching hay onto a truck at a local farm eludes my memory. The fact of a blistering hot sun, aching back, reddened hands did little to dampen the excitement of having my first money-paying job. I felt like a man. There were about five or six of us working the field, gathering hay, putting it in neat bundles, then loading them on a truck. This was a few days summer job for which I was paid 13 United States Dollars, all of which I asked for and begrudgingly got in one dollar bill denominations.

On the last day of work, I rushed into the kitchen at 118 Beech Street holding out the money in one hand and yelling to my mother "Ma, look all the money I got."

"Bene, Bene," was her response. I sat at the table and told my mother to come and see as I counted the money. After doing so several times to assure myself it was all there, I placed the bills in a neat pack, picked it up and held it out to my mother. "For you Ma."

She looked at me and said, "No, no, its yours you earned it." But I insisted she take it. Seeing how sincere and intent I was she said she would take it to hold for me and that whenever I wanted some of it she could give it to me, however, I was not to spend it foolishly. I said no, it was for her to keep for herself and Pa.

That evening my father came up with a Salomonic solution. The money was to be split equally, $6.50 for me and $6.50 for my parents. I nodded in agreement.

If that brief summer job made me feel good about earning my own money causing me to grow at least one foot in self-esteem, it also convinced me outdoor work was not for me. And so it was that at 13 years old I had already eliminated one possible future career.

****

From farm work where all I was required to provide was my physical strength I moved on to what normally would be the classical American boy's first employment. For this job in addition to my personal services I was required to contribute capital in the form of a bike. The job consisted of going to the Sentinel production plant on Main Street and picking up my clearly marked bundle of newspapers. With the papers in a basket in the front part of the bike off I went up and down Beech Street delivering the Fitchburg Sentinel.

Whenever I got to my house at 118 Beech Street my dog Blackie would run alongside the bike. At first this was fun but it soon became a problem. At many of the houses I simply threw the folded newspaper into unfenced front yards and Blackie would run after the paper and bring it back to me. Tying him to a tree in our yard whenever I was delivering papers provided negative results as he almost choked himself attempting to get loose. Though he was an outside dog we tried keeping him indoors while I worked my route. But that didn't turn out to be a good idea for when he sensed I was near the house he ran around barking and jumping up on the windows and curtains. As a result of these failures, I had no choice but let him follow me and to get off the bike and hand deliver the Sentinel to the subscribers' porches.

One day I was going down steep Beech Street towards the Hillside Café when the bike's brakes gave out and off I went flying down the street with absolutely no control other than my feet which soon proved inadequate. I ended up in Mike Lasarra's yard with a broken wheel and me on my back. The loss of this mode of transportation meant the end of my career as a newspaper delivery boy. The pay had not been anything to brag about but I loved the fringe benefits, especially the cookies, candy and other goodies the customers sometimes gave me. I recall an "American" lady in the house at the end of Beech Street who sometimes rewarded me with a big slice of watermelon with the explanation that, "This young man needs some cooling off." I must have been some sight as I maneuvered my bike with one hand, eating watermelon with the other and trying to balance the newspaper load at the same time. I've often thought how marvelous it would be if I could have a perpetual summer and remain that young kid riding his bike down Beech Street with a cool slice of watermelon in his hands.

****

My third employment differed from the first two in that it was performed indoors at Rikers Lunch owned by the Greek Blepyros brothers and located on Fitchburg's Main Street. I started as a dishwasher and worked my way to part-time short-order cook, master of hamburgers — with and without cheese — grilled cheese, tuna salad, ham and cheese sandwiches, salisbury steak and the pork chop special.

My mentor at Rikers was a skinny, bow-legged short-order cook named Patsy who taught me just about all I learned about cooking. Patsy had two loves besides cooking – music and whiskey. Whenever he was cooking he had music on the radio. To music with a beat he danced small steps around the kitchen or in place which he could do while flipping eggs over. During these dances I was never convinced his arched legs would not collapse on him.

Patsy kept a whiskey bottle in a lower shelf behind the oils and vinegar from which he would occasionally take a swig. By the end of some days he was noticeably feeling no pain and the owner would be obliged to send him home. Patsy said he was married and had two kids, but whenever the owners called the home telephone number he gave for someone to pick up the intoxicated Patsy there was never an answer. Neither did his wife and kids ever come to Rikers.

After I had been there a couple of weeks a new waitress was hired. She was in her mid-thirties with a handsome face, what we called bedroom eyes and a slim well proportioned body of which my hormones were not insensitive. When she wasn't busy waiting on customers she sometimes came to the kitchen and we would chat. This Patsy didn't like and he did nothing to hide his distaste for her going so far as to intentionally bumping into her when she entered the kitchen.

One evening after closing time, I went downstairs where I kept my bike, my means of transportation. As I was about to leave from the back door I was startled by the waitress who appeared seemingly out of the shadows. She asked whether I was going straight home or would I like to leave my bike and she would drive me home and suggested that on the way we might stop for a drink at her place. She reached over to the bike's handle bars as if to take it from me when suddenly the lights flicked off and on. I heard footsteps on the stairs and I instinctively jumped on my bike and was gone.

The following afternoon Patsy came to me and with a stern expression that admitted of no question said I should stay away from the waitress because she was a sick bitch and if I didn't stay away from her I was going to get her sickness. My young, inexperienced mind was overwhelmed with concern. Had she touched me? What sickness did she have? I didn't dare ask Patsy any questions because the way he spoke led me to believe I should have known what he was talking about. I didn't want to appear stupid so I retreated into my imagination. It proved easy to stay away from her because within a few days she was gone. Not a word passed between us from that evening in the basement to the time she left, only an occasional wry smile from her. For some time after that what Patsy had said about her being sick stuck with me and made me wary about getting too close to any woman who looked to be as old as the waitress.

Several years later while I was home on leave from the Navy, I went to Riker's Lunch hoping to see some of the folks I knew from the old days. Charley Blepyros remembered me and we sat at a table. During the course of our conversation I inquired about Patsy. At first he didn't seem to remember him but when I mentioned the music and the whiskey he knew who I was talking about. Charley said Patsy got liver cancer, real bad. It must have been too much for him to bear so he hanged himself in his room.

I told him I seemed to remember Patsy saying he lived with his wife and kids on Summer Street and that it must have been rough on them.

According to Charley it was all a made up story for Patsy lived by himself in a tiny postage stamp room next to the Simon Mill. No one came forward to claim his body and he was buried as a pauper. Charley said that after I left he recalled Patsy saying I was a good kid and that some day I would become a good short-order cook. As it turned out Patsy was a far better chef than soothsayer.

****

During a summer vacation I answered a Help Wanted ad in the Boston Globe –college students welcome. I went to an interview, was hired and attended three days of training. The job was to sell door-to-door a chemical spray product treatment for homes which it was claimed instantly killed all bacteria in the air. The company was called, something like "United States Sanitation Services," a name surely calculated to induce a homeowner into believing there was some connection with the Government.

"Knock, knock."
"Who is it?"
"I'm with the United States Sanitation Services."
(Door immediately opens)
"Yes, what is it you want."

I would quickly flash an identification card and say, "I'm here to help you maintain an infection-free home." This would unfailingly get me into the house or apartment.

I had been on the job only a week when I quit. I made no sales but left some people in a dither about deadly bacteria in their homes, but who were unable to pay the cost of the service. On my way out of office on my last day I noticed there was a map of the Boston area on the wall with pins indicating where the salesmen were working. The pinned areas were in the poorest sectors of the city.

Of all the jobs I've held this is the only one that left me feeling culpable for it was obvious I had been part of an obnoxious scheme to take advantage of the intellectually vulnerable. A few months before I took on this job there had been a rather serious outbreak of some kind of infectious disease in the area. The guys who owned company must have known about this and it seemed pretty obvious to me they had decided to capitalize on the public's fears. The sales pitch we were given to memorize said nothing about scientific or other proof that the product in fact was effective against this disease. Nor were we prepared to respond to any questions along this line. The emphasis was on how menacing this disease was, how much suffering there would be, and how the medical expense of treating it could be devastating with no guarantee of survival. It took me some time to overcome my sense of guilt for having been a part of what I was convinced was a nefariously opportunistic business, if not an outright scam.

****

During another summer, I found redemption from my stint with United Sanitation Services as I got a job as a tutor for young children with reading problems. This was a service performed at the children's homes. Out of about ten students I had one who proved to be special. She was a black girl of around 9 years old. Once a week for several months I worked with her and she was showing progress. She had a strong desire to improve and was the most polite and sweetest of all my students. Her mother was aware of the progress but unfortunately money, or better the lack thereof, got in the way and I was told she would have to end the tutoring.

On the last day I gave the girl a brief exam in the presence of the mother. Throughout the hour I detected a strong fragrance and realized it came from the girl. At the end of the hour as I was about to leave the girl came to me, gave me a kiss and ran into another room. The mother asked me whether I noticed the strong perfume the girl was wearing. She put it on for you because this was to be her last lesson and she wanted to smell good for you. Apparently in doing so she had emptied the remains of a tiny bottle of her mother's perfume on herself. "Looks like she got a crush on you," smiled the mother.

This was definitely a feel-good kind of job in contrast to the one for United States Sanitation Services, for I actually helped kids to improve their reading which better prepared them for the future. I concluded that what kids needed in order to enjoy reading was to get them to relate in some way to what was being read. To do this I often had the students imagine themselves as one of the story's characters and then asked how they would act in certain of the situations depicted in the story. Along with improving their reading skills the children were re-writing the story and being creative.

****

My final early years job found me in a liquor store on Massachusetts Avenue in Boston, not the greatest part of town by any stretch of the imagination. In addition to waiting on customers the job called for me to make home deliveries. This proved to involve the scariest experiences I had ever had as it often meant going into the most run-down and dilapidated areas.

There were a number of bizarre situations I ran into but one in particular stood out. There was a never-fail delivery to be made every Friday evening to an apartment on Mass Avenue. The building was dingy and run-down. The apartment was located on the third floor to which I often had to climb stairs to reach since the elevator was seldom operating. The halls were dark, hardly helped by low-watt bulbs strategically placed so as to be as ineffective as possible. The stairwell was dirty and dank with the indescribable smell of human waste. I was sure I would be mugged one day.

I never got a good look at the person who was receiving the fifth of Gordon's Gin week after week. My ringing of the doorbell produced a "Come in the door's open." Oddly enough it was always open though it had at least four different types of locks on it. The apartment had a heavy musty odor about it, the furniture over-stuffed and out-sized and belonging to another era. The occupant never made herself totally visible, unfailingly sitting somewhere in the shadowy corner of the room.

She appeared to have a substantial body judging from what I could make out and from the huskiness of her voice. She often sat with her hands on her knees. Occasionally I thought I saw her nose, mouth or eyes but these quickly shifted as if under water giving me the impression I was imagining them. One part of her body was often clearly visible, a large swollen, uncovered leg which she kept extended. The sight gave me goose pimples, it seemed to be covered with red welts. It was almost as if she intentionally had light reflect on it though I never saw the possible source of the light.

"Put the gin on the table and pick up the money, there's a tip there for you," were, with one exception, the only words she directed to me during the eight or ten times I made my Gordon's Gin deliveries. The exception was on my second visit when she asked me my name. "Are you a student, what are you studying, where do you go to school?" I had the impression she looked forward to my short visits.

Whenever I went to the apartment I did so with a queasy uneasiness. My attempts to get information about her from the manager of the liquor store were unavailing. All he knew was that she called in faithfully every Friday for her Gordon's Gin and that was just fine with him. After I explained what the lady was like, he said if I thought she was strange I should stick around a while and I would see some real freaky of-the-wall cases, adding that all he cared about was the fact they bought his booze.

PART TWO

PEOPLE

NEIGHBORHOOD PERSONALITIES

When the mind is reduced to its final embers the images that arise are often not those of beloved ones but of obscure, isolated figures long stored somewhere in the deep recesses of memory. (anonymous origin)

Our neighborhood had its share of colorful characters, perhaps a little more than its share. In reminiscing over this period faces of certain unique characters flicker across my vision. Some were humorous, others pathetic, still others creepy, but all entertaining in their own way. They helped to add color and spice to the scenes of daily life in our neighborhood.

Matty was a slightly built, quiet sort of guy with an oversized family. His kids were known for their good manners, always polite and never seemed to get into trouble. While otherwise quite normal Matty had one peculiarity, he always, that is to say every day both day and night, wore a cap. During the day it was a baseball cap type of headgear and in the evening, so went the story, he wore a night-cap to bed. The explanation in general circulation for his cap hang-up was that he had had some kind of scalp problem when he was young which left him bald. Ashamed of this he kept his condition under wraps. It was said that as time passed his scalp got whiter and whiter and his embarrassment grew in tandem so he continued to wear a cap. When he went to church on Sundays he stood outside the door so he wouldn't have to remove his cap. People jokingly offered him money to remove his cap which he steadfastly refused.

One Saturday afternoon a group of fellows from the neighborhood were at the Hillside Cafe drinking beer, talking and generally having amiable fun. Among them was Matty. He wasn't much of a drinker nor did he particularly like being around when the guys began "feeling their beers." This particular afternoon many lagers had been downed and the customers were getting increasingly boisterous. Matty got up from the table when without forewarning a drunken customer who was horsing around with several others practically threw himself at him and in the act grabbed Matty's cap and pulled it off. Whether this was intentional or the result of the drunkard's imbalance was anybody's guess. Matty's normal voice – when he spoke at all – matched his small frame, and was weak and high-pitched-womanly. But when his cap came off a howl bellowed from his throat that was so loud and deep that the bar became instantly silent. The drunkard was so taken by the outraged howl that the cap fell from his hands. Matty pounced on it, placed it back on his head and quick-paced it out of the café mumbling indistinguishable words. For a few moments there was silence in the bar as the patrons looked at each other with disbelief.

As time passed this event became a popular subject of discussion at the Hillside. During those confusing few moments when Matty's cap lay on the floor did anyone get a look at his head? Many had their own *on-my-mother's-grave* sworn descriptions: He had patches of yellowish hair. He had huge wrinkles on this noggin, almost like trenches. You're all wrong, he didn't have any top to his head, only some kind of funny looking skin. The more time elapsed from that Saturday afternoon the more bizarre became the opinions.

Some four years later he died. Out of respect for what seemed his life-long wish his children decided he should be buried with his cap on. If anyone, anywhere ever knew for certain what in fact lay beneath Matty's cap he or she never came forward to reveal the secret. His wife remained tight-lipped on the subject and carried the secret with her to her grave.

****

Not unlike Matty, Bruno Rosano was a slightly built and soft spoken neighbor. He was the type of guy who could easily go through life without attracting much attention except for one personal trait – he loved his wine, or as far as that goes, anyone's wine. Since our neighborhood was almost pure Italian, homemade wine was ubiquitous, bestowing on Bruno the delight of a mosquito in a nudist camp.

Bruno's surrender to his addiction was so complete that he gradually convinced himself that he loved his neighbors so much that he was part of just about every household in the immediate area, giving him the right to help himself to any wine around the house. This he did though there was no one at home and the house door was left open, which was customary in those times. Not that he wouldn't help himself if there was someone at home and an offer of a glass of wine was too delayed in coming.

In a neatly shingled one story nearby house lived Malena with her son Johnny. I never saw Malena's husband and according to back-yard scripture the idea of his existence was a figment of Malena's imagination. What was not a figment of anyone's imagination was the attitude of the neighborhood's married women towards Malena. In their opinion, men, particularly those wearing a wedding band, should stay away from that woman, for with her wiles she could ensnarl and tempt them into the world of sinful lust, and down the slippery slope of perdition. Reason. Malena was a tall, stately woman, full breasted with a very shapely figure, high cheek bones supporting soulful dark eyes. A sort of poor man's Sophia Loren.

Though there were no reported incidences of Malena bewitching or luring men into her web of passion, still there was a nervous spousal concern about the lurking risk to any weak, pleasure-seeking husband. After all, Malena lived alone, assuredly a formula for trouble.

On a fall afternoon a neighbor knocked anxiously on Mrs. Rosano's door to inform her she was sure she had just seen her husband Bruno enter Malena's house. What? You saw what?

There were a few more questions, each in a louder and more agitated tone. By this time the Rosano children were at the door asking what was the matter. I knew Bruno fairly well for my father's wine seemed to be one of his favorites. Occasionally, after a few glasses he flipped a couple of pennies or even a nickel at me. It was not clear whether he was paying for the wine or simply being generous to me, I conveniently assumed the latter to be the case.

When Mrs. Rosano came out of the house with the informer, I was playing catch with a neighbor in front of her house. It didn't take me long to realize what was going on. Mrs. Rosano's friends and family gathered on the sidewalk in front of her house and were angrily looking in the direction of Malena's house. I ran to Malena's house through her back yard to warn Bruno. I found him sitting at the kitchen table with a half-empty bottle of wine while Malena was cleaning her stove. No sooner had I told him what was happening when

51

we heard the voices of Mrs. Rosano and her entourage of indignant women angrily approaching. Bruno told Johnny and me to go out and pretend we were going to play and that if we were asked about him to say he had left.

Peeking from behind the kitchen curtains Bruno saw his wife – who had not been convinced by my statement regarding his departure – open the front gate and with headless broomstick in-hand walk towards the front door. Without hesitation he ran to the back bedroom, opened the window, squeezed his way out and dashed down the yard towards Rockland Street. One of the neighbors shouted out to Mrs. Rosano that Bruno was running down the yard. Crouching behind bushes at the bottom of the yard Bruno lost his footing and slid down the embankment into Mrs. Canora's backyard, landing just barely beyond the reach of a less than cordial barking German Sheppard who was straining against the rope that mercifully tethered him to a tree.

Mrs. Canora came out to see what was happening. Bruno managed to hurriedly string enough words together to give a general explanation. Come with me, she said as she led him into her kitchen and helped him squeeze into a space under the sink and then drew the curtains which served to close off the space. No sooner had he crammed himself into the enclosure when shouts came from the top of the embankment. Canora went out and told Mrs. Rosano she had not seen her husband but that if she did see him she would let her know. After Mrs. Rosano and friends left Canora returned to the kitchen, pulled the curtain aside to help Alfonso out but found only empty space. He was gone. It took Canora some time and scrubbing to rid the space of the smell of urine.

Later that evening Bruno was reported to have been seen with grimy shirt, torn pants and bleeding elbow sitting on a bench in the park across from Cucciara's store. His two older sons and my father went to the park and after a lengthy conversation the four returned home. Bruno was exiled to his front porch where he slept every night for a week. From that eventful day on whenever he passed Malena's house his pace quickened to a quasi-trot, eyes fixed straight ahead. As for me, for weeks thereafter I was given a stern look by Mrs. Rosano which I supposed was for having lied to her about Bruno's whereabouts. She once frightened the wits out of me by telling me that the tongues of those who lie will someday fall out of their mouths and that they will never again be able to speak a word.

****

Everyone called her "Canora." Whether this was her first or surname I never did know. What I do know is that she looked ancient – some claimed she was over 100 years old and that she was born old. Her frame was emaciated and bent encompassing as it did all of her less than five feet. Remove her skin and you would have had a skeleton. The wrinkles on her face were in large folds, so much so her eyes appeared at times to vanish into them. Then there were her long, thick woolen socks without which she was never seen, be it winter, summer or in between. Her fingers were long for her diminutive size giving her hands a claw-like appearance.

Canora lived on Rockland Street in a small house with her son Tony, who though well into his thirties had never worked a day in his life, preferring to hang around local barrooms. It was a mystery as to how they managed to cover their living expenses. Certainly she was not indifferent to her son's indolence for she often referred to him as her "bum son." Canora was known in all of the bars in the vicinity, not as a patron but as a mom looking for her son. When she found him he would obediently follow her home.

When not out looking for her son, Carnora could be found at home smoking powerful Parodi cigars accompanied by a glass of red wine. This was obvious upon entering her house for the two complementary odors seemed to have been absorbed by the walls of her rooms. An errand kids looked forward to with relish was to buy her Parodi cigars from Cucciara's store which got them a 5 ¢ tip. She never took a regular mouthful of wine, preferring to sip it much like one would sip tea. Jokingly people said she was either a British Lady in an Italian body or she was an Italian signora with an illusion of being British.

Canora had no known close friends though her visitors were not infrequent. Young and not so young went to her seeking advise on their problems for which she had earned a reputation of being a wise woman. Then there were those who saw her as a sorceress and as proof pointed out her alleged resort to the use of strange cards, tiny stone-pebbles and trances in dispensing her counsel. Regardless, many who turned to her for help swore by her and claimed she was wonderfully helpful.

There was one particular instance which did little to dispel the dark beliefs about her. A young girl, not known in the immediate neighborhood, came running out of Canora's house one day and upon reaching the street threw herself on the ground and began screaming as her body shook violently in convulsions. People came out from their houses to see what was happening. No one dared approach let alone offer to help until Canora came walking down the steps of her house with an agitated pace went to the girl and said something to her that calmed her convulsions. Canora led her back into the house. Though people waited for some time for the girl to come out, it was said she never did.

When I was attending elementary school I got an infection in the thumb of my right hand. It got so bad that it had ballooned out almost to the size of a ping-pong ball. My thumb was operated on at Burbank Hospital and to this day I bear the ugly scar-reminder of that hospital stay.

Less than two years later my left hand thumb decided to do a replay of the experience of the right hand thumb. Same pain, same puffing out to ping-pong dimension. Up to there the histories of the thumbs were identical but from that point on things would be quite different. Pay doctor Backman so that he can butcher your other thumb, never was my Mother's response to the suggestion that I be taken to a doctor. We are going to see Canora that's what we'll do.

Come here Domenico, let me see your thumb. Canora touched the thumb and placed it against her cheek. She told me to follow her as she led me towards her kitchen. Passing through the kitchen I noticed a shelf space containing an array of empty bottles of different sizes and shapes, leaves, bottles filled with colorful liquids as well as an assortment of trays. Noticing that I was looking at this collection of items Canora stopped, pointed to them and said I wouldn't need any of them. We went out into her back yard where her German Sheppard stood barking at us. "STOP" she shouted at the dog. He reacted as if he had run into a wall, gave a little ground, stood still for a moment then begrudgingly dropped to the ground where he lay watching us. She went over and snipped off a fairly large leaf from the grass and went back into the kitchen. We followed. She took my hand, rubbed the leaf over the thumb, then placed the leaf around the thumb and tied a strip of cloth around the leaf-covered thumb. She told my mother she would find these same leaves in her yard. Once a day I was to repeat what she did with a fresh leaf. Two days later my bandages were soaked in puss. Four days later my thumb had returned to its normal size.

After Canora's death, there were all nature of theories about who she really was. It was observed that unlike the other Italian homes there were no religious pictures or icons in her home. Her neighbors across the street swore that on some nights they could see what appeared to be a transparent, luminous blue haze hovering over her house.

Following Canora's funeral Tony was hospitalized and later placed in a retirement home where he became permanently bedridden. His body progressively emaciated and he spoke less and less until he stopped completely. It is said that when he died his body had shrunk to the size of his mother's when she died - a virtual skeleton. A picture of his mother which had been placed on the headboard of his bed during his entire stay at the retirement house was placed in his coffin. A piece of paper was found under his mattress with three words in Italian written by an unsteady hand and repeated several times. "Sorry Mama."

****

The Cristanos house was diagonally across the street from Malena's house. Generally considered rather eccentric there was little socializing between them and their neighbors. The family consisted of husband Pietro, wife Rosa and six daughters. From their early years the Cristanos girls were guarded by Piero as one would care for a cherished treasure. Something not to be touched nor looked at in a certain way.

Piero's all consuming concern were boys i.e. all boys, those "Indecent, trouble-seeking wise guys who were always on the prowl for young innocent girls." As a result, the girls were allowed out of their house only for school, church and occasional trips to stores but always accompanied by one of the parents. The girls were not allowed to talk to boys unless they were visitors and then only under the watchful eye of the father or the mother. On one occasion Piero caught a daughter at an open window talking to a boy standing on the street. Within one week the house was surrounded by a six-foot wooden fence with all views of the street cut off.

It was rumored that after the father's death two of the girls became pregnant *sans* husbands. The headstone on Piero's grave must have trembled violently.

****

I was fond of Rino. He was a good guy and an excellent tailor. He regularly went to Boston to pick up work. He used to tell me stories about his life in Italy and how he decided to become a tailor when his tailor father lost both of his gangrened arms.

Rino was as close as one could get to being a clone of Hollywood's Gary Cooper. Tall, erect, slow talker, good looking, shy, compassionate and as honest as they came. His wife Sia, many years his junior, was young, restless and very pretty. They were as incongruous a couple as could be imagined, a real study in contrast. She had become pregnant several times but was never able to fulfill the biological promise, so the couple remained childless much to Rino's disillusionment.

Rino never gave any indications in public that he blamed Sia for their childlessness, to the contrary, over the years he seemed to wax increasingly doting and indulging perhaps hoping this would induce family effects. It had become a platitude to hear people comment on how fortunate Sia was to have such an ideal husband. Apparently, these comments never reached Sia's ears for one day while Rino was at work she packed a suitcase and walked away.

Rino took this as one who had just been told by his days on this earth were numbered, understandable for a guy whose life revolved around his wife. After that he was seldom seen outside his house. On some evenings no lights at all shone from his house. Most of the people who tried to visit were left knocking at his door.

One Saturday morning a powerful odor of gas was detected around the front of Rino's house. Firemen broke the windows and climbed in. There in the kitchen slumped on a chair next to the gas stove was the lifeless body of Rino with one end of a rube on his lap and the other end connected to the gas stove.

Sia never showed her face at Rino's funeral. Several months later she married Giorgio Carone, the wealthy owner of the Carone Food Stores. As in the case of Rino, Giorgio too was much older than Sia, but in his case a widower with several children. It was rumored that Sia mistreated the children and soon became the object of their wrath. But despite the domestic hostility she managed to extract as many material benefits as she could from the marriage. And in a spirit of exhibitionism and presumably to spite wagging tongues she drove up Beech Street flaunting her new cars.

Within less than five years Giorgio fell seriously ill, was hospitalized and diagnosed as having terminal cancer. Learning of this Sia made several trips to the hospital with papers for Giorgio's signature which he refused to sign. Sia became desperate and attempted to deceive him into signing what she claimed were hospital-required documents. Eventually, Giorgio gave in and signed what turned out to be his Last Will and Testament in which it was stated he left all his estate to Sia including all his Food Stores. After his death Sia learned that before dying Giorgio had legally transferred all his assets to his children leaving Sia with a worthless piece of paper. For the people on Beech Street this was poetic justice.

****

Pablo Neruda, the famous Chilean poet, said in his Memoirs that his mission was to, "go singing through the world." Reduce the world to Beech Street and the same can be said of Angela. Music was her passion. But the comparison ends there for she was also the most unkempt woman on our street identifiable by her messy, desperate hair. She wore the same dress for days on end complemented by shoes in need of attention.

She was illiterate and had no inclination to change that. What she knew was gleaned from personal experience and from anecdotal information and stories heard over the years.

She began her daily trek up Beech Street just after lunch, stopping often along the way to chat and laugh with neighbors. And laugh she did a lot of for she had talent for turning a conversation into humor, always looking for the lighter side of events and poking fun at people who she thought took life too seriously. One of her favorite sayings was, "Life is too short to be wasted on serious thoughts." I once heard her also say that too much learning dried up the heart. Not bad for an illiterate. Angela loved wine, red wine that is. Several glasses were consumed during her daily trips up Beech Street. She was well known by everyone on the street so that when she stopped at a house it was customary for the neighbor to serve her a glass of red wine. Drunk-drunk she never got just ever enough to allow free-reign of her light-hearted and buoyant personality.

She was equally well known for her love of singing Italian songs which she belted out with the deepest of gusto. Her voice was passable and what it lacked in aesthetic quality was made up in volume and feeling. Sometimes her singing was contagious and she would be joined by those around her. When there was a long break in a conversation in which she was not particularly interested, Angela would start humming. In the summer she could often be found sitting on a neighbor's front porch and there, joined by two or three other housewives and a bottle of wine, sing and laugh part of the afternoon away. Passerbys were hard put not to smile in amusement and appreciation of the free concert.

Angela died at the early age of 50, leaving children who could neither sing nor who enjoyed red wine. After her death her husband, a strong contender for the title of Mr. Silence of the World, spent the rest of his life walking the streets of Fitchburg, some said in search of his troubadour wife.

****

Not all of the characters in our neighborhood were from outside the Perenzin family. We had our own very special one, his name was Blackie our canine mongrel. I don't recall how he came to us it seems to me he was just always there just like the rest of the family. His name is a giveaway as to his color, pure black from head to tail except for a conspicuous brown spot the size of a half-dollar coin above his right eye. What breeds contributed to his mixed ancestral status were impossible to determine, perhaps because of too many past dilutions. I doubt any respectable canine breed would admit to being a part of Blackie's mixture, he was that mongrel-looking. This fact did nothing to deter him from being promiscuously active around the neighborhood as confirmed by the occasional appearance of black puppies with single brown spots.

Blackie was an "outside" dog, seldom if ever allowed in the house This he didn't seem to mind at all for he enjoyed the outdoors and was my faithful companion wherever I went, particularly up in the quarry and surrounding woods. It was probably his enjoyment of the outdoors and all that it contained which led to our biggest Blackie drama.

I remember that morning vividly. My mother had been in the backyard and entered the kitchen holding her nose saying, "My God there has been a skunk here." Soon the smell made its way into our house and around the neighborhood.

My father who was searching around the back of the house yelled, "this dog stinks," as he backed away from Blackie. In response to our yelling at him Blackie ran to the side of the back porch and squeezed his way underneath. My father tried to look inside through a horizontal opening just large enough for the dog to get through. Unable to see into the interior darkness he got a flashlight. "Oh Hell!" there's a dead skunk in there." The only way to get the animal out proved to be to remove planks from the back porch which my father did all the while cursing Blackie.

When a couple of months later Blackie found and killed another skunk and dragged it too underneath the back porch, my father decided to seal the opening. We were puzzled by the fact that Blackie was able to withstand the revolting, sickening skunk odor in order to kill the animal. It wasn't that

Blackie had lost his sense of smell which he proved whenever my mother was cooking. Perhaps we should have had a postmortem conducted on his olfactory system. Who knows we might have discovered scientific medical information useful to mankind.

I recall our neighbor Mr. Battistela yelling at me from across the street, *"Domenico, I'ma gonna keel your dog, I gotta gun here."* Blackie had been caught several times digging holes in Mr. Battistella's garden, a thing he never did in our or other people's gardens. My father told me we would have to get rid of Blackie. Distressed, I took him to the back of our shed and there, where my mother found us, I sat holding him in my arms and crying. All that was missing from this *tableau* was some background music, perhaps an aria from a Puccini opera. Moved by the scene she convinced my father to let him stay. This proved to be the first of a number of reprieves Blackie would receive. His fatal downfall came as a result of bites from a struggle with a woodchuck.

ANTONIO AND ANTONIA

There was a standard joke around our neighborhood that I was really the milkman's son. At first I didn't get the double *entendre* for in a sense Antonio had indeed been a milkman back in Italy.

Story telling was not one of his favorite activities and his repertoire, as it were, was quite limited. Favorite among his stories and the one he told and re-told with the greatest relish was about his experiences in the First World War. At the time of the War in 1914 he was married and had his residence in the USA, however, he was visiting Italy with my mother when the war began. Before he fully understood what was happening he was wearing the uniform of the Italian Army for he was still an Italian citizen.

The First World War was perhaps one of the bloodiest ever fought. Armies engaged each other in hand–to-hand combat. Soldiers spent days and weeks in trenches filled with mud, with rain and bone-chilling dampness their constant companions. Soldiers carried rifles, knives, hand-grenades and pistols. When arm-to-arm combat was imminent bayonets were fixed to rifles converting them into dual - purpose instruments of combat.

My father was involved in one hand-to-hand combat where his right arm was cut by a German bayonet. He bore the scar from that wound the rest of his life.

Whenever in years later my father told the story of his hand-to-hand combat he would, as indisputable evidence of what happened, roll up the sleeve of his right arm to show the permanent scar left by the German's bayonet. It was far from a pretty sight but all the kids in the neighborhood wanted to see Tonyo's scar. While some vets proudly exhibited their medals father just as proudly showed his scar.

Antonio Perenzin basked in the joy of living, a full-fledged extrovert who relished being with people. At get-togethers his sonorous voice could be heard above all the rest. Like my grandfather he was a soft touch and often helped friends with financial problems. Not that his money coffers were overflowing but he could always find a way to spare something for a friend, not infrequently to my mother's visible chagrin as she did her best to reign in any excesses.

Father was a worker of boundless energy. I can't recall a single time when he missed a day of work because of illness. As far back as my memory is able to stretch he was always a foundry worker. His daily work-week routine was rigid. Up at 5:30 a.m. Mother got up to make coffee and prepare his lunch box, always the same black metal container resembling a mailbox. He broke off the top of an egg, poured a little red wine into the egg and drank the raw mixture. Next, a large bowl of coffee and milk into which he would put a man-size chunk of Italian bread. By 6:15 he left the house with the black lunch box under his arm and went down Beech Street to the corner of Kimbal next to the Hillside Café.

At 4:30 the co-worker dropped father off at the same corner. Tired and grimy from the day's labor he would climb Beech Street to our house. My sister Mary and I awaited anxiously for him on our front porch for we knew his black lunch box contained a candy bar for us. Always the same candy bar. Always the same argument about one or the other having gotten the biggest piece. No sooner was he in the house when he took a bath – we had no shower – with little talking between arrival and bath. In the summer, with the forever present glass of wine in his hand he would walk out into his beloved garden to check on his tomato plants, bean stalks, cabbages and whatever other vegetable he may have planted that spring. Dinner finished back he went into the garden, this time to do a little gentle re-arranging of the earth mounds around the plants, nipping off leaves here and there and finally out came the water hose. During this gardening he sometimes interrupted his work to go to the fence to talk to a neighbor or actually go to the neighbor's garden to give or get advise on proper husbandry. It was from my father that I first learned to appreciate the wonder of nature as exposed in the things that grew in our garden and how important it was that humans help nature fulfill its promise.

Garden work finished he visited or received a visit from a neighbor. Socializing concluded, he would sit in his favorite rocking chair to read the Italian newspaper delivered daily from New York. Then to bed – no radio, no TV (didn't have the latter) – for a good night's sleep so as to be able to start his daily routine afresh at dawn.

My participation in this daily pattern came in three stages, the candy bar episodes, helping with the watering of the garden and in the course of his Italian newspaper reading listening to his report about interesting items. I don't recall father ever speaking to me in English.

Father was never one to get involved in my life, particularly when it came to matters of education. At times I felt it was because he didn't want to be embarrassed by not understanding what I was studying, for while his formal education was short-lived, his broader education was obtained from his day-to-day real life experiences. It proved unnecessary to embarrass him with questions about my homework, because as far as I recall there was none. Neither were there any books in our house. Whatever I did or did not do up through high school was done on my own initiative or unhampered indifference. This lack of home supplement to school learning placed me at a disadvantage with kids who didn't have such a vacuum at home, particularly the kids whose parents were English speaking. This stark personal experience as well as similar experiences of others I have known has done much to convince me of the vital importance of a supportive home environment in establishing the foundation for future success of children. No question about this.

The Italian men from our neighborhood formed the Venitan Club which had its physical location in the basement of Alfred Stroparro's house which opened up to a huge backyard. Each member was required to either donate several gallons of wine or in lieu thereof to make a cash contribution. My father always contributed from his home-made wine which was the hands-down favorite. On the wall behind the bar a sign read, "*IN VINO VERITAS*" (in wine there is truth).

During the summer, tables and chairs were moved outside into the backyard under the richly foliaged trees. Here on weekends members drank wine, played cards and bocce. On special occasions there was singing to the accompaniment of Mr. Bianchini's accordion. The men had created a wonderfully warm and friendly ambience, a tiny microcosm of *La Bella Italia.*

During the late forties father had his first heart attack. He was never the same after that. Pale, listless and disoriented, he moped around the house. At that time by-pass and angioplasty operations were unknown as were the marvelous drugs that would come to market some 15 years later. Too late for him.

****

How does one go about writing dispassionately about one's mother, particularly if one is Italian. My greatest shock was to hear a friend say he hated his mother and wanted nothing to do with her. This fell on my ears like barbaric blasphemy. For the life of me I could not comprehend how a person could feel that way and concluded he must have been mentally deranged or a visitor from a distant planet. Paradoxically, I had considered the guy who said this to otherwise be a good, kind, and self-effacing person.

The mother figure permeates Italian life. Every year popular songs are written about *"la Mama." Mama Mia* is the most common exclamation among Italians. Wounded soldiers even those who are married often call out for their mothers. The next most common exclamation is "Madonna" the spiritual equivalent of mother, and the universal symbol of suffering and self-sacrificing womanhood. The Catholic Church itself has promoted this national tendency. It has been rightly observed that for Italians Jesus Christ shares His supreme standing with His Mother, almost with equal ranking.

In contrast to her husband, Antonia was a quiet and very private person, one of few words. Her life revolved around the home. Her universe was her family and her neighbors. She took pleasure in being alone, to sit, relax and think. She reminded me of a poignant saying by the philosopher Blaise Pascal:

> *All Man's miseries derive from not*
> *being able to sit quietly in a room alone.*

Though neither she nor those who knew her closely ever used the word "meditation", that was in fact what she was doing. It came to her as the natural order of things and not as a learned discipline. She would sit comfortably erect, close her eyes and remain silent and unmoving. I learned not to disturb her at these times.

Mother ran a tight ship. From an early age we were taught to keep our rooms neat and orderly, a practice I never forgot. Dinner was at 5 p.m. not a single minute earlier or later. Sunday Mass was at 10:30 a.m. and I was expected to sit next to her, regardless of where my father sat. The weekly menu seldom saw any variation as to certain core dishes. Thursday was veal day – my mother didn't like veal but father did. Fridays was *pasta fagioli* day. For Sunday lunch it was chicken and *polenta* or *risotto*.

Delectable magic was what she worked in the kitchen. A simple item such as steak was prepared in a combination of olive oil and butter that filled the kitchen with waves of an aroma that made one's mouth salivate Pavlovian-like, a delight that ended only when the last bite was taken and the last spot of the steak juices had been sopped from the cooking pan with a piece of Italian bread. Ravioli were seldom if ever purchased, they were made from scratch with the pasta itself hand made by mother. I remember the sheets of thin pasta spread on a cloth-covered table and mother spacing balls of meat, spinach and cheese in neat orderly rows on half of the sheet and then covering them by folding over the other half. From this the individual ravioli were cut. Pasta sauces were made at home using tomato sauces prepared by her from home grown tomatoes. All ingredients were fresh and savory. The tomatoes flaming red, plump and garden juicy, the tomato paste thick and rich.

At Christmas time mother would bake her own version of Italian Christmas cookies. Again the aroma wafting from the kitchen convinced me Christmas should be every week. Long before the Miami Youth Fair people ever thought of elephant ears, mother Perenzin was making their precursor first-cousin called *"crostoli"* in her kitchen. Many years later when I was in the Navy I often thought of her *crostoli* and my mouth watered as did my eyes.

Seldom if ever did mother remove her apron when at home, except for those times when we had visitors, but only special visitors. Perhaps she looked on the apparel as a kind of chevron of honor as a devoted housewife and mother. She loved the two pockets in her aprons for it was there that she carried the accoutrements of her trade; tiny scissors, a truncated pencil and half a folded sheet of paper, a handkerchief, some change, a thimble and a few safety pins. Her aprons were so much a part of her that whenever her birthday or Christmas gift-time came around at least one gift would be an apron. When my mother died the only item I took from her home was an apron which I still have. The quintessential keepsake of Mama.

For a while mother's life was harsh. Up at 5:30 a.m., coffee and lunchbox for father. Breakfast for herself, lunchbox for herself and me. Out of the house by 6:30 and to my aunt Angela's house where I would remain until I left for school at 7:30. She then punched her card in the time clock of the Fitchburg Yarn Company where she worked until three in the afternoon. She picked me up at 3:30, went home and began her housewife duties, washing, cleaning, preparing dinner. Then there was the making of home preserves, the caring of her flower garden. This routine underwent changes when I was about 8 years old and she had become a full time homemaker.

Again unlike my father, mother devoted a lot of time to me. I recall joyful hours listening to her stories about life in Italy, tales replete with magic, witches, angels and animals. Often her stories were about people who fell from great heights of fame and fortune by some totally unexpected, fortuitous turn of events – sometimes with a humorous twist or giggle at her own story endings. There was one particular story she told me several times which she said had been told to her by her grandmother:

> *A huge bird swooped down from the sky, caught a chicken and flew away. An Italian fox was watching and wanted the chicken for himself, so he followed the bird for miles and miles. The bird was aware of the fox's pursuit and kept trying to lose him. Finally, he gave up and alighted on a tree. The fox arrived and said "I guess you're wondering why I'm following you right?"*
> *"The bird remained silent, the chicken still in its mouth."* *Well I'll tell you why. Its because you're the most beautiful bird these eyes of mine have ever seen. Lovely feathers, great colors. And I hear your voice is the most beautiful in this kingdom, you must be the king of all birds. Will you sing for me?" So thrilled at hearing this the bird opened his mouth to sing and the chicken fell from his mouth. The fox caught the chicken and ran off.*

"Be careful of people who pay you compliments and then ask a favor," was her warning.

"Mother, was the big bird Italian too?" I asked.

"No," she said, "he was French." I didn't get it.

"Do you want to know how I know the fox was Italian?"

"Why," I asked.

"Well the reason is that when the fox reached home with the chicken Mrs. Fox was there waiting with a big pot of *polenta*." Then she would burst out laughing.

When I was in college one of our assignments in English was to study Aesop, among his fables was the story of The Fox and The Crow. I asked my mother one day about her grandmother. She said her grandmother lost the use of both legs in an accident, after which she spent her days in a kind of wheelchair. She took up reading, particularly two books which she read and re-read many times. I asked her about the story she told me about the big bird and the chicken. She admitted to having changed the story a little to make it more humorous. She had added the part about the fox being Italian. I asked myself whether her grandmother living on a meager farm in the early 1800's could have read Aesop or was it an amazing coincidence.

Mother's greatest love outside the family was her flower garden where she spent many hours. During the summer it was a common sight to see her bent over her flowers clearing away weeds and sprinkling water over them. She spoke to her flowers complimenting them, blandishing the younger and fragile while cursing the intruding weeds. All a labor of love for this, her second family. She never cut any of the flowers to adorn the inside of the house nor would she consider doing so for this would have been a sacrilege, a felony, an unspeakable crime.

Antonia was a very private person. Though she enjoyed having company visit she also didn't appreciate them staying long. If people overstayed their welcome – which could be measured in minutes not hours – she would let them know, not by rudely saying so, but by conveying the message by subtle gestures such as voice modulations, eye movements and nervous shifting of her sitting position. She enjoyed quiet moments alone.

If my mother was ever ill she kept this to herself. To picture her in bed anytime between 6 a.m. and 8 p.m. would have required a powerful imagination. There was one exception to this which occurred when I could not have been more than four or five years old. We were alone in the kitchen, I was sitting at the table and she in a rocking chair near the window. She was sewing. There was a knock at the kitchen door, then a second and third knock. I looked over to mother who had dropped her sewing materials and was gesturing with her hand for me to open the door. Strange noises came from her mouth, it was as if she had a large object in there and was trying to talk around it. I climbed down from the chair, went to the door and after several efforts managed to open it. It was our neighbor Mrs. Quarella, mother's cousin. She stepped into the kitchen and exclaimed, "*Madonna Mia*, Antonia what's wrong?" for she appeared to be chocking and her eyes were being sucked into their sockets. Mother tried to extend her arms to her cousin but collapsed in the effort. Mrs. Quarella ran to her, lifted up her head and repeated "*Madonna mia* she's swallowed her tongue its gone, its gone." The next thing I remember was my mother in bed upstairs, doctor Morgan at her side and my father sitting in a chair, unwashed from his day in the foundry. She was up and active the next day as if nothing had happened. Never again would I see her in bed sick until the very end-years of her life.

This incident did not leave me unaffected. I recall my father saying to me for weeks after to stop sticking my tongue out, and asking what was wrong with me. Though I never answered this question I knew dam well I would never let happen to me what happened to my mother. I was going to make sure I didn't swallow my tongue.

On a more positive note, an event which represented a major high point in mother's life was the day she traveled to Washington, D.C. to take the oath of citizenship. She began preparing for the trip – which was to last three days – a week before. Selecting clothing, arranging for bills to be paid, making sure we would not starve during her absence, figuring and refiguring how much money she would need. Though she had successfully taken her citizenship exam and despite the fact she would not be asked any more questions, she insisted on reviewing her exam notes, "Just in case someone asks me a question in Washington." Then there was the matter of a dress. Mother was showing my father the clothes she had set aside for the trip when he commented that for such an important occasion she should have a new dress. Her reaction was immediate. "We should not add another expense to this trip." But as the departure date approached closer she showed signs of a mind-change. Did father really think we could afford a new dress. In the end she gave in and bought herself a new dress, the first one in years.

Her visit to Washington was dream-like as she saw most of the landmarks she had read about – the Capitol Building, White House, Lincoln Memorial and Washington Monument. The climax came when a U.S. Supreme Court Justice administered the oath. She said she had tears in her eyes, remembering the day years ago when she received the letter from her brother urging her to come to America. When asked which Justice had granted oath she said she didn't remember but that he was a "Nysa-man."

When she returned home there was no stopping her from describing the details of the trip as she proudly exhibited her naturalization papers. Every so often she would pause to say "*Mama mia*, now I am an American citizen." She was convinced that the certificate of citizenship was in fact her citizenship so she bought a metal box with a lock where she kept the certificate, out of fear that if she lost it she would lose her citizenship. After we explained the real nature of the certificate and that she would not lose her citizenship if she lost it she said she understood, yet she kept it locked up just in case.

SIBLINGS

My brother and sister were involved in my life in different degrees. Leno less so than was Mary. When Leno (whose real name was Bartolino) married I must have been around 4 or 5 years old, which helps explain why my memories of him living in our house are practically non-existent. I do recall the cherry episode mentioned earlier but not much else.

In certain ways Leno was a physical and personality image of my father, nail-tough, strong, ready to argue and to fight anyone at any time, yet he had a ton of friends. Occasionally, their strong characters would collide leading into semi-violent clashes. Although I don't recall my father ever striking my mother, I do remember a particularly heated altercation between him and Leno in which Leno warned, "If you ever lay a hand on my mother you'll be sorry, and I won't care that you are my father." I'm sure he meant it.

Leno was always athletic – softball, bocce, bowling, ice skating and horseshoes. You name it he played it. His best softball was played for the Hillside Café team which was often City Champions. He played all positions and did so with talent. Whenever things didn't go the way he wanted them to his favorite exclamation was, "Oh Misery!" This he repeated so often that the players began calling him "Oh Misery." I can hear the infielders yelling encouragement to him when he was on the mound, "Come on Oh Misery you can do it, strike the bum out." Many times that's exactly what Oh Misery did – strike them out.

Though he played at many sports they were not enough to consume his enormous reserve of energy. He frequently changed jobs; he worked for the Boston and Maine railroad and in factories, drove a cab in Chicago and Shirley Massachusetts. He boasted he knew the Big Guys in the Chicago, but never claimed to have worked for them.

Like my father Leno had an oversize warm heart and friends who were in need could always count on him for help. But unlike my father he seldom had money in his pocket for very long. Ironically, when he found himself in need few friends stepped forward to help, yet he never gave any signs indicating he was miffed by this. Father and son loved wine, cards, bocce and shared the feeling of *camaraderie* with a wide range of friends.

Between the two of us there was little contact, owing in large part the gulf of 15 years separating us. His children were closer to me than he was. I suffered a sense of frustration in dealing with him because of his penchant for over-exaggeration and fabrications. For one reason or another he preferred not to tell things as they were. This was odd because neither of our parents had this trait. It was taxing to converse with him at times because in order to get the underlying truth of what he was saying it was necessary to diminish what he claimed was great and augment what be said was unimportant. By the same token, at times it was entertaining to engage him in a dialogue of exaggeration-one-up-man-ship.

I don't believe Leno lied or exaggerated with the intent of hurting anyone, though at times that was the result. It appeared to me he engaged in that behavior in order to avoid certain consequences or to impress people with how much he knew about a given situation. Did he believe what he was saying? I suspect at times he managed to convince himself.

One thing was sure about Leno, being with him for any length of time was never boring. Left alone with a group of people, regardless of who they were he would eventually either antagonize someone, get into an argument, cause looks of incredulity or provoke laughter.

He never learned to dance nor did he have any sense of rhythm, yet he was never bashful about getting out on the dance floor and enjoying himself by jumping around wildly, often leaving his partner at a loss as to what to do.

True, Leno was often irritating, impossible to reason with, frustrating to deal with and at times infuriating, but it was equally true that people loved him realizing that in his idiosyncrasies he meant no evil, just playing out his life in the only way he knew, with color, humor and unpredictability and blessed with the ability to turn a dull day around.

Later in life I developed a sincere fondness for my brother. Not that we agreed on much, it was more of a late developing genetic bonding.

Returning to Leno's penchant for embellishing the facts, I have sometimes considered the possibility that he really wasn't at fault but that he was culture-genetically programmed to behave as he did. Compared to all the other European countries, in Italy life has many features of a grand spectacle. It is picturesque and animated. Theatrics can make boring and insignificant moments in life dignified and entertaining.

This mindset manifests itself in various ways in Italy. For instance, it has been alleged that at one time measuring instruments that gauged certain external phenomena were adjusted to fib for the pleasure of the populace; car speedometers indicated speeds in excess of the actual speed of the car; clocks in some railroad stations were set a few minutes fast with the purpose of encouraging people to move faster; while clocks in trains were set a few minutes behind the real time in order to create the impression the train would arrive on time.

In so many ways Italy ran in my brother's veins more so than in Mary's. As a matter of fact, I would have wished to have had a more generous share of his Italian traits.

****

While Leno was an extrovert and gregarious, Mary was an introvert. At about the time she realized the opposite sex could be interesting, she fell in love with Bobby Parisi whom she later married. There was never any other man in her life. While Mary loved Bobby my parents were deadly opposed to her having anything to do with him, not because of any faults they found in him but because his parents were Sicilians. I recall my father coming home from work one afternoon only to find my mother in the kitchen with tears in her eyes. "What's the matter he asked?"

"It is Mary, she wants to get married to that Parisi boy and wants to do it right now."

"Where is she?"

"She's upstairs"

I quietly and inconspicuously followed my father up the stairs as he entered Mary's room. After realizing I could see only shoes by looking underneath the door I pressed my ears against the door and listened hard as my father calmly explained his objections to her intended marriage. Getting nowhere with his exhortations he switched tactics and asked her to not rush into marriage but to wait a while and he would give her a very nice wedding. She remained silent. Two days later without a word to anyone she was nowhere to be found, she had packed her clothes and undetected by my mother left the house. She got married by a justice of peace.

Over the following two years there was no contact between Mary and our parents. She managed to get word to me as to where she and Bobby were living, and I often visited her but never leaked a word of this to my parents although I suspect my mother knew about it all along. During the third year, Leno concluded that it was time to bring daughter and parents together so he invited my parents to his house. When they arrived and walked into the living room there was Mary. A total and sudden silence enveloped the room as if someone had turned off the audio system. The kids who were there were aware of what was happening and crowded around the door to get a better view. The Italian melodrama was about to begin.

Both parents stood there in surprise, unprepared to deal with this situation. They looked at each other as if to ask what they should do. Father looked around the room and saw the nervous expectancy in the faces of those gathered there as if waiting for him to do or say something. Meanwhile, mother brought her hands together as if in prayer in the hope of receiving divine enlightenment in this moment of conflicting emotions. Mary, equally stunned by the appearance of her parents, kept her head lowered as if awaiting an indulgence of some kind.

Father with his gaze directed straight at Mary finally broke the leadened silence. "Are you happy now?"

"Yes pa, I am. I am sorry if what I did has caused you unhappiness but felt I had no choice. This is what I've always wanted."

Again an anxious silence. Mother began to cry. My father walked slowly over to Mary lifted her head, then looking at her as if trying to come to terms with the situation took her in his arms without saying a word. Audible sighs of relief followed by applause from all corners of the room. My mother walked up behind my father, and uttered "Oh, Maria, Maria," and she too embraced her. It was not until much later in the evening that a sheepish Bobby showed up. Ironically, years later Bobby, the Sicilian, became like a loving son to my mother.

Mary has always been a quiet person when it came to conversation, but she was strong of character. It wasn't long before it became clear who called the shots in her house. Bobby to the contrary had an easygoing personality that despised confrontations or arguments. Nevertheless, in a strange and inexplicable way Mary's life revolved around Bobby to the exclusion of everything else, the consequences of which weighed heavy on her when he passed away.

Ask Mary about the early years when she and Leno were still at home and she will tell you the first thought that comes to mind is Leno constantly teasing her or trying to set her up as a scapegoat. She recalls a particular incident that she will never forget.

Leno had taken money from my mother's room and bought cigarettes. Later in the day noticing the missing money mother reported this to my father. Mary and Leno were called to the living room. Both staunchly denied having taken the money. Suddenly Leno – with a surprised look on his face – cried out "Look, look," as he reached into the pocket of Mary's dress, "here's the money she took it, she took it." Unnoticed by anyone he had slipped the money into her pocket while my father was explaining why they had been called to the living room. Mary cried saying it was a lie. My mother went over to Leno and told him to empty out his pockets. He resisted saying, "We've caught the thief, isn't that enough?" My father went to him and did the emptying out. The contents included a half-full pack of cigarettes. In a tone of wounded trust Leno said that Mary had put them there. My father took him by his shoulders and led him off to the proverbial back-of-the-house.

Mary is still alive at the age of 83. Almost totally house-confined because of a severe arthritic condition affecting her legs, she continues to live at 118 Beech Street with her son Ronald. The lone survivor of what once was our Italian neighborhood.

PART THREE

MUSIC & BOOTS

The day starts out like any other day, nothing special on your agenda, no wish entertained that something out of the ordinary occur, no recent event suggesting it might spew forth consequences, in other words, the type of plain ordinary day that will soon be irretrievably dismissed by your memory. Then it happens, the unexpected, an event that shakes your being down to its very foundation and in the course of doing so alters your life forever.

MUSIC ON A SUMMER NIGHT

All music is what awakens from you
when you are reminded by instruments.
(Walt Whitman – Leaves of Grass)

Mother had just finished lining up a row of shoes on her bed when I walked into her bedroom. "Bring me the shoe polish box," she asked. She was unquestionably one of the most orderly persons I knew, everything in its place. No uncertainly at 118 Beech Street as to where things were. I handed her the box which she opened, pulled out and looked into the black polish can and exclaimed, "Ah, *Madona mia*, there is nothing left." She picked up and examined samples from the shoe line-up and shook her head as she put them back. Looks like I'll have to go down Cleghorn and buy some she polish; come Domenico I'll buy you ice cream.

It was around seven Saturday night on what had been a very hot summer day in 1943. But the heat had receded somewhat at the insistence of a welcomed breeze. I didn't have anything in particular to do, no interesting radio shows that time of the year and I was a pushover for ice cream.

There were people doing what people did on warm early Saturday summer evenings. Women were in Salas Market doing some late-day grocery shopping; Mr. Salas behind the counter with his white apron, spotted in places with splattered blood from the meats he had butchered and trimmed during the day. Across the street at Leger's Barbershop a couple of guys waiting their turn, browsing through last year's magazines, people walking out of *Cucciara's* store

78

with ice cream cones, and heading towards the Strand Theater for the Saturday night movie. Others could be seen coming down the hill from St. Joseph's Church, feeling good and at peace after confessions. A relaxed Saturday night full of a sort of "Our Town" contentment. Mother went to Pete's Shoe Shine Parlor to get a couple of cans of black shoe polish — all of our shoes were black—while I went to Cucciara's for my chocolate flavored inducement. There I ran into Paul who had just paid for a bag of assorted candies. "Walk with me to my house and I'll give you some candy" was the second proposition of the night. Mother said OK, that I shouldn't take too long and that she would see me at home.

Paul lived in a tenement house along the Nashua River. We strolled along the river bank, stopping occasionally to heave stones into the summer-lethargic stream.

The Nashua has always been a reminder of the gentle summers of my youth. Bordering the river stood the Town Talk Bakery that baked the greatest bread in the world. On any given morning at around 7 a.m. place a nickel on the counter and walk away with a hot just-out-of-the-oven loaf of bread. Sit along the river bank break off a piece from the still warm bread and watch the steam rise. Once in a while toss a stone in the river and watch the ripples expand outward until reclaimed by the mainstream.

The Nashua in those pre-pollution days was hospitable to life of all kinds, fish, frogs, turtles and river rats. The latter gave us a chance to test and sharpen our marksmanship as we tried to hit them with our B-B-guns. Some folks caught fish from the river. I was never that lucky. Perhaps my poor showing was the result of a lack of talent aided and abetted by my shortness of patience for sitting quietly for long stretches waiting for a nibble on my line.

"Must be a dance at the Arena," commented Paul as we saw couples strolling along the street now closed to traffic and heading for the Arena where people had already gathered at the main entrance.

We climbed up the bank in front of Paul's house where we parted. Guess I'll climb up the wall behind the Arena and short-cut it home, I thought. The Arena was an elongated building sitting along the bottom of a 30-foot embankment at the top of which were the backyards of several Beech Street houses. Between the Arena and the embankment stood a cement wall some 10 feet tall and about 3 feet wide. The Arena was at that time used, as far as I recall, only for dances, the regular Saturday night dances and occasional

Monday night dances when big-name bands such as those of Benny Goodman, Harry James, Stan Kenton and Woody Herman came to town.

I climbed to the top of the wall and slowly ambled my way from one end towards the other. As I approached the opposite side the sound of musicians warming up their instruments came wafting towards me. There was the guttural sound of the saxophones, trombones with their velvet notes, trumpets sounding their brassy arpeggios, the drummer hitting cymbals and the base drum and then a rush of syncopated rhythms. I stopped and stood there listening. Then over sounds of the instruments a voice, "OK fellows let's get going, ready, let's go." The instruments fell silent, then the same voice. "One-Two-Three-Four," and the orchestra began playing its theme song. Then it happened, I felt a tingle under my skin as waves of lovely sounds came streaming from the bandstand. For over an hour I sat there feet dangling over the side of the wall enthralled in a trance-like state.

So moving and overwhelming was this experience that I look back at it as my personal epiphany, for from that moment on my world changed, little of what I had previously thought, wanted and liked remained untouched. This new world and this love affair with music was to last some ten years, years which shall always be remembered as among the most fantastic I would ever experience. To this day thoughts of those moments sitting on the wall behind the Arena produce an emotional warmth through my body.

I walked home without touching the ground and straight to bed with the music still lingering in my head. The next day I told mother and dad I wanted to learn to play a saxophone. Though they had no idea what had suddenly come over me, one week later I was the owner of a tenor saxophone and had made arrangements to take lessons from Eddie Hamilton, the same Eddie Hamilton whose orchestra was playing that Saturday evening at the Arena and whose voice I could still hear saying, "OK fellows lets get going, ready lets go-One-Two-Three-Four." My lessons were given at the Fitchburg Music Store on Main Street, the same store whose street window was the one through which my father once punched a guy after being taunted with the derisive "hey guiney warp."

Within two years I was playing with a small combo, mostly at weddings, anniversaries, first communions and birthdays. The group was comprised of two alto saxes, the tenor sax which I played, a trumpet, piano, and drums.

Sheldon Smith one of the alto sax players was also a student of Eddie Hamilton which is how we met. Reddish blond hair, light complexioned,

80

abundantly freckled, and a good sax player. John Parker a trumpet planer was a quiet guy who did a fine job as the only brass-instrument player in the group. Any mistakes he made would be obvious and heard by everyone.

There were about ten numbers in our repertoire so we usually had to play each number at least twice. Not that it mattered much at the gigs we were playing since by the time we worked our way through the ten or so numbers people had either emptied too many glasses to know what was happening or the noise level had reached such a high decibel level that the music was merely a faint backdrop.

One experience was new for me. None of the musicians were Italian. Our rehearsals were at Bill Walsh's house whose mother was very un-Italian. She spoke only English and she served lemonade and cookies. I felt like I had suddenly stepped into a real American home, the same one depicted on the radio shows I regularly listened to like "Henry Aldrich" and "Jack Armstrong The All American Boy." The group was together for about a year after which we broke up and I lost contact with all except Sheldon Smith.

I practiced, practiced and practiced. Sitting in the third room upstairs at 118 Beech Street I went on for hours. Occasionally, I would go to my mother's bedroom and played while looking at my full figure in her large mirror and picturing myself playing with one of the famous big bands of the time. Many were the times when mother would cry out to me to come to eat and put the sax down for a minute. This I would do but no sooner I had swallowed my last bite when I was back upstairs to my personal concert hall.

I was in high school when all of this was occurring. Though I never flunked a course neither were my grades anything to brag about. Whenever possible I picked the desks farthest from the teachers so that they would not notice I was doing my harmony lessons or looking over a band arrangement. Academics were of no interest to me for what need would I have of all those English classes since I intended to communicate with people with my saxophone. Why would a famous musician need to know anything about history and math, just a waste of time thought my know-it-all teenage brain, for I intended to make history and the only math I needed would be addition so I could count the money I expected to make.

It was during my middle high school years that I joined the Ricky Launders brimming-with-Italian-musicians orchestra. WOW!, four saxophones, three trumpets, two trombones, piano, bass, and drums and two vocalists – girl and boy. To sit in the sax section, to be the part of such a big band and playing those fine arrangements proved to be even more thrilling than I ever imagined.

With the Launder's orchestra I got my first experience as a professional. We played around New England, mostly on weekends and holidays. Big dance halls, hundreds of couples dancing, me on the bandstand, playing late into the night, getting paid on the spot. At times we were so far from home we stayed over at hotels. A different experience all together were the theater stage shows we played – at that time theaters showed two movies and the better theaters presented stage shows between the movies. At very classy theaters like the RKO in Boston there could be only one movie and a stage show. The shows – which probably evolved from vandeville – had the usual dancers, comedians, singers and magicians.

One show in particular stands out. The orchestra had been booked to play three shows a day for three days at the Cummings Theater in Fitchburg. A couple of days before our first show one of our trombone players was hospitalized, to make matters worse he was the one who played the trombone solos. One of the musicians said he might have the solution for he had recently seen Milt Lodger walking down Main Street, perhaps he would be willing to sit in for the hospitalized player. Lodger was one of the best trombone players or, for that matter, jazz musicians to come out of Fitchburg.

He had played with some of the very famous orchestras in the country. The strenuous schedule of one night stands got to him and he began drinking heavily until he started losing jobs because of his addiction. Between jobs he often returned to Fitchburg to dry out. We located Milt and he agreed to play the shows with us.

Our first stage show at 2 p.m. went just great. We played a lot of swing arrangements for which the young kids in the audience applauded loudly number after number. Some started jitterbugging in the aisles but were stopped by the ushers. Milt's solo improvisations were great, wonderful technique and interesting flows of ideas.

Playing stage shows was much more demanding than playing for dances because in the former the audience's attention was focused completely on the stage and not on their dance partners. Also, unlike at dances the band didn't have the luxury of playing a few warm up numbers.

The second show went on at 5:00. The orchestra was seated in three rows, saxophones in the front, one level up where the trombones and a third level up were the trumpets. We were well into a swing number and the part where Milt had a solo. He got up started to improvise, tripped and fell off the side of the bandstand. The piano player alertly began playing a fill-in solo but could hardly compete with the laughter from the audience. Milt was drunk, a condition which probably spared him a broken neck or limb. He was helped to his feet and to a backstage dressing room. After the show we splashed cold water on his head, poured coffee into him and managed to get him into fairly respectable shape for the last show. As an insurance policy we made sure Milt had the inside chair away from the edge of the bandstand.

Our dance gigs usually lasted about 4 ½ hours. Half way through which we had a customary half-hour break. A few of the musicians stayed around the bandstand to converse and just relax. When we played in an amusement park they could be found walking around, taking in the sights or grabbing a bite to eat. Some of the musicians suffered from a condition called roving eyeballs. These were the guys who while playing divided their attention between the music and the pretty faces on the dance floor. If by chance a dancer's eyes met those of the musician he was sure to search her out during the break. One night one of our flirtatious trumpet players got hit in the mouth by a jealous boyfriend. A trumpet player with a swollen lip is useful as a car without wheels so the band played the second half of the evening with two trumpets. A number of calendars later I caught the eyes of a dancer and I was drawn into one of the toughest periods of my life. But that's material for a later chapter.

During my stay with the Ricky Launder's band, I decided to get a broader experience in jazz and swing music so I enrolled at the Schillinger House in Boston, a jazz music school. Joseph Schillinger had come developed a theory of music based on mathematics. It was said George Gershwin had studied with Schillinger and that his famous musical "Porgy and Bess" was composed based on Schillinger's mathematics. I was still living in Fitchburg at the time and took a daily 7 a.m. milk train to Boston with my saxophone. There I took sax lessons from Joe Viola, a great saxophonist. I had classes in the history of music and in arranging as well. The best part was playing with the different school bands. The musicians were top caliber. So much so that it was not odd to have one of the big name band leaders come to the school to listen and hire away special talents. Some musicians at the school went on to become famous in the jazz world such as was the case of Charley Mariano a baritone sax player. The Schillinger House School survived to become today's Berkley School of Music, the largest and most respected school of its type in the country.

One Thursday evening after arriving home from Boston I got a phone call from Eddie Hamilton, my first sax teacher. He had a dance date Saturday night in Leominster and his tenor sax man would not be able to play. Could I take his place? I called Ricky Launders and was told he had no gig for Saturday so it was alright to help Hamilton out.

It was one of the most esteem building and immensely satisfying evenings I have ever had. The band was just fine. As the evening rolled on my mind journeyed back to that summer evening behind the Arena when I first heard the Eddie Hamilton orchestra, and now here I was sitting and playing in the sax section. I felt and relived the warmth of the sounds of that summer evening which were the sounds all around me and of which I was now a part. I felt a deep sense of gratitude to Eddie Hamilton for having been my teacher and then allowing me the opportunity to play with his orchestra. Rogers and Hammerstein must have had that night in mind when they wrote *Some Enchanted Evening*.

In 1950 my music career led me down a different path, one that propelled the course of my life in a new direction. This I'll pick up in a later chapter but first there are the amazing 1940's to look at.

THE GREAT WAR

The music was loud, the hall of the Turners Club in Fitchburg was packed well beyond capacity. Some people were dancing while others formed small groups conversing or just looking on. All joined in singing a song over and over again, one whose first line was, "Let's remember Pearl Harbor." It was all about what had happened exactly one week earlier on December 7, 1941, the repercussions of which continued to reverberate across the country.

The purpose of this dance-social was to bring the community together in the face of the embarrassment and losses of Pearl Harbor. A mixture of emotions pervaded the hall. There was concern over the future, questions as to what all of this meant, but mostly there was anger over what the cowardly and "sneaky" Japanese had done and a bristling determination to obtain revenge.

Through the heavy cigarette smoke-filled hall I saw myself a week earlier as I was lying on the floor in front of our big Zenith radio listening to my favorite Sunday night show, "The Jack Benny Hour." It was around 7:15 in the evening and in the kitchen my mother was brewing coffee; my aunt Zia Checa was visiting us. Suddenly the show went off the air and there was silence. Not wanting to miss any of the show I jumped up and began playing with the dial. Then the unmistakable voice of President Franklin D. Roosevelt who announced that the Japanese had attacked our naval installations at Pearl Harbor.

I couldn't believe what I had heard, excited I leaped to my feet and ran into the kitchen shouting, "We're at war, the Japs have attacked us we're at war, we're at war, the president just said so."

How ironic because here we were one week later at the Turners Club shouting in song our patriotic anger at the Japanese and during the same week the United States had declared war not only against Japan but also Germany – the irony lay in the fact the Turners was part of the city's German-American Club.

The years between 1941 and 1945 were unlike any ever experienced by the United States in all its history. As I look back, those years were very special for me and I feel privileged to have lived through and witnessed the greatest moments in the history of the United States as the country's spirit and courage were put to acid test. Yes, there were rivers of tears shed, young lives obliterated and harsh times endured, but there were also the tidal surges of nationalistic unity, of sacrifices willingly made, of a common bond bringing together all Americans from every social and economic strata, a pouring forth of prodigious energy and determination directed at a single national objective – defeating the enemy. A complete subjugation of personal interests, hopes, plans and aspirations to the overriding need for national mobilization.

My first exposure to the impact of the Great War was my attendance at a going–away reception given for my cousin Santo Zanin who had just been drafted into the Army. Relatives and neighbors had gathered at my aunt's house that evening. There was wine and efforts made to give the affair a lighter tone which fell short of veiling the deep sadness in my aunt's eyes or the undercurrent of concern that pervaded the house. When the gathering was over and people began leaving, handshakes had a way of lingering into sympathetic hand-holding, pats on the back morphed into warm embraces. Versions of this emotional scene was to be repeated many times across the Land as thousands of young Americans left home for military duty. Being a young eleven years I didn't comprehend the seriousness and pathos of the scene. My mind was busy entertaining thoughts of Santo shooting down Jap airplanes, of mowing down dozens of German soldiers. Why wasn't I old enough to fight the dirty, sneaky Japs!

The national effort to win the War was truly prodigious, everyone's life was touched in some way:

Money: The government's need for money to finance the war effort was vast as weapons, planes, tanks and warships had to be built, military and the burgeoning federal administrative departments needed to support the War effort had to be financed. All of these urgent needs were accomplished in large measure by selling War Bonds and War Stamps. In elementary school I remember buying War Stamps at 25¢ each, pasting them in a book which when full could be exchanged for a War Bond. We kids did this with same enthusiasm we had shown for collecting baseball cards for we were told each stamp we bought meant another bullet fired against the dirty Japs.

Rationing: Scarcities of all kinds occurred, compelling the government to put rationing into effect, food, gasoline, heating oil were among the rationed goods. To implement the program families were given monthly food and gas stamps which were necessary in order to buy these products. Once the stamps were used up so was the chance of buying the products. As a result everyone had to do his or her calculations carefully so that the stamps would last for the entire month. Rationing gave rise to the proliferation of "Victory Gardens" which provided another source of food.

Scrap Collections: People were asked to collect and turn over to the government all kinds of items. Used silk stocking were needed for processing into gun powder. Scrap metal and tires were badly needed, and used cooking fats could be used to make explosives. I recall going around with a small wagon looking for any kind of metal I could find on the street or in someone's backyard and delivering the load to one of many collection depots scattered around town. I recall the pride felt when telling my parents about the scrap metal I had collected to help our boys win the War.

Movies: Hollywood turned out scores of movies involving the War. The favorite theme was the War in the Pacific against the Japanese. How we kids would yell and stamp our feet as the movie hero shot down Japanese airplanes. Our big hero of course was John Wayne the bigger-than-life star of many War movies. Movie stars also did their bit off-screen to help with the War effort. I recall stars coming to Fitchburg on War Bond drives – one in particular was Bruce Cabot, a main character in the movie "King Kong."

Music Industry: The popular songs of those years often had War connections, some boldly referred to the fighting as did "Praise the Lord and Pass the Ammunition." Others were plaintive. How can any of us who lived at that time forget ever Frank Sinatra singing "I'll Be Seeing You In All the Old Familiar Places." There was "I Cried for You," "Saturday Night Is the Loneliest Night of the Week," and on and on.

At a time in their lives when their days and nights should have been filled with innocent adventure, romance and the experiences of the work-a-day world, American boys were fighting, often hand-to-hand, under unimaginably hostile conditions across the bloodied landscapes of France, Belgium, Italy and around the necklace of South Pacific Islands. They were in the air every day in skies filled with horror, they went to sea in submarine-infested waters far removed from the shores of their homeland. While at home uncomplaining civilians worked long hard hours in support of our military. Housewives put away their aprons for work clothes and their kitchen utensils for riveting guns.

At home we obviously were exposed to the same effects that the War produced across the country. Mother got adept at using our food stamps wisely so that they would last the entire month. The closest that military service came to us was the drafting of my Zanin cousins.

There were moments when we became apprehensive about our safety. We had heard that the Germans had submarines off our Atlantic Coast. Posters reminded Americans about spies among us and to be alert to suspicious looking or acting persons. In the end Americans were fortunate that not a single bomb was dropped on this country in vivid contrast to the large swaths of devastation stretching across Europe.

On the bedroom walls of youngsters picture posters of sports celebrities were replaced by wartime heroes. Pictures of baseball stadiums were replaced by scenes of air battles with Japanese planes falling in flames. No more Cowboys-and-Indians games, now it was Us-Against-The-Japs games with the major difference that while there always someone who agreed to be an Indian in our Cowboy and Indian games it took a lot of convincing to get someone to play the role of a "Jap" in our War Games.

With the end of the War came heartwarming reunions of sons and parents, boys and long-waiting girlfriends, husbands and wives. In many cases the joy of reunion overshadowed the fact of missing limbs, and deep psychological scars. Much of this was poignantly depicted in the Academy Award winning movie, "The Best Years of Our Lives." Then there were the homes to which fathers, husbands and sons never returned, whose bodies were either never found or rested beneath the soil of some Pacific Island or European town.

In 1942 there was a knock on the front door of the Philadelphia home of Alfio and Mary Bonanno. No longer would they be able to listen to the voice of Enrique Caruso and other music from the native Italy. Federal agents under government orders confiscated all short-wave radios possessed by enemy aliens

- Italians, Germans and Japanese. The Bonanno's son Sam didn't know this had occurred for, ironically, as a U.S. marine he was occupied in fighting the Japanese in the Pacific.

The Bonannos never got their radio back. They were among the 600,000 other Italian American citizens who had been classified "enemy aliens" and as such subjected to property confiscation, curfew, forced registrations and worse.

During the War the five million Italian-Americans were the largest foreign born group in the USA. A large number were fingerprinted and required to carry special identification cards and had their travel restricted. Hundreds were interned and thousands were arrested or detained.

On the West Coast more than 10,000 Italian-Americans were forced to leave their homes and were prohibited from entering coastal areas. In seaports from Boston to Monterrey, Italian-American fishermen had their boats confiscated and were banned from coastlines and wharves.

Frankly, I don't recall any of these measures being applied to the Italians in our neighborhood. As far as I can remember during the War there were no restrictions, registrations, arrests or limitations imposed on any of us. In retrospect what other Italian-Americans had to endure seems unjust and uncalled for. Many of those who were humiliated had, like the Bonannos, sons fighting in the U.S. military forces. Nevertheless, it is understandable that harsh measures would be imposed by a country engaged in the heat of what was perceived to be a life and death struggle. Fears abounded that the enemy had planted spies among us, that the Japanese had submarines patrolling our East Coast. It certainly seemed like prudent caution to keep close control over aliens from belligerent and expansionist Germany and Japan who were in positions to do harm but arguably less so as to Italian-Americans. I knew of no Italian in my neighborhood who gave the slightest evidence of being biased or sympathetic to Italy in the War. It was as if Italy was a non-entity in the conflict. The battle lines were clearly drawn, it was us versus the Germans and the Japanese. Italy's case was much more complicated for the Italian families of Beech Street each of which had at least one member in the American military.

POST-WAR TRANSITION

I've often thought how marvelous it would be if we were able to look in a crystal ball and see how certain decisions about to be taken will play out. My five fingers would probably suffice to count the direction-altering decisions made by me during my life. One such decision occurred during the years between 1945-50, the intervening years between the end of World War II and the Korean War.

During that period, I attended the Schillinger House in Boston; I held down a full time factory job; I went dancing, played music and made a Korean War decision. Before going into these a few words about the temper of America during this period.

The surviving World War II soldiers, sailors, marines and air force guys were now home and determined to leave the nightmarish memories of the Big War behind. There were those who came back physically or mentally disabled for whom life would never return to what it was, but for the fortunate it was time to get on with the activities of a normal life–raise a family, get a job, make money, buy things so long denied. "KEEP THINGS SIMPLE," could have been the motto of the day. The popular movies were sweet and innocent. No railing against society or the system. Time now to build a comfortable house and become a member of the contented middle class. Avoid stress, conflict, confrontation.

World War II got Americans used to working productively and even creatively in large organizations. Big business, big labor and big government produced a bountiful economy. Post-war Americans were organization men and conformists – beautifully depicted in "The Man In the Gray Flannel Suit" starring Gregory Peck – and it was they who sired the Baby Boom. The customs of the expanding middle class were depicted in a new universal culture of the 1950's television. Crime rarely raised its ugly head, church membership reached new highs. Suburbia became the desirable place to live offering tranquil peaceful surroundings, sanitation and the perceived ideal environment for raising a family.

****

On the world stage seminal events were taking place which were to spawn consequences extending beyond the pale of both their time and place, some of which to this day continue to be major foci of concern.

On May 15, 1948, through the decision of the United Nations, the Jewish State of Israel was born in Palestine. The United States, which had opposed the establishment of a Jewish State at that time, surprised the world by immediately giving formal recognition of its existence. Both the Soviet Union and the Arab States immediately denounced the United States for its sudden and unexpected change of position. The Arab countries threatened to take things into their own hands and invade Israel thereby *de facto* undoing what the United Nations had decreed. The newly created United Nations failed to provide the military persuasion necessary to maintain peace in the region. The up-shot was that the fate of Palestine would be decided by the impending conflict between Jews on one side and Palestinians and Arabs on the other. Now some 53 years, a Middle East War, hundreds of terrorist attacks, and thousands of deaths later the conflict over Palestine between the same protagonists continues while the United Nations remains on the sidelines.

On January 20 of the year of my high school graduation Mohandus K. Gandhi the 78 year old spiritual leader of hundreds of million Indians was cut down by an assassin's bullet. He was India's renown apostle of peace, a peace achieved through the medium of passive resistance. It was the disciplined practice of this philosophy that was instrumental in convincing the British to grant India its independence. Years later in the United States it was the influence and spirit of Mahatma the Great Teacher that inspired and accompanied Doctor Martin Luther King during the days of the American Civil Rights Movement.

On September 20, 1950 Mao Tzetung was elected Chairman of the new Central Government of the Peoples' Republic of China and was to become

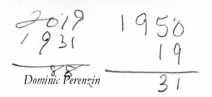

one of the most brutal leaders in the years to follow, being responsible for the death of millions of Chinese and a feared protagonist in the Cold War. Mao ushered in the most tragic and bloody period in the history of China.

Korean War 1950

***********   yrs old 90

I was working at the Independent Lock Company when the Korean War broke out. The place was abuzz with talk about the upcoming draft and who might be called. At 19 years of age I was prime fodder for the Army. Then came my rationalizations: why risk getting my head blown off when my country's security was not at stake? Why go across the globe to intervene in a war between orientals? I felt no patriotic, emotional or other compulsion to enter the Army.

It was at this time that one of the molders at the plant approached me with an idea – it was Bill Johnson a black tenor saxophone player. He suggested I look into the possibility of joining the Navy, but to do so in a particular way. The Navy had a school of music in Washington D.C. to which musician recruits were sent for a year course, be given the rating of USNM (United States Navy Musician) and then assigned to play in one of the Navy's bands.

I discussed this possibility with my parents and friends all of whom encouraged me to do it. Feeling the breath of the draft on the back of my neck, I went to a Navy recruiting station to verify what Johnson had told me which turned out to be true. I enlisted and in the process unintentionally vindicated my father's innocent faux pas with the Italian Navy uniform.

It was a cold, damp November afternoon in 1950 and I was sitting at the kitchen table at 118 Beech Street. My mother had just served me my favorite soup. My aunt Zia Checa was also there to wish me well, for in a few hours I would depart for Springfied where I was to undergo a physical exam to determine whether I was physically fit to be a Navy man. I recall my mother telling me that from that moment on my relationship to the house would never be the same. She was right in many ways. I had reached a watershed moment. The history of my life up to that time uninterruptedly revolved around and had its center in the house at 118 Beech Street where I had eaten some 5,632 lunches, where I got my childhood measles, chicken pox and regular winter colds, where over many nights I lay on the floor listening to my favorite radio shows, where on brisk October days I helped my father make wine in the cellar, where I watered my father's gardens, where I shoveled snow in the winter, to where I returned from the movies and, when older, to where I returned after a Saturday night of dancing, where I spent so many, many hours practicing saxophone and clarinet and where I learned about the joys of manhood.

These were the reminiscences floating through my mind as I looked at the passing scenery from the train window on my way to Springfield.

I made two telephone calls home during this episode, the first was to tell my mother I had passed the physical exam and would next go to Washington D.C. to take a music test at the Naval School of Music. The second call was to announce my successful taking of the test and that I was about to depart for the Great Lakes Naval Training Station located near Chicago. During all of this I had with me what would become my faithful companion, my saxophone.

Again, I found myself gazing from the window of a train, this time on my way to Chicago to become U.S. Navy recruit Perenzin. My ping-pong thoughts bounced back and forth between wondering why I ever decided to join the Navy and fantasizing about the new life awaiting me at the end of the line. Sailors have girl friends in all parts of the world don't they, what a fine opportunity to see the whole world – Europe, Asia, South America. I'll probably be assigned to one of the Navy's overseas bases in exotic places like Italy, Greece, Japan, Hawaii and England, places I would never otherwise have the chance to visit. I could see myself playing in a great Navy orchestra at a club overlooking the Mediterranean or in Paris or London. Then the chilling thought – hell, suppose I'm sent to Korea to entertain the troops and because of lack of military personnel I'm handed a rifle and sent to the battlefield?

These were my thoughts as the train raced through the late afternoon dusk on its way to Chicago. The passing scenery underscored my vacillating moods, heavy cloudy skies, lifeless backyards of houses, listless brownish grass, leafless trees, empty motionless swings, abandoned plastic toys. But as darkness asserted itself these melancholy scenes gave way to warmer feelings as lights from the living room windows of passing houses bore messages of a safe, secure world. Perhaps things would work out just fine after all.

The 1940's began with the U.S. entering World War II throughout which I was to be a civilian, the 1950s began with me entering military service as the Korean War was underway.

Interlude One

Refreshments

Drink wine and live here, blitheful while ye may; The morrow's life too late is, live today.

Oliver Hestford - Allea

Each year in the month of October a truck ritually backs into the driveway at 118 Beech Street. As a couple of men get out of the vehicle and open its back door my father opens the driveway-level window to our cellar. Soon the men begin unloading wooden boxes of grapes and hand them down through the open window to my father. Being too short to reach the window but wanting to help I am satisfied with my father occasionally handing me a box which I then add to the growing stack on the floor. In the cellar my father randomly selects boxes, pries open their tops and tastes a grape or two. A slight nodding of the head indicates approval, a pursing of the lips means unacceptable causing the box to be handed back out the window.

This is the beginning of the wine making season at 118 Beech Street, an activity which I eagerly anticipate. The occasion takes on a festive-like atmosphere. Some of our Italian neighbors drop over to lend a hand at different times and stages. There's plenty of laughter and good cheer as the winemakers immerse themselves in a labor of love. The first step in the wine making process is to crush the grapes – skin, seeds and pulp – into a barrel by use of a hand-powered grinder made up of two parallel rollers covered by sharp grinding teeth which when turned neatly interlace to tear open the grapes sending the resulting juicy mush down into the barrel. This can be a risky operation as it is often necessary to push reluctant grapes into the grinding teeth. At this stage my task is to open the boxes so their contents can easily be dumped into the grinder.

The next step is to cover the barrels, turn them on their sides and allow the crushed grapes to ferment. If there is any doubt about fermentation happening it is quickly dispelled by placing an ear on the barrel and listening to the phenomenon in process. Technically what is occurring is that fuel molecules are being broken down anaerobically by enzyme catalyzation. But to me it sounds like a noisy party going on in someone's stomach, a continuous gurgling noise, the rushing waters of a river, a conversation between wordless voices. I skittishly back away. No doubt there is an operation occurring, a process of transformation from simple grape juice to a complex new genus. This experience helped me in later years to appreciate the saying that wine is alive and breaths.

When father is satisfied – I never can figure out how he knows when the right time had elapsed - that enough fermentation has taken place, he unlids the barrels, places the contents into a press and squeezes out the young wine which is then re-barreled. But in order to do this the previously used barrels have to be washed out. Eager to help I once asked my father if I could clean one of the barrels. Without giving my request much thought he told me to go ahead. I took him literally for that was exactly what I did, I put my head in a barrel and begin cleaning. Within a few minutes I was not feeling that great and my washing motions gradually came to a halt. I felt giddy, a big grin took possession of my face as I stumbled around the cellar. My father helped me up the stairs to the kitchen laughing all the way. I was drunk and my mother upset at my father for allowing me to do a man's work.

Once brought to the point of perfection these Wines of October are ready to undertake their splendid mission of bringing joy and pleasure to the world and warmth to the body and soul. The love and the *joie de vivre* with which they were produced is imparted to and became embodied in the Wines themselves, in many ways a living metaphor for the human and artistic products of the Italian culture of love, joy, creativeness and beauty which are sent out from Italy and then from America's Little Italys into the world bearing their uplifting message that *La Vita e Bella*

****

This was to be my first formal date. Her name was Janet Lindsey a high school classmate. She was in two of my classes. I thought she was impossibly cute, most importantly she was an American girl, meaning her parents were not Italian, in my eyes a big plus back then. Just imagine the young son of Italian immigrants dating a real American girl. It was like advancing up from urchin status in a Dicken's novel. On a couple of occasions I had come close to asking her for a date only to back off. Suppose she were to say no? How embarrassing. Better not expose myself to humiliation.

One day, as we ran into each other on our way to class, the subject of a newly released movie came up and without any premeditation; I asked if she wanted to see it with me. She said that would be great. During the class my head was spinning, I really did it and she actually accepted. WOW! I gave myself a mental kick in the butt for having waited so long and I kept repeating that lovely name, a name that didn't end in a vowel, Janet Lindsey, Janet Lindsey, Janet Lindsey, how American can one be.

Wanting to make the most of the Big Night I planned to take Janet to dinner after the movie at a nice restaurant, not to a diner, but to Romanos, an Italian restaurant where I could proudly show off my American prize. At our table we were talking about the movie when the waiter approached and asked whether we wanted anything to drink before ordering our food. I was caught by surprise for it hadn't figured in my preparations for the evening. Janet said she would have a coke. But I wanted to impress her with my suaveness and sophistication, so I decided to do what I thought the likes of Humphrey Bogart and Cary Grant would do, I asked for a scotch and soda. The waiter smiled and said I was not of legal age for such a drink. I was embarrassed and my face showed it. My attempt to appear suave had backfired. Janet was silent and turned her attention to other tables as if to indicate she wasn't a part of what just happened. I spotted Nick Romano — one of the restaurant's owners — at the cashiers. Nick was a friend of my brother Leno so I got up and went to him. I explained this was my first date with Janet and that I really wanted to impress her. He suggested the waiter take my order for a scotch and soda but that I be served ginger ale. No, to dicey I thought, she might be able to smell the difference or even want to taste it. That would be disastrous. Smiling, Nick acquiesced to my importuning but said he would have it served in a small glass.

Back at the table I explained with a touch of braggadocio that Nick the owner was a friend and that this was not the first time I would be allowed to have a scotch and soda because he knew I was mature enough to handle it, our waiter was new at the job and didn't know about this. The waiter brought our drinks. Cheers as we touched glasses and I took my first sip. My eyes must have popped out as if the spring holding them in their sockets had snapped. I couldn't believe the disgusting taste. So bad was it that my mind went into disarray and I was no longer able to focus on my date or on what she was saying. While Janet continued sipping her coke, I courageously brought my glass to my lips but to wet them only. Excusing myself I went to the men's room and came to the point of vomiting. Nick, who had been following the events at my table, came to the men's room. We arranged for the waiter to say he would freshen-up my drink and substitute a ginger ale for it. He salvaged the night. Ironically, I later found out that Jane's mother maiden name was Cardinale, Antonella Cardinale.

****

The Big War was over and my cousins had returned home having been spared of any injuries though two of them, Angelo and Nello, were in major battles in Europe. Following the quiet celebrations held at their home, it was decided we younger folks would enjoy our own homecoming party for our heroes. We reserved a table, a large table, at a dinner-dance hall in neighboring Clinton, Massachusetts. I remember it had the appearance of an airport hangar with bright, incongruous aluminum panels making up its outside walls. Hardly the place one would expect to find a dinner-dance place.

Though there was music and couples dancing, at our table all attention was focused on our heroes. Gradually, one couple after another did leave for the dance floor. I was much too engrossed in the stories about the War to even consider dancing as bottles of champagne were uncorked. After an hour or so one of the girls at our table took me by the arm and said it was about time for me to get out on the dance floor. Reluctantly, I put down my nth glass of champagne and stood up. Then it happened. Some prankster decided to spin the room and everything in it around in dizzying circles and I found myself in a mental tailspin, lost my balance and knocked over chairs on my way to the floor. I remember looking up and seeing a mosaic of blurry faces looking down at me and a slew of life-preserver arms extended in my direction.

Helped into a chair, I sat with my head resting on my arms. "He'll be alright, let him rest. Someone order black coffee. Maybe he should be taken home. Not a good idea, his parents will get upset," were fragments of conversation I heard. Some Jerry Lewis manqué suggested they call what happened "The Downfall of the Champagne Kid."

****

PART FOUR

THANK YOU
VOLTAIRE

BOOT CAMP PLUS

We got off the bus and were herded into one of the low-lying gray buildings which lined the street, just inside the entrance of the Great Lakes Naval Training Center. It was late November and Chicago cold. Once inside we went into a classroom and were immediately reminded that we were now in the military and that we should sit, listen and do what we were told. "Guys, you are now in the U.S. Navy but you're not yet sailors and its our job to make you into one. Listen and obey and you'll be alright, don't listen, don't obey and you'll regret you ever joined the Navy. Go into the next room pick up your uniforms, place the clothes and shoes in the bag you'll be given. You won't need them for a while."

A guy next to me said in *sotto voce,* "He ain't ah nice fella, izee."

I got in line and received my new wardrobe, most of the articles of which as in Abbot and Costello movies weren't the right size. Goodbye civilian shirt, pants, socks, belt, jacket, sweater, see you in a few years, I whispered to myself as I regretfully placed them in a bag. Next the barber's chair and *chao* to my long hair as it showered to the floor. When the barber finished I looked in the mirror and blinked several times, perhaps hoping that by doing so the image looking back at the me would change, but it didn't. Crewcut Perenzin, how revolting.

Aside from this preface to my training at Great Lakes, I have few precise memories of those six weeks, only foggy recollections of marching, standing in lines, eating, cleaning, cleaning, and:

Weather: Bitterly cold.   Chicago-style winds making a liar out of the thermometer and where I learned first-hand what the the wind-chill factor meant.

Training: Very little that seemed practical to me.   Never fired a gun.   Never taken aboard a ship.   Physical exercises limited.

Mail: Mail time was anticipated with great eagerness – letters from home. Unquestionably, the most unusual piece of mail to reach us was one sent by my mother – a whole pizza – which she did in response to my having mentioned in a letter that I really missed having pizza.   It was ice-cold so I put it on top of one of the room radiators.   When it was acceptably warm we pounced on it. Almost everyone at my end of the barracks got a taste of it, reminding me of the biblical story of Jesus feeding thousands from a few loaves of bread.

Health: If there was one single, abiding concern of the Navy it was that none of us contract a disease, virus or infection and to guarantee that this not occur we were given shot after shot in the arms, on our thighs and on our butts.   Those who gave the shots showed irrefutable evidence that they were working on their Masters in Sadism.   Step up, roll up your sleeve and, "Look Mom, with my eyes closed."

Recruits: None of the recruits in my company was sufficiently unique as to find a place in the folds of my memory.   Perhaps the fact we all sported crew cuts, wore the same clothes and occupied the same generation tended towards homogenization.   They came from all parts of the country judging from their varied accents.   We got along well.

Bacchanalia: During the six weeks spent at Great Lakes we were given only one weekend of liberty.   Chicago was our general destination and its many clubs the specific targets.   I heard a lot of jazz that weekend.   In giving vent to whatever they had repressed some guys got real stinko.   How some ever got back to the Base anatomically complete was close to a miracle.   It was messy. Some guys had lost their wallets, hats, jackets, one guy lost a shoe.   Others didn't get back by curfew and had to face disciplinary measures.

Six weeks passed quickly and again I found myself on a train, this time carrying me to the next stage of my military career, Anacosta, Virginia, located on the outskirts of Washington.   I was on my way to the Naval School of Music where I would spend the next several months before being assigned to an orchestra somewhere in the wide-wide-world of the United States Navy.

The school proved to be a non-event, I learned nothing new.

On graduation day our group met in a classroom, the Big Moment we were waiting for had arrived – Assignment Day. John Smith you are to report to Aircraft Carrier Midway. Ralph Burke you are to report to Naval Center in San Diego, California – and on and on. No mention of Dominic Perenzin. A guy next to me who had received his assignment distracted me by telling me how happy he was that he had not been assigned to a ship when I heard, "Perenzin are you deaf?"

"No sir, sorry,"

"You are to report to Norfolk Naval Base in Virginia where you will catch a ship to Guantanamo Bay, Cuba. You are assigned to the orchestra of the Admiral of the Caribbean Command."

I was dumb-struck and blurted out, "Where the hell is Cuba?"

"It's an Island in the Caribbean," came an answer from someone. After everyone had been given his assignment and as we were walking out of the room, one of the instructors approached me and told me he had spent several years in Guantanamo, a quiet place he said, not much to do for excitement except to go to the mainland where the "girls are." The orchestra there had some good musicians. His advice was to try to find something to do, a hobby, anything at all or I would go nuts down there, the sun is brutal and the boredom brain-numbing.

And so it was that for the second time in my life I was about to embark on a voyage and to new experiences. I was on my way to Cuba, the Pearl of the Antilles.

****

During the months I spent at the Music School I often went home for weekends. Obviously, I didn't have my own set of wheels. Neither would my tight financial condition allow me to fly or take the other form of public transportation to get to Fitchburg. So I did what many sailors did in similar situations, I used my thumb.

Rides were fairly easy to get for we were again at war and I was wearing a sympathy-evoking military uniform. Most of the rides were uneventful.

Questions about where I was from, where was I going, had I been in the War Zone, my family, long stretches of silence and a lot of dozing off.

There were a few rides which broke the mold and were enough to keep me wondering what I might experience upon stepping into the next car. After one of these unusual rides whenever a car stopped to offer me a ride I would do a rapid check of the driver and other passengers to see if I could detect anything odd.

First Ride: The car was a huge Buick, not new but meticulously maintained, the driver a man in his early fifties who asked question after question, some quite personal. He seemed fascinated about the subject of the legendary prowess of sailors in what he called "getting chicks." Did I have a girl in every port? Did I prefer foreign girls to American girls? These he asked though I had told him I had just a few months before joined the Navy. He didn't seem to listen to what I said, being intent in getting his questions out. It was as if he got a vicarious erotic pleasure from the act of asking.

After a while I semi-dozed off when I felt something on my knee and realized it was a hand which was growing bolder by the second. Realizing what was happening I grabbed his arm and twisted it, causing him to momentarily lose control of the steering wheel. "Stop the car, I'm getting out of here," I yelled. He immediately did so but observed that we were out on a dark highway surrounded by nothing but trees and that there were hardly any cars passing. It would be dangerous for me to stand out there. I agreed to stay in the car but that I would sit in the back. I got an occasional glimpse of his face in the rear view mirror, the muscles were taut and it looked as if he were clenching his teeth. I got the impression he was under pressure-cooker tension. I got off at the next town.

Second Ride: "I'm a priest," the driver told me a few minutes after I got into his car. Was I Catholic? He was on his way to Connecticut to visit his terminally ill sister. Did I go to mass regularly? I felt some kind of compunction to lie or exaggerate about the exercise of my faith.

He appeared to be a fairly young 40-ish, pale in complexion and quite thin. He gave off an aura of self-sacrifice like a Medieval monk just emerged from his prayer cell. Other than the time I entered and left the car he rarely looked in my direction. Every so often he would reach over and start searching for something in the glove compartment which he never found. When I offered to help look for whatever it was he was looking for he thanked me but said it wasn't important.

There was a long period of silence which the priest broke when he asked me whether I would join him in saying the rosary for his sister. "A rosary?" As far as I could recall this was something old ladies did when gathered together in church. I had never said a rosary. But, hey, I was getting a free lift so how could I refuse. And so there we were speeding along the darkness of the New Jersey Turnpike at two o'clock in the morning reciting the rosary with a priest on his way to visit a dying sister.

Third Ride: I was tired and disappointed. There were few cars on the road and those that were weren't even slowing down to look me over. Finally, a red sports car stopped, a woman at the wheel said "Hop in sailor." After asking where I was going, where was I stationed was I married, and without any lead-in inquiry by me she informed me she was, as she put it, "an angel of pleasure." It took me a few seconds for the significance to be decoded.

A sailor hitch-hiking can't have enough money to enjoy her pleasures could he? We wouldn't even have money to take a room any place, would we? I said she was right, I was dead broke. She said that was alright because experience had taught her most sailors with a few drinks in them were slobbering pigs anyway. "What's your name, she asked."

"What kind of name is Pernizon?"

"The name is Perenzin and it is Italian."

"Eyetalian!"

I explained that in the region my parents were from it was not unusual for last names to end in an "n." There was a moment of silence, then she launched into a monologue that went something like this:

"There ain't many where I come from but I've known some *Eyetalians*. Hell do they make a gal earn her money. But then its all "I love you, let me rescue you from this cheap life. You're too beauteeful for this." Sometimes I think they were just putting on a show like a soap opera or something, or maybe they were just big overgrown kids. But you know, sometimes they make a gal feel like, well like a woman. You know what I mean. Hell, how would you know. Shit, it doesn't really matter anyway." She turned on the radio and the Symphony Sid Jazz program from New York.

An hour later she left me off at a gas station. As I stepped out of the car she asked me whether I would do her a favor. I told her I would if I could. She handed me what appeared to be labels with adhesive material on one side and asked me to go the men's room and paste them one in each stall. I frowned and asked her to repeat where I was to stick the labels. "On the wall in the stall you know the place where guys take a crap." I stood there holding the labels as she drove off. "Thanks *Eyetelian* sailor boy." I entered the restaurant next to the gas station and had a coffee and pulled the labels from my pocket.

> **RUBY**
> *For an unforgettable time.*
> *Your Desires My pleasures*
> *Telephone (...)......*

A promise is a promise and I went into the four stalls in the men's room and stuck the labels to the walls. "Italian sailor boy", where had I heard that before!

METAMORPHOSIS
IN CUBA

With my course at the Music School completed and my post assignment revealed I was given a 14-day furlough before reporting to Norfolk, Virginia to board a ship that would take me to Guantanamo. I returned to Fitchburg.

It felt good to be back home, to see old friends familiar places and, especially, to savor mama Perenzin's cooking. Many of the people who heard I was going to Cuba echoed my first reaction, "Where's Cuba?" By the time I got back to Fitchburg I had consulted a map and confidently told those country bumpkins that Cuba was an island some 90 miles south of the Florida Keys. It was called the "Pearl of the Antilles." I couldn't resist flaunting my smarts by explaining that Havana was the capital and that many Hollywood stars went there to have fun. People were impressed with how much I knew and were sure that with such worldly knowledge and sophistication I was sure to be a success in life.

I was expectably looking forward to my first trip on a Navy ship. Would it be one of the huge aircraft carriers and would I see fighter jets taking off and landing on the ship? Maybe they'll conduct practice maneuvers on the way to Cuba. That would be great. Perhaps it will be a battleship with all of that armament and canons. It probably wont be a destroyer because though it would be great to go to Cuba on one of those fast, sleek ships, they're probably too small to take on extra personnel.

Arriving at the Norfolk Naval Base, I was told to report to the USS Walker. Never heard of this one, I thought. Must be one of those brand new warships. I was told to go down the pier and that it was about half way down. I glanced at the long line of ships docked at the pier, there was an aircraft carrier and a couple of battleships which, to the best of my calculation, seemed to be about half way down the pier. My excitement began to perculate. I grabbed my overstuffed duffel bag, swung it over my shoulder and with the other hand picked up my saxophone case and began walking past an impressive array of ships, stopping every so often to inquire which was the USS Walker. Not this one, nor the next. Finally, "That's it over there," said a Wave. I stopped in my tracks and blinked a couple of times. There across the bow of the ship in faded letters was the name "USS WALKER," an old bloated transport vessel. Not a canon to be seen on it. This can't be what I trained for can it? But as it turned out this was to be my transportation to Cuba.

The trip to Guantanamo was mostly uneventful. I didn't get seasick and overall, except for one aspect, I enjoyed the voyage. The exception had to do with the rule that all sailors on the ship had to see a movie that was shown just before the ship arrived at a foreign port. This particular tape must have been shown a million times for the audio was bad, the color faded and the actors seemed to have come from a prior era like some Paleolithic Mexican movie. The movie was called, "What all Navy Men Should Know." A better name would have been "The Macabre Side of the Birds and the Bees Tale." It was about what happens to sailors who don't take proper precautions before participating in the pleasures of the flesh. There were endless and very graphic pictures of sailors who had contracted syphilis or gonorrhea and explanations on how these sexually transmitted diseases rotted away parts of their bodies, particularly the genital organs and how they could cause death. After seeing this film for the first time one could end up regretting he had not chosen the priesthood as a vocation.

The ship docked at Guantanamo mid-week in mid-summer but there was nothing mid about the scorching heat. A welcoming committee, banners and band were conspicuously absent. I was taken by bus to the foot of a hill and told that up there in that gray building were my barracks, just go up the road. Duffel bag slung over my shoulder, saxophone case in my other hand and sweat pouring down my face I began the climb to the barracks. As I was getting close some guys appeared on one of the balconies and began yelling, "We've got a replacement." These, I later learned, were some of the band members whose tours of duty were over and who were awaiting replacements.

"What's he carrying, looks like a saxophone case. Hey Scherma, come out here your replacement has arrived."

****

The band I found was mediocre. There were a few good players like trumpet player Joe Ferreccia but there were also cobwebbed career musicians who had been in the Navy for too many years. Scherma, the tenor sax player whom I was to replace, was an inveterate alcoholic. Night after night within one hour after the band began playing Scherma was drunk and by the end of the night he was completely out of it. If the effects of his drunkenness were limited to his personal boundaries all could have been ignored or least tolerated, but his playing suffered and this noticeably affected the band's overall sound.

With the departure of the deadbeats and the arrival of talented new players the band enjoyed a renaissance. Key to the band at this time was Al Maruso (piano), Steve Lungren (drums) Ralph Bavelleri (bass). We Italians were now five. We rehearsed more often which quickly became evident in our playing. We played for dances on the base, in Cuba itself and in some of the nearby islands.

Two hours of rehearsal in the morning and we were free to follow our inclinations for the rest of the day. Some guys took up golf, others swimming, snorkeling or sub-bathing. I tried golf and found it was too snail-like for me. I tried tennis at the invitation of a non-musician friend and discovered it was to my liking. From that first encounter with tennis my love of the sport grew and has lasted to this date.

Shortly after arriving at the base I began attending mass, something I had not done in years. This lasted for about six months. Why this happened at all probably had to do with the fact I was in a foreign land surrounded by strangers and the church and mass were things familiar to me, something linking the present to the past thus giving my life a sense of continuity. The church was poised on a ledge overlooking the ocean some 200 feet below. The view was spectacular and imparted the religious ceremony an even deeper aura of spirituality.

****

I experienced a few first time events while at Guantanamo. I've already mentioned playing tennis. I learned to drive a car. Though I don't recall what

111

kind of car it was, it was definitely not the latest model by any stretch of the imagination. The car was jointly owned by my fellow musician Donald Potts and me, thus mitigating the effect the purchase had on our impoverished wallets. With a speed limit was 30 miles an hour the Base was an ideal place to learn to drive.

I was introduced to my first dry martini which happened at a Toastmasters Club dinner. Before sitting for dinner one night I heard someone ask for a dry martini. Sounded pretty sophisticated to me so why not try one. Loved it though I'm not clear as to whether it was the gin or the gin-soaked olives that first attracted me.

The Toastmasters was a U.S. National Club with a branch at Guantanamo. The Club held regular monthly meetings organized around dinners at which members were expected to take turns at public speaking. This was a totally new experience for me and I managed to deliver at least three talks. The subject matter usually involved music, musicians and related topics. It was a useful exercise, my introduction to standing on my feet before a group of people and talking for 10 or 15 minutes or so and quite a difference from sitting in front of the public and blowing into a saxophone.

I wasn't aware of the use of drugs by anyone in the band and we were certainly close enough that I would have known. There was one occasion in Santiago where we were playing a dance when during an intermission the base player Bavelleri told several of us to join him in our bus. A Cuban had offered him marijuana for free (a loss leader?) and he took it. "What do you say we try it, the guy taught me how to use it." We passed a joint around several times and followed the instructions on how to inhale. Most of the guys said they got a good feeling from it but it did nothing for me. That was the only time I tried any type of drug.

Unquestionably, an event which spawned one of the most profound and enduring changes – a metamorphosis of sorts – in my life occurred while I was in Cuba. To better understand what happened meet our band's piano player Al Maruso who like me was a first generation Italian-American. Al arrived at the Base a couple of months after I did. He was a graduate of Yale and had, as he lamented, made the mistake of signing up with the ROTC or making some similar military commitment which resulted in his being called into service, compliments of the Korean War.

Al could have received an officer's rank had he so chosen but because he didn't want a longer commitment than absolutely necessary, he opted to enter as an regular seaman. Al was a great pianist and his presence in the band made a big-time difference. We were all affected by the emotion and excitement he generated when playing; it made all of us play like never before. Though he was the only band member with a college degree he never flaunted this.

It was quiet in the barracks, the night was breezeless, hot and sticky. Al and I were the only two at our end. It was a night off for the band and rest of the members were out, probably at the movies. I had just returned from taking a shower to help cool off. Al was in a talkative mood and our conversation soon turned our growing up years in our Little Italys. This felt awkward for I had not given any thoughts to the subject since my embarrassing early years. He was from somewhere upstate New York. I believe his father owned a store and was able to realize his dream of seeing his son go to the "best university," which for him was Yale.

Al said he thought he had detected something in me different from the other guys in the band. Had I considered going to a university. I said I had not. Was I willing to do myself a favor and in the process fulfill an obligation, then after pausing a moment said the word obligation was not exactly what was involved it was more of a ethnic-fealty kind of thing, a fulfillment of my family's and all Italian-American communities aspirations and promises. This hit me as pretty heavy stuff and asked him what he had in mind. He reached under his bunk and pulled out a box containing books, rummaged through it and pulled one out, looked at it pensively for a moment then handed it to me and asked me to read it. "When you've finished we'll sit down and talk about it." I looked at the title "CANDID" by Francois Marie Arouet de Voltaire.

Not practiced in reading it took me a week to read the book though it was not long. As planned we got together once I had finished the reading. Our conversation lasted nearly two hours at the end of which he flashed a knowing smile and said I was not on my way to fulfilling the promise. The next day I found another book on my bunk bed it was "Crime and Punishment" by Fyodor Dostoyevski.

The last book which he gave me to read was the Italian novelist Giovanni Verga's "The House by the Medlar Tree," which for some reason was never returned to Al and sits on the shelf of one of my bookcases.

****

It was December 1952 and no chance of any of us going home for Christmas. One morning after mass the Chaplain approached me with a problem. Unless he was able to find someone to play the organ there would be no music for the Christmas Eve mass. The lady who played it in past years had left the Base with her husband, an officer who was transferred to the States. My first reaction was that I really didn't know any organist but I would give it some thought. On my way back to the barracks I recalled that Al Maruso may have commented he had played the organ.

Later that day I explained the situation to Al. He was quick to say he was no longer a practicing Catholic or, for that matter, a Christian. He had not seen the inside of a church for years and was not interested in doing so now. He surprised me by delivering a talk on the fact he doubted the existence of the Christian God. No, he would not play the organ.

Several days had passed without the subject being revisited by us but apparently reconsidered by Al as he came to my table where I was having breakfast and, without sitting down, asked whether I happened to know what kind of organ the church had. I was again taken by surprise and answered that I didn't know. I suggested he go over to the church to take a look at the organ.

"No, I don't think I'll have time," he answered, a little embarrassed since we both knew that if there was one thing we had plenty of it was time.

Unknown to me Al did take a look at the organ and, as a matter of fact, had tried it out. As he was playing the Chaplain heard him and went into the church. That evening Al told me he had agreed to play for the Midnight Mass. There were sheets of organ music on his bunk bed.

The church was absolutely jammed full. All seats were taken, people were standing along the aisles and at the back were standing three deep. Not only were there military personnel there—including the Base Admiral and his family – but also a strong representation of Cubans. The Chaplain was dressed in pure white vestments and attended by six altar boys. The mass was in Latin.

As the mass progressed the music became increasingly moving, so much so that the people were turning their heads and looking up to see who was playing the organ. At one point when the Chaplain sat for a moment he looked up in the direction of the mezzanine and smiled. The music began to swell and engulf the entire church with beautiful sounds; we were witnessing a deeply religious event. Curious as to see close up, I made my way to the stairs leading up to the mezzanine where the organ was located. When I reached near the top I stretched my neck to get a full view of Al's profile at the organ. I shall never forget that scene – one of the most poignant I've ever witnessed.

Al was completely absorbed in his music. It was as if the notes were coming from him rather than the organ. Years later I recalled this scene as an example of what the Toaist mean when they refer to the noun and the verb or the performer and the act being fused into one. I remained there until the mass ended at which time people turned to face the balcony and applauded an organist they could not see. Al did not acknowledge the tribute but sat there with his hands on the organ keyboard, his head bowed back.

It was a few days later when I felt it was alright to talk to Al about that night. Why had he changed his mind about playing for the Mass? His explanation made things fit into place and lent even greater drama to what occurred on the mezzanine that Christmas Eve. Al had only one sibling, a sister name Caterina who was his minor by some five years. He thought the world of her a feeling she reciprocated. Two years ago on Christmas Eve Caterina was on her way to a Midnight Mass in a car driven by a neighbor. Also in the car were two other persons. It was snowing in New York and there already was a considerable amount of the white stuff on the ground. A few blocks from the church as the neighbor turned to make a right at a light an 18-wheeler came barreling from the left through the red light and rammed their car, turning it over several times. Caterina and one of the other passengers were killed instantaneously.

Devastated, Al's immediate reaction was to blame the occurrence on God. Why if she was on her way to church should she be killed? The timeless question of why bad things happen to good people. The bitterness was to fester in him for years. Two days after I had asked him about playing at the Midnight Mass, as if by some curious coincidence, he received a letter from his mother in which she recalled that tragic Christmas Eve two years earlier, how Caterina for sure went to heaven and from there heard the beautiful Midnight Mass on that fatal evening. It was then that Al decided to play the organ which he dedicated to her memory for his mother.

Talking about paradoxes. An Italian-American atheist comes to the rescue of a church by single-handedly turning a Christmas Midnight Mass into a beautiful spiritual event. A church which had never before heard the sound of applause now resounded with applause for an atheist.

Al left Guantanamo some six months later. He was greatly missed by all of us. Characteristic of Al's unpredictable sometimes *outré* behavior it was rumored that he had gotten the Admiral's daughter "in trouble" causing the Admiral to send her back to the States. He also contemplated a campaign to improve the working conditions of the bar girls in Guantanamo and

Caimanera. I've often mused about my encounter with Al Maruso and how random events in one's life can leave deep imprints. A person steps into one's life for a brief moment, turns it upside down then departs never to be seen or heard from again.

****

I don't know how it started but navy man Ken Kornstock became the band's unofficial photographer and one of my closest friends. I had no idea what he did during the day to earn his monthly check but whenever we played at night on the Base there he was. He evolved from photographer to photographer band-boy when he also began helping us set up the bandstand and take it apart at the end of the night.

Ken was from Virginia, good looking in a Cary Grant sort of way. He was soft-spoken, polite and always willing to lend a hand when needed.

We often discussed the idea of traveling around the Island of Cuba. When we learned we both had two week furloughs coming up at the same time, we decided not to go to the States but rather to undertake the trip we had talked about, and perhaps write a book about our experiences, complete with pictures. I would do the writing and Ken the photography.

It was in April of 1953 that we embarked on our venture. We had a two hundred dollar budget so we were compelled to do this on the cheap. Our travels were always by bus, the lowest cost of public transportation. We intended to and did wash our own clothes, seek out low budget hotels – especially those catering to locals – and avoid tourist eating places.

The trip started in Baracoa on the eastern tip of the island, a tiny forgotten fishing village with thatch-roofed huts. Populace dark skinned and friendly. Not much to see only life being lived on its simplest terms. We did enjoy our first tasty fish dinner at the home of the fisherman – there was nothing resembling a restaurant to be found.

Santiago was and still may be the second largest city in Cuba and the major urban center on the eastern end of the Island. Very different from Havana, less cosmopolitan and more of an easy going colonial character. We stayed at the Libertad Hotel which was owned by Chinese, a perfect fit for our tight budget. From our balcony we saw a procession pass the purpose of which learned was to pray for rain for the area was in the grips of a long draught.

The marchers appeared to be more emotionally attuned to the rhythm of the music than to the purpose of the march.

In Camaguey our hotel was the Isle of Cuba, our room was comfortable, private shower, closet, phone and a radio – price $5. We had a dinner at the Subway Bar where in answer to my question as to what the waiter would recommend for food I was told a club sandwich. All the way to Cuba for a club-sandwich! I ordered fish cooked in a great sauce concocted around red peppers.

Throughout our trip we introduced ourselves as two American college students writing a book on Cuba, believing it best not to reveal our true identity fearing it might tend to deprive our mission of seriousness.

In Camaguey we visited a high-school and explained to the director what we were hoping to do. He was delighted we had selected his school to be visited and kindly assigned senior student Maria Elva to be our guide. We sat in on Biology and English classes, both of which we thought were very well conducted and the students impressively bright. Before departing from the school Maria Elva asked if we would have dinner at her house Her mother and father were anxious to meet us. We accepted.

Her house was the first real Cuban house we had ever entered and were impressed. Spacious, airy, beautiful tile floors, huge paintings of local landscapes. We described what we had thus far seen on our trip and received suggestions on places we should include in our itinerary. The father was a physician and the mother an amateur painter, the paintings on the walls were hers.

Our conversations were cordial and with the help of some wine very relaxed. That was until Maria Elva's cousin joined us and began asking questions about the university we were attending. His questions and comments led us to believe he was more curious about us than he was on the purpose of our trip so we decided it was time to thank our hosts and return to our hotel.

In Santa Clara we visited the sight where a new university was being built to be named Universidad Central. Very modern and huge it was calculated that the entire institution would not be completed in less than five years – a virtual community. The school would not have a medical or law school since, we were told, too many doctors and lawyers were being turned out every year by other schools. Universidad Central would emphasize science and engineering. Astutely forward looking we thought.

Santa Clara was a pleasant city with plenty of parks where concerts could be heard at night. The people seemed well dressed and prosperous. On the negative side was the extraordinary amount of traffic, explained by the fact the city was the bus hub for Cienfuegos, Havana, Santiago and Trinidad.

We tried in vain to enter two of the sugar mills that are so ubiquitous in Cuba, the Florida and Agramonte mills, both of which we were told were owned by American interests. Permission for us to enter the mills was denied but we did manage to circle the outside of the mills and view the exterior operations. The sugary stickiness in the air got all over our exposed skin.

Huge trucks were lined up along the mills waiting to disgorge their sweet cargoes. The workers were dark-skinned and slender giving the impression they were really mobile sugar cane stalks waiting to be dumped into the mouths of huge gaping hoppers of grinding machines. Our efforts to engage the workers in conversations were foiled by either the work-leader telling them to get back to work or by our inability to understand the badly bruised Spanish they were mouthing.

Cienfuegos seemed large and bulky but not attractive. Wide streets and parks but not anywhere as attractive as those we had seen in other cities. We were told that being close to Havana it tends to get some of the tourist overflow. It was outside our hotel that we met and became befriended by pint-size Franky, a spunky 12 year-old mulatto. We agreed he could be our guide. The kid did a good job, and seemed to have a lot of information about the city which he uttered in crispy Spanish phrases employing an alphabet from which the letter "s" had been banished, as is customary in Cuban Spanish. The most impressive sight we visited was the 200 year Fort Castillo. We went through the premises, dormitories, battlements and jail. The closest I had seen to this back home was the Strand Theater when movies like The Mark of Zorro were featured.

We had lunch at an open-air café at the foot of the Castillo. The waiters wouldn't allow Franky to sit with us so he sat on a two- foot wall at the entrance of the café. A fairly well-dressed man at an adjoining table asked us where we were from and soon had us engaged in conversation. Almost imperceptibly he moved his chair over to our table. He asked us if we wanted to see something really grotesque, a girl who was born with her head growing out of her shoulder. Franky, in the meantime, was trying to catch our attention and shaking his head in a negative message mode. We declined the invitation and before we could react the man grabbed Ken's camera bag and darted down the street. We attempted in vain to catch him.

Ken's camera was gone as well as several rolls of used film. By the time the police arrived the thief could have reached Buenos Aires, Argentina. Later we asked Franky why he was signaling us. "Because that *chico*, fool *turistas*, he take them to place where he rob the *turistas*," was his explanation. How about the police, dam it, don't they know about this? "*Si*, but they get money, you know."

Ken told him the thief mentioned a freakish girl whose head was located on her shoulders, was he kidding. Franky's face turned aglow with excitement and said his mother knew about that, did we want to talk to her. Ken's first reaction was to dismiss this as a fabrication to get us out of the restaurant perhaps to get us mugged. In answer to our repeated question as to the truth of what the thief had told us what we got was, "my mamá tell you, she know, come you like." I convinced Ken that we might as well go since we had nothing specifically planned for the rest of the day and, anyway, it might help us get over the loss of the camera. So we followed Franky to his house and into one of the weirdest tales we had ever heard.

Franky's house was, predictably, in a poor neighborhood – unpaved roads, half-naked kids, women who looked years older than they should have, soap operas and bongo music blasting from home radios as if competing for the attention of passersby. His mother was on the plump side, with inquisitive dark eyes and high cheek bones. Hearing why we were there she looked down to Franky with a rebuffing stare and told him how many times had he been warned not to do this. She then turned her attention to us and stood there looking into our faces as if studying them for some kind of understanding. "Why do you want to know?" We explained what we were doing in Cuba. Again silence. Then in a scolding voice she said that if we wrote about what she was about to tell not mention her name and that anyway no one would believe us. They will think you made this up. By now we were both intrigued and told her we agreed to her condition of anonymity. This is the story as told to us by Franky's mother and recorded in my trip notes:

> *A number of years ago a woman gave birth to a daughter, in a tiny village in the countryside surrounding Cienfuegos which we'll call "Nago".*

This was the woman's first child though she was already over 40 years old. At her husband's insistence she had consumed all manner of herbs and potions and submitted herself to spells cast by local healers, all in order to become pregnant. When the child was born the midwife-neighbor ran from the house totally distraught, screaming "un monstruo, un monstruo, Dios nos salva, llama el sacerdote, el sacerdote." When asked why she was screaming she tensed up, quivered and said "ugly, ugly, a monster not from this world," and then made repeated signs of the cross.

The mother refused to allow anyone into her house except for one occasion when a priest was allowed to enter. It was said he emerged from the house with his head hung low and his face deathly pale.

The new mother bewildered and desperate for an explanation went to see a woman mystic, some claimed she was really a witch, who warned her that Satanic forces had sent the mother's husband to do evil and produce monsters, a precursor of the Evil One himself who would soon appear in Cuba, one who would control all living things and destroy those who opposed him.

The mother returned home and sometime during that evening took her husband's machete and, while he was asleep, crushed his head. She took her child and left before the sun rose. That morning her body was found along side a dirt road, her eyes bulging out in horror. A pole had been driven into her chest. The child was nowhere to be found. The suitcase she carried with her was lying untouched a few feet away.

The village was terrified with fright after learning of what had happened. Out of fear of what might have occurred in the dead woman's house and believing it could contain evil spirits it was burned to the ground. Several weeks later a sugar field worker returning from work saw something that sent him running full speed until he reached his house. Rushing in the door he told his wife he had seen a monster girl, she was standing under a tree beckoning him to go to her, frightened he ran home as fast as he could. That night the man's house was full of people, as word of what happened got around. When asked what the girl looked like he just shook his head saying parts of her body were in the wrong places. There was a wild look of dread in his eyes he said he had seen inside the belly of Hell itself.

The following day the man was found by his fellow sugar cane workers with a stalk shoved down his throat.

A month later, a cobbler from the neighboring village who made weekly trips to Nago to pick up work came running into Nago out of breath and sweating profusely. He babbled about seeing the girl beckoning him to come to her and that she was a monster with her head in the wrong place. He no sooner reported this than he went into wild convulsions lasting for a few minutes. When these stopped he became totally paralyzed from his neck down and has remained so ever since. He lives with his brother spending most of his time lying on the floor like some kind of domesticated animal. His brother was very poor and all he could afford to help his brother sit in a chair was to tie him with a common everyday rope. People refused to help alleviate his demeaning condition because, it was said, the evil spirit may be in him.

No one had since mentioned seeing the young girl. It was said that anyone who reported seeing her would end up dead or · permanently crippled.

We sat there looking at each other amazed and speechless not knowing whether we believed this tale of horror. If we wanted to see the paralyzed cobbler it could be arranged though we would not be allowed to question him about his experience. We declined. It was already semi-dark when we left for our hotel and were admittedly apprehensive when Franky told us to stop as he pointed to the tree a few yards away where the monster girl had been seen.

Ken and I sat in the outdoor café of our hotel sipping Cuban coffee. Did we believe the story? I was unsure, Ken leaned more towards considering it a fairytale. Franky's mother seemed honest and awfully convincing. But again, we were dealing with uneducated peasants.

By this time our limited funds had been exhausted so we had no choice but to return to the Base. We were pleased with the trip and deeply impressed by the beauty of the Island and of the people we met. The pictures Ken had taken were lost along with the stolen camera case. Over time many of notes I took were also lost and the book we intended to write remained just that, an honest intention.

Years later a young charismatic Fidel Castro led a band of guerrillas out of the Sierra Maestra mountains intent upon overthrowing the regime of President Fulgencio Batista. Shortly thereafter in "The "Godfather II" Michael Carleone – a.k.a. Al Pacino – was attending a high-society New Years Eve party in Havana when the music stopped and there was silence as President Batista stepped to the microphone to announce the fall of his government and his departure from the country. Fidel's Castro's forces were about to enter Havana. The fun-loving laid back, spontaneous Cuba which I had known was to be no more. I thought back to the prediction of the mystic from Nago.

THE FIRST TIME AROUND

There is an aphorism that claims that out of the bad some good often comes. In this instance the bad was my first marriage and the good the continued bond with Latin America.

It was a custom that twice a month a group of young Cuban girls were brought to the Guantanamo Naval Base to meet and dance with the Americans. They came chaperoned and selected by the Cuban American Society of Guantanamo. Our band always played at those dances. At one particular Saturday night dance I spotted a young, very thin, dark-haired girl with the biggest and prettiest eyes I had ever seen. I kept watching her and she noticed and smiled. During the intermission I searched her out. Before the night was over I had her address and telephone number in Guantanamo City.

Within a few days I called her and asked her for a date as I planned to be in Guantanamo. She accepted. Lena Sanchez was from Holguin, Cuba and was in Guantanamo visiting a friend of her mother. The house in Guantanamo was clean, well kept but modest. On our first date we walked around and had dinner. She was less of a conversationalist than a good listener. Nothing complicated about her, simple, straightforward and, I believed, quite naïve.

After a series of decision flip-flops on my part, we were married.

The marriage was plagued almost from its inception with misunderstandings and arguments. As the years passed she became increasingly possessive which is not to imply that the failure of the marriage was to be placed at her doorstep for assuredly I was no innocent victim. But again it's wrong to speak in terms of fault on anybody's part. The marriage was a mismatch-mistake that should never have happened. Eventually, a lack of maturity and the embracing of quixotic expectations collided with the harsh realities of every day life and the marriage shattered.

ACADEMIA

The thought of going to college was the furthest possible from my mind when I was in high school, as a result I missed the opportunity to obtain advice on selecting the college that best suited me. Once I decided to go to college I was more concerned about preparing myself intellectually with little if any thought given as to which college I would attend let alone how I would get admitted. Perhaps I felt the sheer power of my decision to go to college would *ipso facto* suffice to push all doors open to me.

I had heard of Harvard, of course. It was supposed to be one of the best schools in the country. So in full-blown naiveté what did I do but go there to inform this Cambridge school of higher learning of my decision to enroll there. The admissions people were polite and arranged for me to meet an admissions officer. After hearing my story and learning about my high school grades he politely suggested I try another school, several of which he named were in the Boston area. Boston University was one of them. So I crossed the Charles River to BU admissions and arranged to take an entrance exam, which I passed and I was admitted to BU as an economics major. By my sophomore year my mind had settled on the legal profession as what I wanted to be in.

The three years I spent in the undergraduate program were relatively uneventful outside of academics. I enclosed myself in the world of textbooks for I had some catching up to do.

Fortunately, as a Korean War veteran the government helped pay for both my tuition and books. All other expenses were covered from savings, the sale of my saxophone and clarinet, and part-time jobs.

Boston University had – and still has - no campus to speak of, located as it was on one of the Boston's main thoroughfares. Step out the doors of the Liberal Arts College and one found oneself on Commonwealth Avenue. This situation did little to help develop a college social life and remained for me the missing ingredient for a more complete college experience.

The best and closest friend at BU was without question Paul Rakke, who was married to cute Patty Squire whose father was a professional painter. We spent many weekends at Squire's country house in a New Hampshire town just over the Massachusetts border. These were wonderfully, memorable weekends of looking at paintings, watching Squire work, listening to his fascinating stories about his years of apprenticeship in New York and Europe and just relaxing in the quiet surroundings of the New England countryside.

He shared his house with three German shepherds who were great company during our frequent walks through the surrounding woods. It was during a weekend at the New Hampshire house that I was introduced to the poetry of Robert Frost. From that time on my walks in the woods would never be the same.

Squire was one of the very few painters in the world who did portraits in watercolors. He painted his daughter in that medium, an amazingly detailed work that, whenever it was shown to our friends, raised reactions of amazement at the fineness of detail when told the medium was watercolors. This technique was thought to be a lost art.

Why I decided to pursue a legal career is lost in the misty part of my memory. Not that it was hastily decided for I had considered becoming a medical doctor, a psychologist, or following an academic career. Whatever the reason for selecting the law the fact is that the decision proved to be one I would not regret.

The classmate with the most presence was F. Lee Bailey, later to become a famous defense attorney. I believe he graduated at or near the top of the class. During the three years of classes F. Lee continued the work he had been doing as a detective involved in litigation matters. This kept him in touch with courts which must have been an invaluable experience. Like me he was somewhat older than the other students having served as a pilot in the Marines. A year after graduation a defendant's lawyer in a Boston murder trial – for a reason I do not recall – withdrew from the case. F. Lee got himself appointed to replace the attorney. The case sparked national interest. F. Lee won and his meteoric career was now launched.

During my third year I took a class called "Comparative Law" taught by a Doctor Fred Cooley. It was a non-demanding course. However, it proved to be another one of those events which sent my life whirling off into a new direction. The course involved a comparison of U.S. and foreign law.

Mid-way through the year Doctor Cooley asked whether I would be interested in obtaining a fellowship to study foreign law at the Southwestern Legal Foundation's Institute of the Americas, located at the Southern Methodist University in Dallas, Texas. The fellowship covered all school costs plus a small stipend for living expenses. As I gave this thought the prospect worked an attraction on me, as it would combine my experience in Latin America with the practice of law. I was definitely interested. He applied for me and I was granted the fellowship.

While at BU Law I lived in a basement apartment through the windows of which I had a clear view of peoples' feet as they passed on the sidewalk above. The entrance to the apartment was through the garage. It was not long after moving in that we learned we had regular uninvited visitors, large ominous looking black roaches. Whenever we had guests, we were constantly fearful of the possibility that one of those creatures should decide to walk across the room or climb up a wall. This never materialized thanks in no small measure to the fact that whenever possible we prepared for visits by spraying the whole apartment with Black Flag, an olfactory form of self-flagellation.

It was while we were living in these dark subterranean quarters that I returned from my first final exam and flung my books across the room vowing that I would not continue in law school. I had reached the proverbial fork in the road. In the end I didn't quit but I did learn how to take law school exams and later the Massachusetts and New York bar exams.

Interlude Two

Days Of Lament

Like the dew on the mountain

Like the foam in the river

Like the bubble on the fountain

Though art gone, and forever!

Certain past events have been stored intact in my memory, vivid in detail with an almost it-happened-yesterday sensation to them. Perhaps this occurs when the circumstances surrounding the events are strikingly unusual or the time or place have a particular significance.

And so it was in the matter of my father's death. There were no hospital rooms involved, no manifestations of pain, no lingering, agonizing expectations, no doctors bearing distressful news, no funeral home arrangements to be made. It all began one early August afternoon in 1957. I had received my undergraduate degree and was to enter Boston University Law School in a few weeks and feeling quite good about life. I was driving to Boston's Logan Airport to see my father off to Italy. Though – or perhaps because – he had had a heart attack a few years earlier he decided to make what he called his "farewell trip" to the town of his youth, Conegliano, to be with his brothers a while, to walk across the fields of his youth, stroll along the familiar streets and inhale the ambrosial odors of his native land. His brothers had been alerted to his trip and said they were anxious to see him again.

At the airport I asked him to check to make sure he had everything he needed. He showed me his passport, round-trip ticket and, tucked under his shirt around his waist, a money belt. About the latter he commented, "Lets see if anyone can steal this from me."

After he had boarded the plane, I commented how tired and pale he looked and that perhaps he shouldn't have made the trip at this time. Mother said he had made up his mind to go and no one, but no one, could have dissuaded him.

The evening of the day following my father's departure I was lying on the sofa reading when at around 10:30 there was an urgent knocking at our door. "Who is it?"

"It's me Mary" said the voice from the other side. Surprised, I fumbled at the lock until I managed to open the door and there was my sister and her husband Bobby. Mary was visibly upset as she walked in.

"What's wrong?" I asked. Rather than answering she handed me a piece of paper. It was a cable from Italy.

"Well, what does it say," I asked as my Italian had become an almost forgotten language thanks to Spanish. "Looks like it says come quickly Antonio is gravely ill," I ventured. Mary began crying and I knew my understanding was correct. The cable had been sent by a Leno Zanin from Aosta, Italy.

Before leaving for Italy my father had promised my mother he would visit her sister and her family who lived in Aosta, the capitol city of the Valle D'Aosta region located in the northwestern corner of the country just southeast of France and at the foothills of the Alps. His itinerary was to take him Boston-Milan-Aosta -Conegliano.

Within less than 24 hours my mother and I were on a plane flying over the North Atlantic. Mother had been given a sedative and was little talkative during the flight, mostly she napped. When awake she repeated several times, as if talking to my father, "Tonyo, Tonyo why did you insist on this trip!" then she would recite the Hail Mary in Italian. Mother had never been on a plane before which made it easy for me to fob off her question of why we had landed in Iceland by telling her the plane was re-fueling when in fact we had made an emergency landing there because of engine problems. We remained on the ground for two hours and then resumed our flight to Italy.

We arrived in Milan during mid-afternoon and went directly to our hotel. While she rested I headed for the railroad station to get a timetable for Aosta and to purchase tickets. It seemed that upon touching Italian soil a veil lifted from my memory and a lot of my Italian came back not always in pure form since it inter-mingled with Spanish, but good enough to understand and speak the essentials of the moment.

The following morning we were on a train to Aosta. The scenery along the route was spectacular. The Alps loomed almost touchable as we progressed on tracks running alongside mountains which would suddenly dip into gorgeous valleys, pass through verdant countrysides, quaint villages and below what seemed like stately castles perched along the mountain sides. I was wide-eyed with awe. It was as if I had suddenly been transported to a wonderland, like Dorothy in the Wizard of Oz. How can people be so blessed and fortunate to live in this area I thought. Imagined waking up every morning to the splendor of these surroundings. In thinking back to this experience it was given to me to sooth and strengthen my spirit in preparation for what awaited me.

We pulled into the Aosta train station and took a cab. I gave the driver a slip of paper with my aunt's address and off we went into the outskirts of the city. Hills, hills, and more hills. Finally, three quarters up a particularly steep one the driver stopped. That's the house he said as he pointed out a cute house with a freshly painted fence enclosing it. Behind it not more than some 50 yards stood the base of the towering Alps.

As we were getting our bags from the cab's trunk, people came out of the house. They took our bags as a lady I later learned was my aunt embraced and kissed my mother. A young woman took my arm and led me hurriedly into the house. "I'm your cousin Elena, you must be strong, your mother will need your help more than ever Domenico – your father is dead," she said as she squeezed my hands as if to underline her exhortations. Seeing my mother heading towards us holding her sister's hand, Elena pulled me into another room followed by cable-sender Leno Zanin, my cousin.

They proceeded to explain what had happened. My father rather than taking a cab or other form of transportation up the steep hill to my aunt's house decided to climb the hill on foot carrying his heavy suitcase. Arriving at the house and opening the gate to the front yard he shouted "Maria, Maria, your brother-in-law has arrived from America." As Leno opened the front door to see what all the shouting as about my father dropped the suitcase, clutched his chest and fell to the ground. A doctor who was rushed to the house said he had died instantly.

"Where's my father now?"

"His brothers came here from Conegliano and took your father's body with them. That was this very morning."

The train trip to Conegliano with mother the following day was for the most part uneventful. What I found interesting was that at the Aosta train station I heard a number of people speaking Italian with French accents. Being next door to the French border this was understandable but nonetheless odd to my ears. During the trip itself what impressed me mostly were the number of religious we saw, priests, brothers and nuns. This was so not only on the train itself but also along the route and on the platforms of train stations. It felt like the Church had occupied the country.

During the trip I recalled being told that the only article found on father was his wallet. Apparently his money belt had been stolen.

We were met at the Conegliano train station by several of my cousins and taken to the home of my uncle Angelo Perenzin, today occupied by Arturo Perenzin, where we would remain for the remainder of our stay in Italy. My father's body was in the living room of the house; the funeral was to take place the following morning.

As soon as we freshened up, we went downstairs to where my father was. Everyone was asked to leave the room so that we could be alone, only my uncle Angelo remained. To our surprise the coffin was closed. Too much time had elapsed to allow it to remain open. I remained standing next to the coffin. Why couldn't I see his face for the last time. Why had I never said to my father, "Pa, I love you." Because men don't say that to each other? Why wasn't I closer to him over all these years? Why didn't we talk to each other at any length? Why had I waited until he was gone before I felt the need to express my feelings for him? Was it because had a subconscious belief he was immortal and would always be with me?"

That night I wrote in my dairy:

> *A man who loved and was full of life, whose jovial personality was hard to resist, whose smiles and laughter were contagious. To bear a grudge was beyond his ability as was being unreliable to his friends. He always stood tall, honest and sincere and proud to be who he was. The memory of my father will be with me forever as an inspiration to emulate his goodness even if in a small way. To have known my father was to have loved him. (September 2, 1957)*

Before departing from Italy, we witnessed what for us was a bizzare series of events. It started when a local communist newspaper reported my father's death with a perverse spin. According to the article my father had spent many years in the U.S. working hard but had gotten nowhere. So sad was his misfortune in that country that he decided to return to Italy. The humiliation of having to return a failure – another victim of the oppressive American capitalist system – was too much for him to bear. He died of a broken heart.

News of this article circulated among the Perenzins of Conegliano. Shortly thereafter two of my cousins drove to Venice and straight to the offices of the communist newspaper which had published the article. They inquired about who had written the report and were told who he was but that he had not yet arrived. My cousins sat in the reception area to await the reporter's arrival.

Some twenty minutes later two men entered the offices. My cousins asked the receptionist if the reporter they were looking for was one of them. She said yes, the taller one. The cousins went up behind him and tapped him on his shoulder. When he turned around they said what loosely translates into

"You're a rat liar and scum, the Perenzins want to respond to your lying column about Antonio Perenzin." The reporter started to back away with his hands outstretched before him as if to ward off any trouble. While my cousin let go with a blow to the reporter's stomach, the other one hit him square on his cheek. The reporter fell back against a door which flung open sending him to the floor in the next office. They crumpled up a copy of the newspaper containing his column and threw it at him and walked away as people were running and yelling for the police.

****

Twenty eight years after Mary had knocked at my door in Boston with the news of my father she phoned me in Colombia to again convey sad news, my 94 year-old mother was in the hospital and, according to her doctors, was fading quickly. No particular malady just a general weakening of the vital organs attributable to her age, what the Chinese would call a depletion of the body's vital energies. Alicia and I immediately flew north and directly to the Burbank Hospital. Mother did not appear to be conscious, the only movements from her were occasional feeble attempts to change her position in bed which in the end was only accomplished with the help of a nurse. There was no outward sign she understood the nurse when she told her we had arrived and were standing next to her bed. She seemed peaceful and free of pain. As I looked at her face scenes from my youth and 118 Beech Street flashed by and warmed my heart. After a while, Alicia and I decided to go to Mary's house for a few hours of sleep.

At 6 a.m. we received a call from the hospital saying mother had passed away. Leno, Mary and her husband Bobby, Alicia, a nurse and I were standing at the foot of her bed in a silence occasionally broken by sighs and quiet sobbing. We were all deep in our own private thoughts as we looked at the now peaceful face of Antonia. Leno stepped forward and went to the side of mother's bed. With a broken, tremulous voice he held her hand before his face and as if speaking to it said, "Never again will this hand take a pencil and write notes for me, never again." He brought her hand to his cheek and sobbed with his entire body. He was referring to my mother's custom in the late years of meticulously putting a tiny pencil to a small scrap of paper and writing a list of items she needed from the grocery store which Leno would pick up and bring home to her. Judging from its size the last time I saw it, the pencil she used must have been around for years as much sharpening with a regular kitchen knife had reduced it to a mere three inches. Small gestures representative of who mother was and in what she believed. If she had a credo she lived by it would have been to keep thinks simple, stay close to nature and the natural order of things.

We were all deeply moved by what we had just witnessed as we held hands in a gesture of shared grief. Mamá the Grand Italian Lady was gone leaving me as custodian of so many tender memories and with a woeful sense of having lost a reliable anchor in the vast and ever changing world. Later in her apartment I recalled the story she told me about the morning of January 17, 1930 when she looked up at the picture of Saint Anthony and was comforted. I looked over at his statue next to her bed and gave thanks for allowing me to have had her over the past 65 years. I believe he smiled at me.

****

I pulled a CD from the bag and showed it to Leno as he laid in bed in his daughter's improvised sick room. Did he want to hear it. He flashed a brief smile through his pain. We brought a CD player into the room and the music started. Italian music, Italian singers, arias from operas took over the silence. As it reached Leno's ears the muscles in his face gradually eased giving way to an expression of serenity. Leno had always loved operatic arias and singers especially those from his native land. Though he had no idea of the name of the operas or the arias they were an integral part of is emotional life, unaided by any intellectual understanding. I mentioned the name of the singers and the musical pieces that were playing but he wasn't listening to my words only to the music. What soothing memories did the music awaken as it reached deep into his fading life?

Three weeks later Leon Perenzin died in his sleep. He was 84 years old.

I experience Leno's death much more intimately and directly than those of my father and mother. Not that it was more deeply felt or of greater significance. In my parents' situations I never saw death's shadow in their faces. Father looked a little pale when he departed on his final trip to Italy but nothing more, after which I never saw him again. Mother died without ever showing signs that her end was near, her body slowly and imperceptibly surrendering under the weight of her years – she was 94 years old. Leno's case was sadly very different. We had been told by his daughter Theresa that he was very ill, that he had terminal cancer. Unable to get food into his stomach he was losing weight and was in pain. Alicia and I flew to Fitchburg to see him. When he walked into my sister's house where we were staying I was stunned with what I saw. His face had taken on the mask of death, thin, sallow with that all too familiar distant, absent look in his eyes. A few months later we returned to Fitchburg after being told he was now permanently bed-ridden and able to speak only at intervals and with painful difficulty. The robust Leno, the talented athlete, the lively debater, the lover of life and possessor of boundless energy was no more. It was during this visit that I played the Italian music, for I knew that this music which had been so loved during his life would help mollify the pain and anguish of the final days.

As I look back at these three deaths, I am struck by the presence of a *leit motif*, they died as they lived. Father's last words were in a loud, happy shouting to his sister-in-law announcing his arrival. This was jovial father exactly in character. Mother's last hours were spent in calmness, as if in wait for the approaching finality, a reflection of the quiet, meditative person she had always been. Leno had been pugnacious and quick of temper and tongue when displeased. Facing death he often remonstrated in anger, at times striking out at those who were attempting to east his circumstances. Perhaps he saw them as heralds of Death itself and determined he would give them battle, the final one of this life.

****

PART FIVE

BREATHLESS IN THE SIXTIES

Peering back over the years there is little question but that some of the most variegated experiences of my life occurred during the decade of the 60's. The period began with me heading south to Dallas and ended with me heading further south to Colombia. What happened in between never fails to amaze me. These were the years of the Hippies, of the tumultuous national agonizing over the Vietnam War, of Beatlemania, the years of dissent and of challenge to the comfortable social milieu of the Post-War years, an about face from the unity and national pride of the 1940s.

DALLAS

It was a pleasant August morning when with my law degree in one pocket and a fellowship in the other, I got into my car and headed for Dallas, Texas. Before departing I took the Massachusetts Bar Exam – the passing of which is a *sine-qua-non* for practicing law – but did not wait for the results. These I received while in Dallas – I had passed. I returned briefly to Boston to be sworn in as an Officer of the Court.

The fellowship awarded me came from the Southwestern Legal Foundation's Institute of the Americas, physically a part of the Southern Methodist University Law School. Our lawyer-student body was divided into two groups, one comprised of foreign lawyers studying American law and the other made up of Americans and two Canadians studying foreign i.e. Latin American law.

Professor Carmitz – who taught Conflict of laws – was an intriguing figure having served on the prosecution team at the Nuremberg War Crime Trials that put the Nazis on trial after the Second World War. Unlike other professors, Carmitz was seldom seen around school except during his classes. All the more surprising when one Friday evening when I was in the library doing homework Carmitz came to me and said, "Perenzin you're not going to learn anything important from that book, come join a couple of your classmates at my apartment for some wine." Surprised, I went along. The students he was referring to were Glenn Croksey and Tim Jomon who were outside the library waiting.

We were fascinated by his exposition on the different aspects of the Nuremberg proceedings. The arrogance of some of the German defendants such as Herman Goering created a salt-on-the-wound reaction among many at the trial. The defendants claimed that only a state and not individuals could be found guilty of war crimes, an argument that was rejected by the court. After 216 fatiguing court sessions, on October 1, 1946 the verdicts on 22 of the 24 defendants were handed down. Only three were acquitted. Carmitz was at his best describing the efforts of the Germans to convert the trial into a circus and how the Russian General Nikitchenko, one of the justices, little disguised his "hang them all" attitude.

After discoursing for some time and leading us to focus on legal and moral issues of the trial Carmitz made a quick change of subject which he introduced by saying he wanted us to listen to the most beautiful and plaintive voice that ever was, causing us to switch from the left to the right side of our brains. He proceeded to play records of Edith Piaf the French singer whose tragic life in many ways paralleled that of Billy Holiday the American jazz singer. After a number or two there was no more talking, no movement except for the occasional sipping of the wine, everyone seemed lost in his own thoughts. With her raspy-thick French voice, Piaf had a way of absorbing a listener into the soulfullness of her songs. There were melancholy songs and others with a lightly lilting qualify but all deeply felt. Carmitz told us he often spent an hour or so in the evening with a glass of wine and Edith Piaf. Wherever his thoughts were at that instant his facial expressions spoke volumes about the bliss he was experiencing.

From time to time, I have thought back to that evening in the good professor's apartment and considered how wonderful it would be if everyone had his or her own quiet place, a respite from life's hectic pace and demands, where he or she can sit back with one of the good Wines of October and be carried away by his or her own Edith Piaf. A few months ago I saw a television biography of Edith Piaf. The next day I rushed out to find one of her CDs and luckily found what was probably the only one in Miami. I rushed home and played it, played it again and once more, all the while wondering whether Professor Carmitz was still out there somewhere listening to his beloved Edith Piaf.

We had student lawyers from around the world with a heavy emphasis on Europe and Latin America. The European students were smart but generally aloof and little likeable. They associated mostly among themselves. The Latin Americans were friendlier but not as well prepared as the Europeans and not strangers to cutting corners.

Of the Latin Americans unquestionably my closest friend was Oscar Tanifaz from Cochabamba, Bolivia. Oscar and his wife Susana became our best friends.

Oscar was officially a lawyer but for me and in his heart-of-hearts he was really a philosopher/social scientist. We spent long hours talking about geo-politics, psychology, religion and other heavy topics. I remember one cold winter evening when Oscar came knocking at our door. I opened it and there he stood in a heavy coat, woolen scarf around the bottom half of his face and steamed-up eyeglasses. In our apartment over a cup of coffee he told me about an experience he had just had which left him dismayed and in a deep funk. He said he had that evening decided to take a bus downtown, just to get away from his apartment, the school and all of his daily pressures.

Downtown he walked and walked. It began to snow and it felt good. To take a break from the cold he stopped at a coffee shop. He was the only person in the place and decided to sit at the counter. He ordered a coffee though he would have liked a donut too but was afraid he wouldn't have enough money to get back home if he bought one. The girl behind the counter was friendly. She spoke about how bad the winters were becoming in Dallas. Realizing from his English that he was a foreigner she asked him where he was from. When he told her it was Bolivia she raised her eyebrows in surprise and asked him how could he live with all those blacks. Was he a missionary or something? He told her in Bolivia everyone was white or Indian to which she asked, "Isn't Bolivia in Africa?"

He left the shop and continued walking down Main Street a little more comfortable now with the warm coffee inside him. Then it happened. There it was, the storefront window of the Neiman Marcus store. Wow, eye-popping clothes and accessories. He decided to enter the store and began browsing around, inside he spotted a beautiful fur coat and thought that some day he would buy one for Susana. He asked the salesgirl the price of the coat and she said $8,000. He left with his mouth agape, got on the bus and came straight to my apartment.

I told him it must have been a beautiful coat. Oscar was silent then spoke in a soft measured tone. "You missed the point *mi querido* Dominic. Do you know in my country this very evening there are children in bed with empty stomachs, that there are men who do backbreaking work for less than a dollar a day, that there are families so destitute that they sell their children? All of this happens while there is a country where some people believe Bolivia is in Africa and women are able to buy $8,000 fur coats. It would take a man fortunate enough to be earning a dollar a day working seven days a week more than 21 years to buy that coat. Where is justice? Where is God? Not even in the animal kingdom do we find such an abomination."

I understood his anger and depression. My rationalizations did little to assuage his feelings. He reiterated that there was something fundamentally wrong with the system the powerful had imposed on the rest of humanity. I could not avoid feeling this was a case of a long held belief and the Neiman Marcus incident was held up as substantiation.

We became close friends though we sometimes ardently disagreed on certain subjects. But Oscar made me revisit subjects to which I had not given much thought since my sophomore year at Boston University. We are going to meet Oscar again later and learn of the key role he played in bringing about a major change of direction in my life.

While in Dallas I maintained regular contact with my mother. On one occasion she asked what Texas was like, were there any cowboys there. I picked up on this and asked her whether she would come to Dallas and visit us, we had an extra bedroom. "Oh no, I'm too old for that," was her first response. But later she gave in and agreed to make the trip provided she could see cowboys.

She spent two weeks with us. We took her around Dallas and to smaller towns where she actually saw a 1960s version of cowboys. She thoroughly enjoyed herself.

One of her favorite pastimes was to sit in the Rotonda between the law school building and other school buildings. After a while she became known to many of my classmates who when passing by waived or said, "Hi, Mrs. Perenzin" or "Como está señora." She just loved this attention. She was particularly pleased when we were visited at home by foreign students. She would sometimes whisper in my ear, "Where is he (or she) from?"

For years mother spoke of her trip to Texas, an event almost equal in importance to her trip to Washington to be sworn in as an American citizen. In a way it was a complement to becoming a citizen, for what she saw in Texas was, as she put it "the real America."

As I mentioned earlier, I developed a close relationship with Professor Mozolcheck. As we were approaching the end of the school year he called me to his office to explain that he had worked out an arrangement with the Universidad Autónoma de Mexico Law School whereby the Institute of the Americas would be allowed to send one student a year to study for a doctorate. There was one condition attached by the Mexicans, that the person sent would not, upon completing his studies, remain in Mexico to practice law. Did I want to be the first person from the Institute of the Americas to go to Mexico for the doctorate. All my expenses would be covered by the Institute, both school and living expenses. It was to be a two-school-year program starting in January of 1961. The Institute added its own condition to the offer, namely, that upon completing the studies in Mexico I would return to the SMU to teach for one year minimum. Goris urged me to give the offer serious consideration.

Classes were ending in Dallas and I had no job awaiting me and Latin American law interested me. Wouldn't it be great to be able to practice law in the States as a specialist in Latin American law. A doctorate from a Mexican law school would be an impressive addition to my professional credentials. It was decided, I told Goris I accepted the offer.

My move to Mexico began to occupy more and more of my attention. I often spent a few evening hours listening to radio stations from Mexico. I learned about what was happening locally, and what the best beers were – Tres XXX and Corona. I listened to Mexican newscasts, soap operas and ranchero music. I spoke to the Mexican student at the Institute about the Mexican law school I would be attending. In the midst of all of this my thoughts hit a speed bump as I realized classes would start in Mexico in January 1962 but that I would finish in Dallas in June of 1961. What was I to do between graduation in Dallas in June and the next January? Why go back to Boston, of course, wasn't that where I was from.

Back in Boston, I soon discovered it was no easy task to obtain work for seven months. Law firms were not interested on taking in an associate for such a short period.

The end of July was quickly approaching and the bottom of our money coffers were in plain view. Go to Fitchburg and live with my parents was an option but I would do so only as a last resort.

The situation was quickly spinning out of control. I didn't have the rent money for the next month. We would have to cut down on our food expenses which were already scraping rock bottom.

I fired off a letter to Goris Mozolchek explaining the predicament. Goris' response was not long in arriving. "Come to Dallas and help me research for a book I'm writing on Mexican Commercial Law. Dean Heims has agreed to pay you a salary." Within a few days with suitcases in the car we were again heading southwest.

SOUTH OF RIO GRANDE

Immediately after the Christmas and New Years holidays the suitcases were in the car and we began my long trip to Mexico City. This meant we would cross all of Texas from north to south. I had not seen much of Texas beyond the Dallas area and enjoyed the new experience of small rural towns. Never had I seen so many boots, spurs and horses. Cowboy hats were the dress *de rigueur* for all males.

The fact I was in rural Texas became vividly clear when we stopped at a restaurant along the highway. As we were eating, three cowboys came riding up to the restaurant, hitched up their horses and walked in. They were tall and tanned – as all cowboys should be – ordered sandwiches and beers, ate without talking much, got up and walked out tipping their hats to us. For a moment I thought I was back in the Strand Theater in Fitchburg watching a Western. But this was no tinsel-town production.

Of all of the towns and cities I saw, San Antonio was the one which most impressed me. Perhaps because it was so Mexican and different from the other places I had seen. There was the lovely canal that meanders through the heart of the city. A summer evening stroll along the canal was a relaxing experience, a soothing interlude. Then there was the food, best Mexican food I had yet had. Though later I learned it was really good Texas-Mexican food. The fact I was gradually approaching Mexico was confirmed by the progressive changes in the panorama of faces, language and the spicy-hotness of the food.

The entrance point into Mexico was to be through Laredo Texas, then across the International Bridge into Nuevo Laredo on the Mexican side. It was here at this twin-city juncture that I encountered my first Mexican experience. I crossed the bridge and approached the immigration-customs gates on the Mexican side behind a long queue of cars and trucks waiting to cross the border. An eternity later I handed our passports to the elaborately mustached Mexican immigration officer. The ensuing conversation went something like this:

Agent   So you are going to study in Mexico City, *si*.

DP   Yes that's right, to the Universidad Autónoma

Agent   How do I know that's true?

DP   I just handed you a letter from the Southwestern Legal Foundation in Spanish, it says that I'm going there to study and that I have a fellowship.

Agent   But there's nothing here from the Universidad Autónoma. We must have a letter from the Autónoma.

DP   But I don't have one and I've got to be there in three days. I can't get a letter fast enough to arrive here on time.

Agent   We'll accept a telegram.

I turned the car around and back into Laredo and to the nearest telephone. Luckily, I got through to Goris Mozolchek at the school. He said I should check into a hotel, let him know where I was and he would call me once he had cleared this matter up. Laredo is hardly a large city so our hotel and motel choices were limited. We checked into what we hoped presaged what lay ahead, the *New Horizon Motel*.

The motel's newly painted exterior belied the experience we were to have on the inside. Tired and sweaty and in need of a good shower off came my clothes and into the shower I went. I turned on the spigot and got a few drops of water, tried again, a few more drops. After banging the pipe several times I coaxed a thin stream of warm water to pour out. It took me a few minutes to just get my whole body wet, and much longer to get the soap off. In answer to my complaint the front desk clerk said the whole town was suffering from a water power shortage. Sorry señor.

Not to be inconsistent with the state of the water supply the air conditioning soon gave out. We were sent two surrogates in the form of 12-inch electric fans which did a creditable job of circulating the hot suffocating air. So hot and uncomfortable was the room that we decided to go out and walk around.

Not an attractive town by any sane standard, but again why would it be after all it was a border town. Lots of garages with old model cars. Stores overflowing the cheap clothes, plastic souvenirs, liquor, and plenty of Marlboro cigarettes. The streets were hot and dusty causing us to stop at what looked like a relatively clean café for a cool drink. In the short time we were in there we were offered watches, mini-flashlights, pictures of the Virgin of Guadalupe, and special services to help us get things past the Mexican authorities. We were asked if we were going to Mexico to adopt a baby. If so we could get a good healthy one right here in town with all the papers we would need. In the event we weren't in a buying mode, there were those who were willing to buy our dollars for pesos at a great rate.

I waived everyone off. Then I made the mistake of opening a window of opportunity by asking the baby-for-sale guy what he meant by all the papers we would need, which was all he needed to hear as an authorization to pull up a chair and unleash the full fury of his salesmanship. "You no want be investigated, you reputation, you moral, you money, you everything and den wait and wait for answer? Our way fast, no expensive and más completo. You see, you no dopt nothing you go back to States with you own keed, get it," which he repeated with special emphasis on "you own."

While his tongue was wagging away he pulled a stack of plastic picture cards of babies from his shirt pocket and spread them out on the table. "Look at deez, you like?" Irritated, I looked away and said, "Not interested, and anyway how can a couple prove he child is theirs, surely the U.S. authorities will want proof."

"*Fácil hombre*," was his pre-packaged answer, "you see, you have a doctor certificato say he deliver baby. Nobody question him. Then baby register registry. When you leave States and enter Mexico no one know if you wife be pregnant. You understand Señor."

It took sometime to convince the baby salesman we were not interested. Finally, I was able to get rid of him by saying we already had three children of our own. Apparently accustomed to failing to make a transaction, he got up and matter-of-factly said if we knew of anyone who wanted a keed of their own come here and ask for Benito. Throughout this scene Benito acted no differently that the hucksters who were peddling watches and fake jewelry, just another piece of merchandise.

This was my introduction to two features of Mexican life. First, the fact that everything is obtainable in Mexico, it's a question of finding the right supplier. Second, that "no" is not always definitive, and "yes" means perhaps, a place where many things are not what they seem to be but only facades, approximations, halt-truths, surrogates, figments.

Back to the New Horizon and a sweaty evening of tossing and turning. At 7:30 am the phone rang. It was Goris Mozolcheck to tell me the dean of the Universidad Autonoma Law School had contacted the immigration people in Nuevo Laredo and had cleared our way through. A glass of orange juice, a cup of coffee and toast and off we went across the bridge and into Los Estados Unidos de Mexico.

The trip to Mexico City being the first for me was expectedly interesting. First, there was the winding road over the hilly terrain to Monterrey. A few miles south to Saltillo and my first taste of roasted goat, a delicacy in the north. I loved it and had it every time I passed the area over the following years. From Saltillo south to San Luis de Potosi, nothing but desert as far as the eyes could see, cactus, cloudless skies and heat, heat, and more heat. Occasionally, I came across someone standing along the side of the road – a mystery as to where he or she came from since there were no signs of houses let alone towns within sight – holding up some kind of animal by its tail. I stopped once to check this out and found the animal to be an iguana. When I asked the boy how he got out there in that solitary place he pointed to a bike lying next to a cactus plant. Where was he from, I asked. He pointed to the horizon behind him.

As I drove, I kept one eye on the road and the other on the car's temperature gauge. My greatest fear was an overheated radiator in the middle of nowhere. There were the waves of heat steaming up from the highway, almost hypnotic in effect.

At times I caught myself starting to doze off and the car veering off the pavement. The bumping snapped me back to wakefulness. I had no map, just instructions to follow the road straight to Mexico City. Wanting badly to get off the highway for a rest and maybe a cold drink, I sometimes turned off and followed feeder roads leading from the highway with no signs indicating where they led. Along one of these roads I spotted a fallen sign which I couldn't read. Hoping it would indicate where I was heading I stopped to lift up the sign only to find in faded colors the mean looking face of a boxer with shaving cream on his face and the words "Gillette Blue Blades" underneath. Unfailingly, after several miles of nothing I turned back to the highway out of fear I would run out of gas before I reached San Luis Potosi. I never found out where these side roads led, perhaps nowhere. There's a saying that if you're going nowhere in particular, any road will take you there. These side roads fitted the bill perfectly.

Arriving in San Luis Potosi was tantamount to coming across a desert oasis. I parked the car and headed straight for cold drinks. My first Mexican beer was quenchingly great. Thirst satisfied but hunger unappeased we had our first real meal in Mexico. After a few forkfuls I knew one aspect of living in Mexico was sure to be great and I was not to be disappointed.

The trip from San Luis Potosi to Ciudad de Mexico was far less monotonous than the prior leg of the trip as it took me through quaint little towns like Tula de Allende, Tepejidel Rio, Coyotepec as well as the larger city of Queretero. As I passed these villages my senses told me that at last I was in Latin American, the place I had seen in movies when I was a young kid. I had been in Cuba but this was different, this stuck me as more genuinely South American – actually Mexico is in North America. While the odors of sugar cane, coffee and tobacco dominated the air in Cuba, here in Mexico the aromas were different, though I could not immediately identify their origins. It didn't take long to realize the predominance of the smell of tortillas or corn. What I didn't see along the whole trajectory of our trip was a Mexican dozing against stucco house with his face hidden beneath a huge sombrero.

****

I lived in Mexico from January 1962 to September 1963, the time passed unnoticed probably because of the novelty of the new surroundings plus the time spent studying. I traveled to various must see places in the country. There was Taxco, Acapulco, Puebla, Veracruz, all interesting and charming in their own ways. I recall driving through a mountain range on my way to Acapulco when suddenly beautiful music came floating across a valley from a small town snuggled along the mountainside – like a scene from The Sound of Music. It was Tasco, a ruby of a town with charmingly narrow, steeply inclined streets where I expected to find Julie Andrews.

On the Gulf of Mexico side was Veracruz, Mexico's answer to Caribbean Islands atmosphere replete with black Mexicans. The city itself had little to recommend itself, certainly not the heat, humidity and lack of sanitation. On the other hand the fish dishes I savored were vindication enough.

Cuernavaca a small town southwest of and a mere fifty odd miles from Mexico City is where many wealthy Mexicans from the capital had summer and weekend homes. Flowers abounded and were everywhere. Cobblestone streets and a delicious year-round climate. I spent a relaxed Sunday at the spacious and tastefully appointed Cuernavaca home of Oscar Morineau, a prominent Mexican lawyer. Professor and Mrs. Thomas from SMU were there as were my new friends Maria and Gustavo Perez.

In Mexico City, I lived in a third-floor apartment on Avenida Insurgentes Sur immediately above the owner of the building who operated the car oil change shop on the street level floor. From my study I had a good view of the distant mountain range from where the clouds and rain came almost every day at around four o'clock in the afternoon.

Across the side street and below my window was a large vacant lot with a small shack on the Insurgentes Avenue side where a woman lived with a brood of children. I enjoyed watching her make the daily supply of tortillas by hand which she did invariably every morning around 7:30. The fresh smell of corn wafted up to my apartment and never failed to awaken my appetite. Equally as consistent a routine were the Sunday morning walks with her kids to the local church. On these religious occasions she combed her long black hair neatly into a bun on top of her head, put on shoes and removed her apron. Her kids each got a good scrubbing and sprucing up with the older scrubbing the next down in the age ladder.

****

I was at the offices of Oscar Morineau doing research when I chanced upon a scene which left a lingering impression on me. Morineau's office occupied the entire floor of the building the rear of which overlooked the backyard of a three-storied Colonial-style house. I was tired of reading and went to one of the windows to relax my eyes and give my brain a respite. My eyes kept coming back to the house directly below. It was an old large orange-tiled roof house whose backyard was landscaped with trees, flowers and bushes all encircled by a diligently manicured six-foot hedge.

Uniformed maids came out of the house carrying and then preparing a long table with plates, dinnerware, glasses and flowers. A woman, seemingly the lady of the house, followed and made minor changes of the items on the table.

As if on cue people emerged from the house. There must have been some ten or more in all. They stood around talking and drinking cocktails which they had carried with them from inside. After a few minutes an elderly man and his equally aged wife gingerly came into the yard supported by the trustworthy arms of two maids. They were led to the biggest and most comfortable chairs. No sooner were they seated when people went to them and one by one kissed the couple. More people, some with children, began arriving, each dutifully but with obviously felt tenderness went directly to the elderly couple, kissed each of them, exchanged a few words and then dissolved into the gathering. There were quiet complacent smiles on the wrinkled faces of the aged couple as they surveyed the family scene.

As I opened the window to capture the sounds from the scene below, I was met by faint background music, tinkling glasses as people were served more cocktails, and the playful but controlled voices of children. The talk seemed light-hearted and punctuated with laughter with the exception of a business-suited couple who seemed to be discussing weighted matters. At some signal undetected by me people made their way to the table to begin what turned out to be two-hour lunch to which time had not been invited.

Here smack in the middle of a grimy urban metropolis not far from the anarchic traffic, aggressive street vendors and snotty beggar kids sat this oasis of abundance and amiable tranquility. It conjured up a tableau of a medieval noble family gathering in a castle perched on a hilltop overlooking a grungy, muddy, peasant village with which the nobles had no dealings other than to receive rental income in the form of crops or of tax revenues. But the scene could also have depicted an effort to preserve the vanishing institution of the Mexican family as a nurturing social unit embellished by the quiet elegance of manners of years past.

I sometimes recall that scene and wonder whether others like it might still be found in Mexico or whether it too has been relegated to the status of a social museum-piece in the wake of Mexico's headlong rush to achieve developed-country status.

****

For days the local newspapers had been announcing and discussing the upcoming official state visit to Mexico of president John F. Kennedy and the first lady.   Apparently, it had been many years since a Head of State of Mexico's northern neighbor had come to Mexico on a official visit. Kennedy was well-liked throughout Latin America (ex-Cuba) and his Alliance For Progress initiative viewed as tangible evidence of Washington's renewed interest in this Hemisphere.   Mexico was no exception.   The warm and enthusiastic reception the Kennedys received was something to behold. I was fortunate in having a good view of the huge crowds that lined the downtown streets as the presidential motorcade passed by. The Kennedys were caught up by the enthusiasm as revealed by their broad smiles and animated waving to the crowds.

A report in Time Magazine poignantly described the scene:

> *By uncontrolled millions, Mexico gave him (President Kennedy) and his pretty wife warmest abrazos. Gnarled old peasant women threw bunches of white flowers at the cavalcade as it passed, urchins broke from the throng squealing, "Mister Kennedy", One youngster even had a reassuring sign which said, "We play touch football"- which the Kennedys were often shown playing at their Hyanisport compound.*

A few days prior to the president's arrival and during one of my classes at the law school the subject of Kennedy's visit came up. First the professor and then segue-like my classmates stood up and went into tirades against the United States, mouthing a litany of evils which supposedly characterized the history of the United States' "imperialistic" relationship to Mexico. These guys were no college sophomores from whom one might expect such attitudes, they were mature men, professionals, married, some holding important posts, both private and public.

I sat there speechless but mostly angry. Several times I was on the verge of speaking up in a one-man defense while at other times I felt I should walk out of the classroom. My waxing uneasiness must have become noticeable as one of the classmates walked over to my desk, placed a hand on my shoulder and with the other asked for quiet; "Let's make one thing clear beyond any question. Nothing that has been said in this room over the last few minutes in any way reflects how we feel about the American people. We have been criticizing the past governments of the United States, not the people (a distinction I was to hear often in my contacts with Latin Americans). Much less have we meant to denigrate or offend our dear colleague Dominic for

155

whom we all have huge respect and whom we consider one of our own." Signs of approval swept across the room as I tight-smiled uneasily.

Following Kennedy's visit, I asked some of my classmates to explain the fact that throughout the President's stay in Mexico there were no demonstrations against him. From what I had heard in class I would have expected people to pour into the streets in mass protest. The explanation is simple I was told. On the day before the president's arrival the Mexican government's security forces fanned out across the city visiting known as well as suspected leftist and extremists, including powerful labor leaders and academic figures bearing a simple message; stay home for three days i.e. until Kennedy leaves the country. It was not necessary to make overt threats as to the nature of the consequences for failure to heed the government's "request." And so those who would have been expected to organize demonstrations remained at home and with clenched teeth and white knuckles watched the events on television.

The enthusiastic reception, the classroom diatribes and the lack of anti-American demonstrations were another example of the internal contradictions of Mexico in those days, of how appearances were not always the messengers of reality, how manifestations of democracy often masked a wholly different underlying realpolitik. They revealed how cruelty and amiability can co-habit in a single human event with no feelings of contradiction.

****

Raul Guarin was a youngish looking lawyer in one of my classes, thoroughly likable and friendly. His roots were from a small town in southern Mexico (the name of which I do not recall but will call "Tulupcin") where his family enjoyed strong political power. Raul invited five of us classmates to visit his hometown for a special festive event to take place over a weekend. We were to be the special guests of his uncle, the mayor of the town. For those of us who were married the invitation was for the husbands only, no wives, no children.

The trip was made in two jeeps beginning around 4 p.m. and saw us arrive at Tulupcin at 9:15 p.m. We traveled over mountains, across arid plains, through darkened villages of stucco houses, across streams, and into what seemed like interminable darkness.

Not much happened the night of our arrival except getting us to our respective lodgings. We were not to be together. I had just put on my pajamas when there was a faint knock at my door. I opened the door, standing there with a shy smile on her moon-shaped face was a young native girl. "Chocolate señor?" She was carrying a tray with a steaming cup of hot chocolate, three tortillas and a square of cheese. She didn't wait for an answer, just walked in and placed the tray on a table. She turned, went to the door, turned again smiled and closed the door. I enjoyed the warming effect of the evening snack. I had pleasant anticipations of what lay ahead the next two days as I reached out to turn off the lamps for what in the fresh coolness of night turned out to be a thoroughly relaxing and refreshing sleep.

The following day I was up at around 7:30p.m. No sooner was I out of bed and walking around when I heard the same faint knock at the door. It was the young native girl, same shy smile, but this time holding a basin of hot water. "For shaving señor." This time she handed me the basin and left. I soon discovered why the water delivery was necessary or at least hospitable. The shower had only one knob and in the U.S.A. it would have the letter "C" on it. I absolutely detested cold showers so it took me ages to manage to get my whole body wet, soaped and rinsed. As I was toweling myself I noticed the clean refreshing odor from my body which didn't come from the odorless nondescript piece of soap I found in the shower tray. It had to come from the water. My classmate buddies confirmed having experienced this same phenomenon. I recall our mentioning whether this special water could be the basis of a business venture.

I was picked up by Raul at around nine and we went around gathering the rest of our group. We went straight to the mayor's office located in a two-story building in the center of the town plaza. It was in this plaza that the parade was to pass.

The mayor of Tulupcin was a diminutive figure, small almond shaped eyes, light, thinning brownish hair, features at odds with those of the people of the town, who were clearly of Indian descent. The mayor was particularly pleased to have me present since he could not recall an American ever visiting his town. The mayor's wife soon joined us with her four children. She was somewhat taller than her husband, sharp-nosed, very black hair tied at the back of her head with a red ribbon. Alert eyes and imparting an aura of being very much in command and self-possessed.

Soon others joined us, mostly relatives of the mayor. The proper introductions were made and there were expressions of enthusiasm over having so many distinguished guests, lawyers no less, from the Big City. We were to occupy front seats on the balcony overlooking the town plaza. The

157

mayor was seated in the middle, to his right his wife, his two sisters and one brother. To his left the town treasurer, the parish priest, another public official, then us the visitors or, more accurately, the honored guests.

The parade was colorful, native dresses flowing in the breeze, banners, drums, odd looking flutes and horns, men in native dress mounted on beautiful horses. I turned to Raul to ask what must have seemed a stupid question. I asked what event is the town celebrating. It was the 100th year of the town's official recognition as a separate political sub-division. As the parade was drawing to a close Raul nudged me with his elbow pointing down to the end of the parade. At first I didn't see anything unusual. Noticing I had not spotted what he was pointing at he said to look at what the little girl on the right was carrying. I looked and had to smile and applaud, for she was carrying a small American flag. Surprised by my applause others on the balcony looked in that direction, spotted the flag then looking at me joined in the applause. I must have grown ten feet in stature at that moment. It was later explained that when it was known that an American would witness the parade and with no American flag to be found in town, the mayor's wife had a flag made for the occasion.

Following the parade a sumptuous lunch was served in the main reception room of the mayor's headquarters. Abundance of food and drink. Conversations. Questions about the U.S., about American movies, about Mrs. Kennedy and how beautiful and elegant she was. What was I doing in Mexico. Were Americans really interested in Mexican laws?

After lunch we were given a brief tour of the town. I was particularly impressed by the beauty of the surrounding countryside. Lovely rolling hills, lush verdant vegetation. How I asked can the existence of this town be explained since it seemed to stand alone among the vastness of its peopleless surroundings. Again, in Mexico, what the eyes see is not necessarily what is. Behind several of the hills lay small villages. Tulupcin was the commercial, banking, trading and political center for these villages.

By 4 p.m. we were taken back to our quarters for a highly recommended siesta since the approaching evening's festivities were to be lively.

And so they proved to be. It seemed every house had its own opened-to-the- public party going on. There was also the official party, replete with the inevitable Mariachis, tequila, tequila and more tequila. Tequila in a shot-glass, tequila disguised in orange juice, tequila in daiquiris, tequila salt and lemon wedges everywhere.

We attended the official party as a group. People went out of their way to be friendly, we were made to feel like celebrities. We were invited to private parties and dispersed in different directions. Music flowed from open doors and grated windows and filled the streets with festive sounds. It seemed everyone in town had a party going. I must have visited a handful of houses that night. Before I realized what was happening I was drunk, very much drunk. Somewhere during the festivities apparently I picked up, or was probably assigned a female escort who I was later told accompanied me during my rounds. I was told I danced with her, a claim I had trouble believing since I was born with two left feet. I didn't recall having an escort and much less having danced with her. Apparently she got me to my lodgings and to bed.

The following morning was pure undiluted misery. Surely I had died and was now in the place where one atones for past excesses, an accelerated karma of sorts. My head felt like it was full of exposed nerve ends that fired off waves of pain at the slightest movement or sound. Raul came by and managed to get me to the kitchen where the smiling maid had prepared *huevos rancheros* and tortillas. If there was anything on the face of the planet that could distract me from the head misery it proved to be the hot *huevos rancheros*.

Huevos rancheros in our bellies we crawled into the jeeps and headed back to Mexico City. I dozed most of the way, occasionally dreaming about the mysterious faceless girl of the night before. Why couldn't I remember who she was. Then another dream, a smiling young native girl bringing me a hot chocolate, tortillas and cheese. Could it have been, maybe? But no, I would have noticed. Or would I? Neither Raul nor any of my other companions shed any light on this.

****

In 1963 pretty Joanna was born. Perhaps, I dared hope, Joanna would make the difference needed in our marriage to change its perilous course. At first Joanna consumed a lot of attention and our time leaving less in which we could argue. In the end the dynamics of the impending collapse had too much traction to be overcome by Joanna's arrival but it was allayed for a while. Joanna brought great joy to me and a breath of fresh air to our home.

****

According to my agreement with the Southwestern Legal Foundation upon my completion of studies in Mexico I was to return to teach at the Institute of the Americas. So in 1963 we were on the road again this time heading north on the way to Dallas.

I taught at the Institute through the 1963-1964 school year. Although I found a measure of satisfaction in teaching, it was not an activity I wanted to embrace as a profession. But I was willing to remain at my teaching position for the promised two school year commitment and would have done so had not an unforeseen set of circumstances intervened.

During early Spring of 1964 Dean Heims informed Professor Mozolchek that he would not return to the Law School in September. He was going to New York to join the Mathew-Bender Law Book Publishing Company as a Vice President. Professor Mozolchek, the Dean's fair haired boy on the faculty, soon learned that his contract for the next school year would not be renewed. Almost concomitantly with these announcements I learned I too would not be back in September. The news of my fate was shocking for I had not given any thought, let alone made any plans, to finding employment outside the School. To make things worse I now had a third mouth to feed. Fortunately, a solution soon made its appearance. Dean Heims asked me whether I would accept a job in New York with Mathew Bender. And so it was that during the summer of 1964 I moved to New York to begin what proved to be a period of rocky instability and of exciting new experiences.

Before ringing down the curtain on my brief professorial stint in Dallas, there is a "Where-were-you-when" event to mention. One November 1963 evening I was listening to the evening news and learned that president Kennedy was to visit to Dallas. Upon hearing this I commented that the president seemed to be following me around for he had gone to Mexico when I was there and now here he was coming to Dallas.

November 22 was a regular day at the law school. No one I met mentioned the fact the president was arriving that day. Having finished my 11 o'clock class I was about to head home for lunch when suddenly there was a jolt of commotion in the halls. People scurrying around, others circling radios. "What's wrong?" I asked. "It's the president, he's been shot," came the responses from different directions. I lingered for a few minutes then decided to dash home for the TV news. Outside the school the air was electric with the urgent screaming of sirens and police cars racing by.

That evening I heard the gruesome details of what had occurred, president Kennedy had been hit by a bullet in the throat. He also had a massive, gaping wound in the back right side of the head. Doctor Malcolm Perry – the first physician to treat the president – tried a number of resuscitative measures including oxygen, anesthesia, an indotracheal tube, a tracheotomy, blood and fluids. A closed-chest cardiograph massage was attempted. This produced palpable pulses for a fleeting moment but to no avail. As I heard this I shook my head in disbelief. They're taking about the president, this can't be! The TV newscast switched the scene to Air Force One where Vice President Lyndon Johnson was being sworn in as the nation's new president.

Later that evening, I recalled an incident that occurred when I was a student at the Institute of the Americas a few years earlier. It happened at a gas station in Dallas. The attendant must have noticed the Massachusetts license plates on my car for when he came to be paid he said, "You can tell that red-head president we just don't like him here, tell'm to stay-way from Texas."

Speaking of ironies, President Kennedy visits to Mexico and is greeted by a cascade of flowers from the surrounding buildings. President Kennedy visits Dallas, U.S.A and is greeted with mortal gun fire from a nearby building.

THE BIG APPLE

Off with the damp shirt, my shoes and the cover of the container of Chinese-Cuban food, and filling a glass to the brim with a cold soft drink, I turned on the TV and began eating my dinner. No significant news other than heat-wave related fatalities occurring around the northeast. Kids dancing and jumping around water-spouting fire hydrants in the Inner City. The room felt good and refreshing after a day out in the city. I went over to the window and there it was a slice of the Manhattan skyline and here I was at the Carlyle Hotel, a guest of Mathew Bender Publishing.

I was in an orientation period, getting to know the people I would be working with, the facilities, the books being written and general workplace information. After work I enjoyed taking different routes to my hotel and absorbing as much of the sounds and sights of the city as possible. It was hot but of no consequence to me for I was thrilled to be in New York, the capital of the world, and I had a job, a job in New York mind you. Not that this was a dream realized, for I never seriously contemplated working in New York, but it was a dream I realized I should have had.

I rented an apartment in Bayside a quintessential middle-class neighborhood in Queens. I don't recall why I selected this location, perhaps it was suggested to us by Sheldon Smith my erstwhile musician buddy from Fitchburg who was now married and living in Queens. To get to work I took a bus to Flushing where I boarded an elevated into Manhattan. From the drop off location I took a subway, or sometimes a bus, to Mathew Bender on the East Side which was a short walk from the United Nations Headquarters.

Initially this round-trip was pleasant enough for it was a part of my New York experience. If this is what New Yorkers did then who was I to complain.

As time passed the novelty of the commute petered out and I became aware that not everyone in Manhattan or at Mathew Bender underwent anything like my commute routine. Couldn't I be doing something more useful or interesting during the weekly twelve hours I spent on elevated trains, sub-ways and busses, was a question which kept popping up as I looked out the windows of the elevated.

It was during the months at Bayside that the underlying tensions in my marriage surfaced again this time more acute than ever. Arguments became a daily occurrence and stress increased. I felt trapped and asphyxiated and an urgent need to break out of my confinement. After serious introspection and no small amount of vacillation I decided to move out and to take a small efficiency apartment in down-town Flushing. The aspect of this move which left me with a heavy heart was little Joanna. It was her image that tested my resolve the most severely. But the specter of life with Lena with all that this implied was enough to re-enforce my determination. So I bit my lower lip and weathered the emotional turbulence.

Her name was Carol Simon. Tall, stately, not pretty but femininely handsome and ten years my junior. An insatiable devotee of music, books, movies and the theater; not a hippie but definitely sympathetic to many of the feelings, values, beliefs of that rebellious generation, deeply opposed to the Vietnam War, and convinced of the superior value of personal freedom over social demands for conformity to what in her mind were the dehumanizing and often sclerotic rules of social behavior. She was the first Jewish girl I had ever knowingly met.

She worked at Mathew Bender Publishing, her cubicle was at the other end of the large room in which my workplace was located. We often chatted during coffee breaks and soon I began to sense there was something special about her. One day just before quitting time and in part because of my aversion to going directly to my lonely Flushing efficiency apartment, I asked her whether she would like to take in a movie. Without giving the proposal much thought she said yes, but first, however, she had to drop off shoes to be repaired. I don't know why I remember this shoe thing unless because having shoes repaired rings odd to 21st century ears.

Not knowing Manhattan very well especially as to the location of movie theaters, I asked her to make a choice. We went to Greenwich Village, a place

I had heard of as being known for its resident artists, hippies, followers of the Bohemian and other off-beat life-styles. Judging from the way she got us through the labyrinth of criss-crossing narrow streets of the Village, all with memory-challenging names rather than numbers as in uptown, it was obvious Carol was no stranger to this area. As it turned out it was a section of Manhattan I would re-visit many times.

What happened that night presaged what the following months had in store for me. Since my early years as a frequent customer of the Strand Theater, my interest in movies had faded. The few movies I had seen were the typical kisch Hollywood productions of that period. Carol suggested we see the Italian movie, Le Notte di Cabiria (The Nights of Cabiria) directed by Federico Fellini. This became my introduction to the voguish foreign films of that era, particularly those from Italy, France and Sweden. At this time Hollywood was in serious decline and foreign movies were the in-thing, at least among the more educated urbanities. For me it was catch-up time as I saw such end-of-World-War-II movies of the neo-realist genre as *"Roma, Citta Aperta"* (Open City) Roberto Rosselini's; *La Terra Trema* (The Earth Trembles), Visconti; *Ladri di Biciclette* (Bicycle Thieves), de Sica; *La Strada* (The Road), *la Dolce Vita*, Otto e Mezzo (8 ½), *Guiletta degli Spiriti* (Juliet of the Spirits), Fellini; *Deserto Rosso* (Red Desert) and *"La Notte"* (the Night), Antonioni; *Les Quatre Cents Coups* (The 400 Blows), Truffaut; *Une Femme est une Femme*, Godard; *The Seventh Seal and Wild Strawberries*, Bergman. Through all of these Carol was my knowledgeable guide.

These films belong to the golden era of cinematography when movies were exalted to their rightful status as art in which the theme of the human condition was examined. It was no coincidence that this transformation of the cinema occurred in Europe while Hollywood was struggling to find a new identity. Post-war Europe was a devastated landscape strewn with spiritual, economic and social corpses while in the victorious U.S.A. people were content with jobs, new homes, money to buy all those goodies unavailable during the War, in other words they were in pursuit of the good life.

As history has shown it is during times of adversity that the human spirit soars and masterworks are produced.

I occasionally rent one of these movies and find they have lost little of their essence as classics. Styles in dress, tastes in music, advances in technology and other externals may have changed but the underlying human condition remains as it has been.

Back to the first night. While we were watching *Le Notte di Cabiria* the weather had turned nasty with strong winds and chilling rain. Braving these elements we made our way to a tiny side street restaurant specializing in Middle Eastern style cuisine. Though our clothes were damp our conversation was spirited and lively, as we got to know each other. We agreed we would see more of the Fellini-type movies.

Except for the brief episode involving Al Maruso back in Cuba I had given little if any thought to my Italian background since departing for the Navy in 1950. Seeing the great Italian movies, hearing the praise heaped upon them by sophisticated and educated non-Italians such as Carol and her friends not to mention the New York Times movie critics, I experienced not so much an ethnic re-birth – which Al Maruso had first urged upon me – but more of the beginning of recognition of the artistic genius of the Italian spirit, all thanks to a young Jewish girl.

Carol had the charming ability to derive delight from the simplest of events, a trait I discovered was not uncommon among certain of the iconoclastic youth of that period. Preparing dinner, sipping a glass of wine, seeing a movie, sitting on a bench at the waterfront on the Brooklyn Heights Promenade in the early evening with the shimmering lights of Manhattan reflecting off the water.

Carol devoured books at an amazing clip, a book a day was far from unusual. Since leaving college my reading had been limited to academic legal texts so at first I was rusty in exchanging ideas on fiction, which were her favorites. Though she read across a wide spectrum of fiction writers, even Italian writers which I looked up and had suggested, what she preferred was skewed towards Jewish novelists such as Philip Roth, Normal Mailer and Malamud. Most importantly she got me reading and appreciating good fiction.

Perhaps out of a notion that the flow of new experiences should not be one directional and that I should contribute something to our relationship I introduced her to jazz. I bought a number of records. I took her to Birdland, the Mecca of jazz in Manhattan at that time. We went there twice, once to hear Woody Herman and a second time to hear Gerry Muligan's big band. Neither one nor their combination resulted in generating much enthusiasm in this genre of music.

My efforts in the world of opera did result in at least one very special evening. For many years the Metropolitan Opera Company as well as world famous invited sopranos and tenors had performed on the stage of the Metropolitan Opera House, one of New York's towering cultural landmarks. For some reason it was decided to tear down the Opera House and to shift performances to the new Lincoln Center for the Performing Arts. Wednesday was to be the last performance at the Met and I managed somehow to get two tickets, *albeit*, for seats way up in the balcony. The opera was Puccini's *Tosca*. A spell-binding performance. As Tosca threw herself from the battlement of the palace and the final curtain fell there was wild applause, shouting, whistling and cries of Bravo, Bravo. Not one single person I could see remained seated. So many flowers showered upon it that the stage took on the appearance of a Wizard of Oz landscape. There was curtain call after curtain call.

On the way out people were silent as if still under the spell of the poignant *tour de force* performance they had just experienced. Carol said she enjoyed the different experience. She thought the music was beautiful and the voices superb, though she found the storyline of soap opera quality. We agreed that what made the evening special was the fact that the tragedy unfolding on the stage was matched by the heavy hearts the audience in knowing this was to be the last performance ever again to be heard in this illustrious house of opera.

While I was fortunate to have been enriched by having known Carol and to have taken much of lasting value from our friendship, there was also an enigmatic side to her character. Though for the most part Carol's behavior was perfectly normal, sporadically Carol vanished to be replaced by a very different and disturbed person.

She was known to occasionally lock herself in her room and to refuse to see anyone, losing days of work. I heard that on one occasion her father had to go to her college to convince her to come out of her dorm room. Why this happened and what went awry in her mind was a mystery, one which she was unwilling or unable to explain. As far as I knew she never sought professional help for this condition.

One evening as we were leaving a theater, she suggested we sit on a park bench for a while. We did and began discussing the movie we had just seen. Suddenly with no forewarning of any kind she began shouting, "What are these stupid people doing walking around? Who are these people? Why is that ugly bastard laughing?" It was as if she suddenly felt she was in hostile surroundings. When I reached over to take her arm suggesting I take her home, she stood up and furiously flung her bag to the ground causing the contents to scatter in all directions. After retrieving as many of the items as I could locate, I walked her home. She remained silent the whole way. It was as if the Carol Simon I knew had been replaced by someone else.

Who was the real Carol Simon? Why these occasional outbursts or withdrawals? Whatever the answer to those questions may have been the whole issue was reduced to insignificance by the fact she was a beautiful spirit who guided me through a world previously unknown to me and along the way increased my appreciation of the richness of the life-experience. I was the prime beneficiary of our friendship.

****

I was walking briskly along a main Brooklyn boulevard. It was early autumn and the air had a pleasant nip in it and I was feeling good. I noticed but paid no special attention to a black man walking down the sidewalk towards me. When just a few feet away he stepped in front of me and brandished a long knife with which he proceeded to poke me in the stomach "Give me everything you have" he commanded punctuating his order with a few more knife-jabs. I was shocked and scared to hell. The guy had a distant glassy look in his -eyes which I surmised was the result of too much liquor or drugs.

Analyzing the situation I figured that if I could distract him for even a moment I could turn and get away, so I said, "You're stupid, here comes a police car" and without troubling to see how he had reacted quickly turned to run. As I did so I felt a dull blow to the middle of my back that sent me sprawling to the sidewalk. My pants were torn at my scraped knees and my desensitized attacker was approaching me with knife in hand. He turned and walked away as a police car came down the street toward us. Another black man who apparently had witnessed the incident came from across the street while at the same time hailing the police car. He helped me to my feet and waved the cops over to us.

I was now sitting in the back of the police car with a policeman at my side. We went up and down streets stopping to grab and search anyone who looked even remotely suspicious, pushing them up against the police car and with a strong light focused on their faces repeating the same question over and over again, "Is this the guy?"

"No" it's not him. No, not this one either. No not him".

I was getting woozy as the constant car radio static and the meaningless exchanges between the officers in the car and whoever was at the other end, and the increasing heat came crushing in on me. With no warning pain struck me deep in my chest. I told the officer. He told me to take off my jacket and as I did, he said "This guy's soaked in blood let's get him to a hospital."

In the next frame of my memory I was lying on a gurney in a hall among a sea of beds. I must have again lost consciousness for when I next opened my eyes I was in a room with Carol sitting next to my bed. Her telephone number had been found in my wallet.

Not yet completely conscious or aware of the circumstances, my thoughts drifted back to an incident that happened when I was fifteen or so years old. It was a Saturday afternoon when Al Mastozzi and I were returning home from seeing a movie in downtown Fitchburg. Rather than taking the regular route home along Kimball Street, we elected to walk along the railroad tracks which ran parallel to it. Balancing ourselves on the tracks and throwing peanut shells at each other we were in a relaxed, playful mood. Soon the quiet of the afternoon was broken by the sound of an approaching train which seemed to be coming from the east just around a bend some 30 yards away. Let's put coins on the tracks and see what the train will do to them we commented. But on what track would the train come for there were three separate sets of tracks it could be on. While we talked about this the oncoming train though not yet visible sounded alarmingly close, so we made a run for it. Al went one way into the parking lot of the Finnish Cooperative while I went the opposite way to the foot of a six-foot wall separating the railway from the upper level of Kimball Street.

Al yelled that the train was approaching on the tracks nearest the wall I was at. "Run, run!" he screamed. I made several starts but backed away each time out of fear that Al might have been wrong and the train was in fact coming on the middle or farther tracks rendering it impossible to get across without stumbling and before the train would be upon me. So I tried to climb the wall up to Kimball Street. No luck as I kept slipping back down.

The roar of the train was all around me. I looked up and there was this huge smoke-spouting engine angrily careening around the bend exactly on the tracks next to my wall. A cold chill ran down my body; I could feel my hands trembling and my knees getting weak. There was no choice but to press my body against the wall with as much force as I could muster. I closed my eyes as first the monstrous locomotive and then an endless number of cars passed within a couple of feet from my sweating body. The roar of the passing cars was deafening, obliterating my history so that all was reduced to this moment in time, to this personal holocaust. I was convinced survival was possible only if God answered my prayers. Several times I started to cry only to check myself out of fear that doing so might make my body move even the slightest and cause the train to splatter me against the wall. Finally, the caboose passed and the train disappeared down the tracks as I, reeling from the experience, sat on the ground. Al came running across the tracks yelling, "Dom, are you OK?" I was far from OK for I had just had my first brush with death.

My reverie ended when a guy in a white jacket with a stethoscope dangling from his neck said "Buddy you're lucky, the knife just barely missed your aorta, which would have ended your life pretty dam fast. As it is you've escaped with a punctured lung. Once you leave here you are going to need a few weeks of rest, no lifting, no stressful motions." Carol told the doctor there was no problem and that she would be taking me with her. A few days passed and unable to get any answer from anyone as to my status, Carol said, "I'm taking you out of here." She helped me get dressed and we nonchalantly walked out of the hospital and took a cab to her apartment.

I never told anyone about the monumental stupidity I committed that Sunday evening on a Brooklyn street, for when I was told to hand over all my money what I had in my pocket was $5.00.

★★★★★★★★★★★★

I was pouring myself a cup of coffee in the Mathew Bender lunchroom when one of the lawyer editors came over to tell me that Jack Heims had resigned. Within one week after Jack's departure I was called into the editor's office. "Dominic, I believe your real interest is in international law and, frankly, we have no plans to cover that area of law." In other words I was again to pink-slip and Jack Heims my way out the door, déjà vu all over again.

Thus began another of my famine periods. After a few months of drawing blanks in my search for a job my funds were drying up. Every weekday morning saw me taking a subway to Manhattan to leave off resumes, then return to Carol's apartment and there check the help-wanted ads of the day's newspaper which she unfailingly left for me. I made telephone calls, many telephone calls.

An insidious depression began taking my mind hostage. Drained of self-esteem I fell into a period of self-pity mixed with anger against the world. How could a guy have so much education, know so much and yet be unable to get a job. I felt there surely must have been a conspiracy against me. Dam Jack Heims!

Fortunately, when my unemployment checks ran out I got a job as claims adjuster for the Firemen's Insurance Company. The work was non-challenging but it put some badly needed cash in my pocket and simultaneously rescued a small part of my self-esteem.

I worked at the Hartford for about four months when the big chance, that great dream in the sky, that opportunity of opportunities, that door to the legal big leagues materialized. But before that happened and while I was somnambulating my role as claims adjuster, another part of me went through a wrenching period of emotional distress. Carol and I separated and, as it turned out, were never again to see each other.

The warning signs of the impending break-up were flashing brightly had I been honest enough to notice. Carol had not changed but I had. Shaken by my long futile search for employment post-Mathew Bender I came apart psychologically. I fell prey to feelings of self doubt and inferiority, of loss of self-worth mixed with suspicions that others were now looking down their noses on me, that I was being patronized. Carol was ten years younger than me. How, I brooded, could I compete with guys her age, guys with jobs, guys more naturally attuned to her lifestyle, guys who also believed the Vietnam War was immoral. I saw our relationship in jeopardy and became irrationally jealous. In an effort to prevent my fears from materializing I tried to build a wall around her and in doing so deprived her of the freedom so essential to who she was and which, not so incidentally, was what attracted me to her in the first place. She didn't complain openly but it should have been obvious to me that she was saddened and disconcerted. After accusing her of coquetting on her vacation, I walked out on her never to return.

The weeks following our break-up were emotionally draining. Her face was everywhere, I heard her voice and laughter whenever I was alone. My appetite abandoned me as did my interest in anything I previously enjoyed. It was at this time that angels in the form of two young lady co-workers at the Hartford and who knew of my break-up made their appearance and set about helping me through this emotional ordeal. They invited me to parties, movies and, as I recall vividly, an Arabic restaurant night-club featuring belly-dancers. Though I don't remember their names they are tucked away in a corner of my mind where I store memories which renew my faith in the inherent goodness of people.

One night some ten years later when I was in New York, I picked up the telephone directory in my hotel room and looked up Carol Simon. There she was, but at a different address. I dialed the number. After a few rings I was about to hang up when I heard, "hello". I didn't reply immediately, not knowing whether I should speak or just hang up. "Hello, who's out there?" she said. No question it was Carol's voice.

"Hello, Carol do you recognize my voice?"

"Dominic, of course I know your voice. Where are you?" She said she knew I was living in Colombia and what I was doing there as she regularly received information about law firms. We spoke for some 30-minutes about collective memories and particularly of her life since we separated. No she had not married. Her father, to whom she was devoted and with whom she had a most beautiful relationship, had died. She told me she still had the Stan Kenton records I had bought and played on her stereo, but admitted she didn't play them. No she had not seen any operas but did remember the night we saw Tosca. I inquired about some of her friends from back then. Paul was working with the New York City government, Elaine was now a professor of literature at the NYU, Howney had committed suicide. It was a profoundly satisfying few minutes from which I came away pleased to have learned she had done well for herself.

Several years later I again fingered a New York telephone directory but Carol's name was not to be found.

****

My phone rang at the Firemens, I answered and a voice said, "Mr. Perenzin, this is Albert Pareño of the Curtis-Mallet Prevost Colt & Mosle Law Firm. I would like to talk to you about a position in our firm. My jaw must have reached the floor.

And so it was, Dominic Perenzin from Fitchburg, Massachusetts, the son of Italian immigrants was about to become a lawyer with a big-time Wall Street law firm. A dream I would not have dared to dream. It was now ten years from the date my father proudly attended my graduation from Boston University and told me that that was the proudest day of his life.

This was truly a new world I was entering. Talented lawyers, interesting cases, a refined ambience, great restaurants and private clubs. One of the first things I did upon starting work was to walk over to the Brooks Brothers store

– the dean of professional men's couture – and bought a suit, shirts, ties and the first hat I had ever owned.

Most of my work at the firm involved Latin America, at times requiring travel abroad to places like Mexico and Venezuela. My first week, however, was anything but pleasant as I was literally bombarded with things to do. I felt I had hit the ground running. One of the partners with whom I worked most frequently called me to his office and asked for the memo he had requested I prepare. "Sorry," I said, "I've been doing research for Al Pareño and haven't had time to work on the memo"

"Listen Perenzin," came his sharp rebuke, "you're on Wall Street now, you do two, three, four…things at the same time, get it." And that more or less describes high-powered legal work in New York.

Perhaps one of the most interesting cases I worked involved the designer Oscar de la Renta. It was interesting not only from a strictly multi-layered legal aspects but also from the exposure it afforded me to the whirlwind fashion world. In working on the case we often had to meet de la Renta wherever he happened to be at the time. He never seemed to have time to come to our office. We met him at work overseeing the selection of materials, at his gorgeously appointed Manhattan town house or at the actual designing rooms of his business. We did, however, have a brief get together at the bar of the St. Regis Hotel right after signing the agreements to celebrate the event with champagne.

For the most part the firm's client's were moneyed individuals or families and major corporations. There were also clients promoting new ventures. Quick talking, convincingly glib and at times charming individuals whose mission in life was to put a group of investors together for one project or another, copper in Mexico, oil in Peru, etc…During the time I was with the firm I don't recall hearing of the success of any of the ventures though the promotional material spoke of potentially mouth watering profits. Perhaps they required longer incubation periods.

The 1960's was a decade of mutual funds. We at Curtis-Mallet had our share of setting up funds. It was during this period that I learned a lesson not taught in law school. While working late putting together a new mutual fund a partner commented that at times a lawyer's most useful resources were a pair of scissors and adhesive tape. Funds were basically boilerplate clauses. Do one and with a few additions or deletions you can clone as many as you wish.

It was the year 1970 and I had been on Wall Street some four years and the almost daily work pressure combined with the intensity of living in Manhattan began to weigh on me. The desire to escape from all of this kept nibbling at me. I found the manner in which the firm was conducting Latin American legal work to be unsatisfactory, depending, in my way of thinking, too heavily on what independent attorneys in a given country advised us as to the applicable law and possible solutions to problems. I missed the hands-on approach.

I conveyed these feelings and beliefs to some of my legal brethren in the firm and as a result a chain of events took place that led to a decision which nudged my life into another major change of direction, one that would last no slight 18 years.

It all began when an associate stuck his head in my office one day to tell me he had learned of an international law firm that was in the market for a lawyer to work overseas and that the associate was going to be interviewed. I wished him good luck. The next day he suggested I talk to them about the overseas position because the firm had an operating model that he was sure I would find interesting. He gave me the interviewing partner's card. I did give him a call and did meet him. As a result I was offered the opportunity of opening an office for Kirkwood, Kaplan, Russin & Vecchi in Bogotá. The firm already had offices in Washington, D.C., the Dominican Republic, Thailand and Vietnam. I was impressed by the firm's operating model and agreed to consider the offer.

Bogotá, Colombia? I couldn't remember one case I had worked on in which Colombia was involved, a 1970 version of "where the hell is Cuba." So I went to our firm's index of cases going back ten years and found nothing on Colombia of any substance. None of my associate friends knew of any work we had done involving Colombia, Venezuela, Mexico, Argentina and Brazil yes, but not Colombia.

I discussed the possibility at home with no resulting decision. I read material on Colombia in the hope this would help me arrive at a decision. No luck.

Some time passed and yet I could not make up my mind perhaps my sub-conscious was hoping for a *deus ex machina* solution, instead what I got was a telephone call. My secretary told me there was a gentlemen on the line who claimed to be a good friend who wanted to surprise me. Should she put him through. Alright, I'll pick up.

Perenzin:	Hello
Caller:	Dominic do you remember my voice
Perenzin:	No I don't but talk a little more
Caller	Don't tell me you've forgotten your great friend from Dallas.
Perenzin:	Oscar, Oscar Tanifaz

And so it was, Oscar Tanifaz from Bolivia, my buddy from Institute of the Americas. He was staying at the St. Regis Hotel would be in town for a few days and said he would love to see me. We chatted for a few minutes and agreed to meet at his hotel.

In the cab on my way over to the hotel I wondered how Oscar could afford to stay at such expensive lodgings when some eight years earlier he had to scrape in order to do things which most of us took for granted. As my cab passed a Dunkin Donut shop I was reminded of time Oscar stopped for a cup of coffee in downtown Dallas but didn't have money enough to buy a donut. Perhaps he inherited a tin mine. It began to rain and I sat back as pleasant scenes from Dallas paraded across my mind.

"The room of Oscar Tanifaz" I asked the desk clerk.

"Just a minute sir", as the clerk looked up the name in the registration book. Here it is, "Minister Oscar Tanifaz. Sorry I can't give you his room number but I can call him for you. Your name please".

I sat in the lobby waiting for Oscar to appear. Minister? What's that all about I wondered compounding my curiosity. The elevator door opened and out stepped Oscar Tanifaz. Our embrace was warm and lasting. "Mi querido Dominic," were his first words. Yes it was him, same metal rimmed spectacles, unchanged facial expression of perpetual surprise, hair longer but also grayer than I recalled and still trim as ever.

We sat in the bar for a while over a drink and I wasted little time in asking about the Minister stuff.

"Yes, I'm the Bolivian Minister of Hydrocarbons", he smiled and asked whether I was interested in hearing about the folkloric set of circumstances underlying his appointment. I told him I would and suggested he go home with me, for Lena expected him and was preparing dinner.

On the way to my apartment he explained that the freshly minted government of Bolivia needed a Minister of Hydrocarbons. A friend who was close to the president-elect knowing that Oscar had studied in Texas and had taken a course in oil and gas law recommended Oscar for the post. That was all there was to it.

During the course of that most enjoyable evening of reminiscing about old times, I brought up the matter of Colombia. Oscar said Bogotá was considered the Athens of Latin America and culturally and linguistically a marvelous place to live. He had been there several times and was delighted. If I made the new office successful it would be a feather in my cap and who knows where it might lead me. He urged me to accept the offer.

I pondered Oscar's advise over the next few days. True, I was becoming weary of the stress that was New York but walk away from a good position on Wall Street, interesting case work, international travel, fabulous dry martinis served one of the street's watering holes and all the magic that was New York in exchange for the uncertainties of opening an office in a little known Latin American country? Gradually the enticing challenge of the move overpowered my concerns and I accepted the offer to go to Bogotá, Colombia to open an office for Kirkwood, Kaplan, Russin & Vecchi. In so doing I was about to draw down the curtain on the New York episode of my life. It had been a marvelous experience, so very, very special for things done, things learned and above all else for the fascinating unforgettable people met.

MANHATTAN VIGNETTES

During my flight to Bogotá some of the experiences I had had in New York came to mind and kept me company all the way, and for a few fleeting moments caused me to question my decision to give all that up.

I suppose these vignettes could have occurred in any sizeable metropolitan area yet they do have a certain aura of the diverse, bizarre, tragic, inspiring, heroic, callous, loving, indifferent, mean, whimsical and magic that is New York City.

I had separated from Carol Simon and was living in an apartment off of Riverside Drive. It was mid-summer and still hot that Saturday at 3 a.m. when I got out of bed, poured a glass of orange juice and went to the window. The street was quiet, no traffic or people, no movement at all. The silence was conducive to roaming thoughts such as my new job on Wall Street, the lawyers I had met, those whom I immediately had visceral good feelings about and those whom I was sure I would not like. What's Carol Simon been doing? Will I pass the New York Bar Exam?

About to turn away from the window to make another effort at sleeping, I noticed a light in an apartment across the street, the only lighted window in the whole eight-story building. I saw a figure in the apartment and squinting my eyes half-closed to get a better focus I realized it was a woman scantly dressed in what seemed to be her panties and a brassiere. She stood in a full side view for a few moments, stepped forward out of view, then back into view where she remained with her gaze straight ahead, apparently on some object out of my line of vision. She repeated the motions. She was holding what appeared to be a stick and came to the conclusion that she was probably in the process of painting or sketching something.

What followed was one of those rare times when against his nature a person does something totally out of character like stepping out of who you really are. Not something one would plan to do someday, simply a spontaneous thing.

I stood there watching her for a while when an idea came to me. I put on my pants, hesitated for a moment thinking this is crazy. But why not I thought as I finished dressing. I went down the elevator, out of my building and across the street to building number 295. As I approached the steps leading to the entrance I was startled by a long shadowy object on the bottom row of steps. A car passed and its fleeting lights revealed a human body. I approached cautiously and concluded the body belonged to a drunk judging from the tattered clothing and an empty bottle of wine lying next to his outstretched hand. Careful not to disturb him I stepped over the snoring figure, entered the front door of the building and went to the apartment directory. Before leaving my room I made a note of what floor the painter-in-the night was on. Fourth floor, Mr. & Mrs. James Maculty, Frank Corsico, James Olsen, Peter Rodeo and George Salazar, and finally Beverly Strickland. "Got to be Strickland," I thought.

Again stepping over Rip Van Winkle who had turned over and was now face up, I crossed the street to a telephone booth from which I luckily could see the lighted window. Within a minute I found the name Beverly S. Strickland and her address matched. Good luck so far, I thought. But then a moment of wavering, should I? She'll think I'm a predator or worse she could call the police which would put a peremptory end to my budding career as a Wall Street lawyer. I was still mulling this over when I dropped a quarter in the slot and dialed the number from the directory. The phone rang and rang again and did so for a third time before I heard the sound of the receiver being lifted and a soft voice say, "yes".

Hell, what do I say now, I thought. "Hello, who is this," said the voice, this time with a slightly testy tone.

"Sorry to call you at this insane hour of the morning but..." and I went on to explain what had happened. When I finished there was a suspenseful silence.

"Well now that you've managed to interrupt me, what do you want? Do you realize I could call the cops. Who are you anyway a professional peeping Tom or what." I told her who I was. "Great, so you a hot-shot lawyer from Wall Street and that gives you the right to call a perfect stranger in the middle of the night? What do you want?"

"There is a coffee shop around the corner on Broadway, it's open 24 hours, called Chuck's Coffee Shoppe I think. How about meeting me there in a half-hour. I'll buy you a coffee; I would love to meet you."

Silence at the other end of the line. "You know this is too off-the-wall even for me. How do I know you live across the street? How do I know you're not a screwball? There's certainly enough of them in this town."

Thinking for a moment I offered proof. I would go to my room which was on the third floor, turn on the lights and wave at her from the window. No sound from her end so I improved my offer. "Tell you what, I'll place a personal card in your mailbox right now. How does that sound?"

"Go ahead" was her response, but I don't know why I'm doing this."

Again I stepped over the sprawled-out body, deposited my card, went to my room, stood in the window and waived to her. She didn't reciprocate nor did she give any sign as to whether she was convinced of the veracity of the whole thing. She pulled the window shade down kind of late for that I thought. Without a clue as to whether she would show up I left for the coffee shop which not surprisingly was devoid of patrons. Ordering a cup of coffee I took a seat at a table near the front window. Ten minutes passed and raindrops began striking the window. Hell, I thought, she's not going to show up and I can't blame her. Just making an ass of myself. I'll wait for a few more minutes and that will be it. I picked up the smudged breakfast menu again. I noticed the price for two eggs and bacon cost less that one egg and bacon and I was about to point this obvious misprint to the Puerto Rican behind the counter when the door opened and in a stepped a young lady shaking then folding up an umbrella. Unnoticed by me the rain was now coming down hard.

"Beverly? I asked. She looked at me for a moment as if trying to read me, then looked around the empty coffee shop, only then did she nod yes to my question. As she took off her raincoat, I noticed how slim thin she was. No make-up, hair cut short. I observed how gracefully she moved. I later learned she had taken ballet classes as a sort of surrogate for her mother whose professional dancing career ended by a fall which permanently damaged her spine. We sat and talked until 7 a.m., accompanied by cups of coffee and an occasional bagel or danish. We became good friends as there was an almost instantaneous good chemistry between us and remained so for some eight months.

Beverly was from up-state New York presently a student at an art school in Manhattan. She told me her father was a well-known politician in her hometown, her mother was now a publisher of a magazine covering the world of ballet. Her father would have preferred that Beverly pursue a more practical career but did not hesitate to support her decision to become a painter. She was an only child.

We went out together mostly to museums and art exhibits, walked a lot along Riverside Drive section of the Hudson River. She listened politely to my accounts about recent happenings on my Wall Street job. Though she grasped things quickly she was not impressed by all these Wall Street goings on. She candidly told me she wasn't really turned on by lawyers or by what they did. Lawyers play with words, distort meanings and create false images. Artists, on the other hand, deal with the truth, with what is real. I particularly enjoyed listening to her descriptions of things we saw as we walked or sat on a bench along the Hudson River. She saw things I didn't, infused them with meanings which would not have otherwise occurred to me. All I know about painting and painters I learned from Beverly and Donald Squire up in New Hampshire.

There was an incident involving a famous mural by the Mexican painter Siqueiros which was in a book Beverly lent me. I told her the mural looked familiar but I couldn't place it. Then it occurred to me it was the same one that covered the entire side of a building and the Universidad Autonoma de Mexico which I passed several times a week.

Our friendship was not without its lighter moments. One morning I received a call from Beverly and heard her say we should stop seeing each other." Startled I asked her why, had I done or said something. "No, it's just that being with you has intruded on my professional life." She went on to explain that she had a weird dream that night. In it she finally had the first public exhibition of her paintings at no less a prestigious venue than the New York Museum of Modern Art. There were loads of people in attendance. Cocktails and a reception first, Beverly moving from person to person and group to group chatting mostly banalities about art. As the moment arrived for the crowd to enter the exhibition hall where the paintings were on display, Beverly's nerves took over and she decided not to join the crowd in the exhibition hall. Minutes later the crowd began exiting the hall shaking their heads in disbelief. She ran to the Museum Director to ask what had happened. He also shook his head. "Go look inside," he told her.

She entered the now empty exhibition hall. Her mouth dropped in disbelief. All of the beautiful landscapes and portraits she had hung on the walls were gone. In their place were black and white sketches of law books of all sizes flying through the air with Beverly dressed in a judge's robes riding astride the largest book. We laughed together for a while. Then I commented I was not going to worry about things until my legal memos became landscape scenes.

Not long after we drifted apart as my professional work consumed more and more of my time and Lena and I tried to give our marriage a second try. Beverly helped me see things I had never noticed and to go beyond the veneer of surface appearances, a teaching that certainly enriched my life. I sometimes wonder if she ever became successful in a big way.

****

The adjacent apartment to ours on West 68th Street was occupied by Charley and Betty Rogen. Charley was a professional actor working mostly in off-Broadway productions and Betty worked as an insurance agent. We became as close friends as neighbors can in a place like New York City. What initially brought us together was their Airedale dog Harry. We loved the dog so much that we bought our own Airedale, Timon.

Betty was an unpretentious, no-nonsense, on the move gal. Charlie, though I don't believe he ever had a major role in any well-known play, was filled with himself, utterly vain and opinionated. I recall he had a serious hepatitis health problem from which he suffered frequent attacks causing him to say in bed for days and turning him into a sickly yellow.

One Saturday morning Charlie came to our apartment to ask whether I wanted to see a scene being filmed up the street, the movie was "The Midnight Cowboy" staring Dustin Hoffman and Jon Voight. He knew some of the crew involved in the filming and said he could get us close to where the scenes were being shot.

The scene was to take place in a small coffee shop on Broadway. We were early and were able to see the lengthy preparations being made for what would amount to a no more than five minute scene. After all was readied and as if on cue, Hoffman and Voight showed up. Charlie and I were standing among the extras involved in the filming, some of whom Charlie knew.

When all seemed ready a guy carrying a stack of papers rushed over to where we were standing and motioned us to get inside and take our places. The extras standing near us went into the coffee shop. The paper-carrying guy who had gone to talk to someone behind us now came back to us and started pushing us into the coffee shop angrily asking whether we needed an invitation or what. He had mistaken us for extras.

Surprised, I asked him what I should do. Charlie poked me in the ribs. The guy squinted a stern look and was about to say something nasty when one of the crewmen shouted out saying we were not extras just friends of friends. The scene being filmed involved Hoffman and Voight sitting at the counter talking. Being on the outside I couldn't hear what they were saying. The scene was repeated a number of times. Between takes it was obvious Voight was less than thrilled by so many re-takes. Once the last take had been done the actors walked out of the coffee shop. As Jon Voight passed us, he shook his head and said something nasty which I assumed was meant for the guy who decided to shoot the scene so many times and who I supposed was the director. The Midnight Cowboy not only became a box office hit but it also became a classic of that era and I came close to being in it. But this would not be the end of my big screen story as will be seen later.

****

Sunday morning, mid-December and snow had fallen relentlessly all night and now blanketed everything in sight. At least two feet of white had accumulated. Snow or no snow our dog Timon had to go out to do his thing. I made my way along the sidewalk and towards Central Park. There were absolutely no signs of life. No cars, no people, no animals, no noise, only the sound of my footsteps crunching through the snow.

Central park, what a gorgeous picture-card scene. Virgin snow piled high all around us. Tree branches so laden with snow they bent to the ground as if in genuflection to the author of this beauty. Unleashed Timon went into the Park and tried to run but the deep snow made that impossible. We walked across the Park and back again as I occasionally reached for a branch and shook down the snow triggering a playful barking by Timon.

All of Central Park was ours, every New Yorker, every taxi, every horse-drawn carriage, all signs of life had obligingly exited leaving Timon and me alone to savor the scene without distraction.

At one spot a couple of birds alighted on the branch of a tree I was standing under and the snow came showering on me. Years later I recalled this scene in reading Robert Frost's poem, "Dust of Snow":

> *The way a crow*
> *Shook down on me*
> *The dust of snow*
> *From a hemlock tree*
>
> *Has given my heart*
> *A change of mood*
> *And saved some part*
> *Of a day I had rued*

Upon reaching the street I looked back and there was this broad carpet of white, and across it footprints of a man and his dog. It was as if we had left our imprimatur of approval on Nature's masterpiece.

****

Our neighbor Betty drove us to Kennedy Airport where we checked in with no hitches, patted Timon on the head as a gesture of consolation as he was pushed unwillingly into his crate and taken away. We were about to depart for Bogotá, Colombia our new residence to be.

I was in a newspaper shop on the upper level browsing for reading material when I thought I heard my name being called on the public address system.

"Dominic Perenzin, please report to the Braniff International counter" was the message being piped out.

I got on the escalator wondering why I was being called. As I looked down below I could not believe my eyes for there was Timon running around loose with two airline uniforms in hot pursuit. I instinctively shouted "Timon, here boy," but to no avail as the clamor of voices, carts being pushed and occasional announcements about arrivals and departures conspired against my voice reaching Timon's ears. I vainly tried to push my way down the escalator.

Timon ran from one area to another sniffing everything in sight. Some people amused by the scene tried to pet him as he sometimes stopped for a brief moment before darting off again. A hippie-type looking couple standing in a ticket counter line were in a deep, intimate embrace oblivious to anything or anyone around them. Timon stopped next to them sniffing their backpacks lying on the floor and did the unthinkable as he lifted a back leg and proceeded to relieve his bladder. I felt like going back up the escalator changing my name and denying any knowledge of the dog. A lady standing in the same line a few feet behind the embraced couple seeing what Timon was doing shouted and tried to wave Timon away. The hippie type apparently believing she was yelling at him to leave his girl alone relaxed his embrace enough to give the lady a finger. The now angry lady extended her third finger at him then turned her hand over and pointed the finger to the urinated backpacks.

After a few moments of running and apologizing to people bumped into, I caught up with Timon. The airline employees reached us and explained Timon had demolished his wooden crate. If I wanted the dog to travel I would have to find him another crate. Braniff had none. Our flight was scheduled to depart in about 45 minutes. One of the Braniff representatives volunteered to take me to a different airline hangars by motorized cart in search of a crate. Pan American came to our rescue with a metal crate large enough for Timon at a cost of $120. I met Lena and Joanna at the departure gate. The flight had been held up for us. We boarded the plane uttering a litany of sheepish "I'm sorries" to stern or blank faces along the aisle to our seats. Definitely not an auspicious beginning to my next stage in life.

****

The ship was approaching New York and a group of us were standing on deck straining to catch our first glimpse of the Statue of Liberty. We were all from the Guantanamo Naval Base and on our first home leave. It was a good feeling to know we would soon set our feet on good old U.S.A. soil. Someone had a radio and Tony Bennett was singing "See the pyramids across the Nile..." from the song "You Belong to Me." For a brief moment a collective melancholy descended over us as our thoughts went back to our home towns and those wonderful halcyon days. The mood dissipated with the last notes of the song and, as if the pause button had been released, the group again became lively and talkative.

Two of the fellows with whom I had become friendly during the trip and I decided to spend one night in New York City before heading to our respective hometwon destinations. After checking in at the local YMCA the three of us were walking down Broadway looking for and wide-eyed ready for a good time. We felt relaxed and thrilled to be walking among the towering skyscrapers, fascinated by the store window displays, the bright marquees announcing the newest movies. Suddenly I stopped, grabbed my buddies by their arms causing them to recoil.

"Look over there, see the sign 'Tony Paster's, there across the street about half way down the block," I excitedly pointed out.

"Yea, so what," came the response.

"Tony Paster is an Italian saxophone player who used to play for the Artie Shaw orchestra. Now he has his own band which featured Betty and Rosemary Clooney as singers. I bet he owns that place, maybe his band is playing there."

We crossed the street and entered Tony Paster's and went straight to the bar where we made a preliminary reconnaissance of the place. It was a one-third-full night club with an immense semi-circular cocktail bar, tables, a dance floor and live music (not Tony Pastor though). No military uniforms in sight but ours, girls nicely dressed, but a little older than us, a bartender who looked like a real cool veteran of New York night life. "Where are you guys from?" he asked as he rearranged some of the bottles. "I suppose you're looking for some action right?"

A few minutes later two girls came and sat at the bar some five stools away, partially facing us. "Dam it, those girls are gorgeous aren't they," one of my buddies commented. And he was right, they looked like show girls. It soon became obvious to the three of us that the girls had noticed us and were looking in our direction and exchanging comments which we assumed were about us. When our eyes met the girls smiled a man-you've-got-it-made-in-New-York look. We collectively swooned as our testosterones went into overdrive. Two of us went over to the girls and asked if we could join them. "Sure honey," was the answer.

We chatted a while and ordered a round of drinks for all of us. They asked mostly perfunctory general questions about us and seemed to listen with rapt attention, hardly ever taking their beautiful eyes off of us. A third girl made an appearance so it was suggested we all sit at a table where our odd-man-out buddy could join us.

Lydia, the girl whom it seemed was destined to be my date, called the maitre d' over and asked him to give us a table, which he promptly did. Guess you're well known here, I observed.

Yea, they all know us, they're wonderful people, very accommodating, she smiled.

And so we began what was to become a the long night. We danced and we drank. People dropped by our table, chatted for a while and left, though occasionally some stayed and a new table was joined to ours. Soon our group occupied three tables, everyone laughing, joking, drinking and getting loose. My thoughts were dizzying as I saw myself in this swanky New York night club surrounded by beautiful Hollywood type girls and cool people. And how about this Lydia girl! Imagine taking her home to mama. Man would she ever turn a few heads as I walked around town with her on my arm. Domenico, the son of Italian immigrants and his New York American show girl, important enough to be featured in the Fitchburg Sentinel I thought.

Three in the morning and I was back on the dance floor again. Then things took an unexpected turn. My partner, who by now had had a number of scotch and waters, began to act as if she wanted to lead me during the dances. Not forceful in any way but lightly and only occasionally. I quickly had to assert myself and maintain control. It gradually dawned on me that her body seemed different, more muscular, bigger boned than I had noticed earlier. Then it happened, we were doing a jitterbug when during one of her spins the high dress collar slid down her neck to reveal what I thought was either an Adams apple or the biggest tumor that ever was. She pulled the collar back up. Puzzled I began focusing my alcohol-soaked attention on her features. Her face seemed to be changing shape as if I were gazing at it under water. It was becoming disconcertedly clearer that the face I was looking at showed evidence of wanting to change gender. My awareness must have become obvious to her/him as I began to draw away from body contact.

"You've noticed haven't you?" she smiled at me. "Do you like me sailor?"

I half-smiled nervously, made an excuse to stop dancing and went back to our table. I moved next to my buddies and told them what I had discovered. They already knew for their dates were also not what we thought they were. "This is crazy, let's just get out of here," I said.

185

We asked for the check and when it came it was handed to me. I read it and my jaw dropped. It read $575. I showed it to my friends, equally shocked we called the waiter back to tell him he had made a mistake. No mistake we were told. Explanation, the people sitting at the added-on tables were our guests since they had been invited to join the group by our dates. We argued with no success that we had never invited them.

I told my buddies we had been set up, this was a rip-off, a robbery and that we had better get out of the place but fast. It was agreed we would one at a time go to the men's room and then instead of returning to our table we would just go out the front door. I was to go first. All went as planned until I reached the exit door where I was greeted by a Mr. Hulk who told me there would be no leaving until I settled my account. He gently but with firm command took my arm and escorted me back to the table. When I got there one of my buddies had already headed for the men's room. He too was escorted back to our table.

By this time most of the people at the table had become aware of the problem. What had been loud chatter and laughing had now given way to silence interrupted by occasional whispers. We asked to see the manager who turned out to be a hard-as-nails looking red-head. She – or was it he? – accepted no excuses or explanations. I told her/him we collectively had only about $160. She/he was or pretended to be irate. "What else do you have of value," she demanded. Nothing said one of my buddies who in a lapse of memory opened up his wallet to show he had nothing more when a travelers checkbook he had forgotten about fell out on the table. There were three checks each for $25.

We turned over our money and travelers checks and left after threatening to call the police to report this rip-off. I never did find out what the connection was, if any, between this place and Tony Paster the musician. Not long after that incident Rosemary Clooney went out on her own singing and acting career. The pain of coughing up all my money would have been much assuaged had lovely Rosemary Clooney been there singing with the Tony Pastor orchestra.

****

PART SIX

THINGS THAT HAPPEN
IN HOTEL ROOMS

Normally our experiences with hotel rooms are limited to having a place to sleep after a day of vacation fun, of business meetings or conventions. Seldom if ever do we recall a particular stay in a hotel, after all, seldom does anything particularly out of the ordinary ever happen there meriting recollection years later. But I do recall four memorable events that occurred to me in hotel rooms.

It had been a dragged out day of work topped off by a cocktail reception at the Waldorf Astoria in New York where I was staying. The reception was sponsored by our firm Kirkwood, Kaplan, Russin & Vecchi for the purpose of promoting our image and bringing in more clients. It was well attended by existing and potential clients. One of the persons I had invited to the reception was Robert Stuller, in-house counsel with an important client of mine for many years whose friendship went as far back as the time I was with the Curtis-Mallet law firm. Bob gave the impression of being the picture-perfect example of that species of men who are all professional, dependable, stable, serious, weekend golfers and family-devoted.

I was on my way to the men's room when Bob stepped out of the elevator accompanied by an eye-arresting blonde. We exchanged greetings and he and the girl disappeared into the reception hall. Later that evening Bob in a confidential tone told me he had just left his wife and had moved in with his girlfriend. No explanation was offered beyond a smugness around the mouth. I couldn't shake off the feeling that stability and predictability on the planet had been dealt a serious blow, a harbinger of what was to happen later that evening.

Comfortably settled in my room my mind flitted between admiring the rich appointments of the room and the Robert Stuller surprise. As I entered the bathroom thoughts about Bob vanished as I took in the golden luxuriousness. The ornate tub was surrounded by a multitude of creams, shampoos, salts and oils, all with the singular mission of pampering the human body which this evening would be the appreciative one I had been dragging around with me since my birth. The whole scene was one that would have made an Egyptian pharaoh or a Roman patrician salivate.

By the time I had finished my bath, had dried off with thick, pampering-soft towels and had slipped into my pajamas, it was around 1:00 a.m. One last smoke and I would call it a day. I couldn't get the Bob Stuller matter of my mind as I looked for a cigarette. My jacket pockets failed to produce a pack of cigarettes. My pants and shirt sadly did no better. I spotted an empty pack on the chest of drawers. Oh well, I thought, I'll buy some tomorrow. No sooner had the synapses of my brain fired this decision when it was vetoed by a biological craving for a nicotine so intense that I found myself dialing room service hoping it would send me a life-saver. No luck, too late, no room service. By now the craving had surged like a tidal wave compelling me to get dressed and to go downstairs in a late night search for calming nicotine. I found no place in the hotel to purchase cigarettes nor was I any more successful in finding a store with its lights on within a two-block radius of the hotel.

Back in my hotel room, a sweeping search for a cigarette from which no item of apparel escaped scrutiny turned up nothing. Growing more anxious by the minute I spotted what remained of a cigarette butt in a wastepaper basket which turned out to be mostly the filter. Never mind, I lit it up and holding it securely but gingerly between my thumb and index finger took a short puff simultaneously looking into the mirror. The sight of that person taking a drag on the cigarette butt as if it were his life-line to existence caused me to literally freeze. I stood there glaring at the stranger. Is this what I had been reduced to?

I had a disturbing night of tossing about, freaky dreams, and perspiration. In one of my dreams I was a teenager hiding in an alley between two buildings covertly smoking a cigarette which soon began expanding in size. Soon it had swallowed my hand and was progressively sucking me into it. Struggling, I hobbled towards the street end of the alley but as I approached the walls at that end converged so that there remained only a tiny eight-inch opening. Pressing my face against the eight inches I screamed for help. The ghost-like passersby didn't seem to hear or simply ignored my pleas. As my head, the last part of my body remaining outside the now gigantic cigarette, began to be sucked in, I awoke in a sweat.

Some twenty years have passed since that grotesque Waldorf Astoria evening and I have yet to bring another cigarette to my lips.

****

The Double Tree Hotel in Kansas City is where my Colombian client and I were staying in May of 1995 while negotiating with a company regarding its decision to discontinue using my client's services in connection with a bid on a large Colombian project for which the company was ultimately awarded the contract. Our meetings over the past days were not going well with the company's lawyers. The thrust of their arguments was that my client had agreed and consented to end his bid efforts on the company's behalf. My client was of little help as all I could pry out of him and his sudden siege of amnesia was a repetitive, "I don't remember." The lawyers produced copies of letters and faxes in which my client appeared to be consenting.

It was Thursday and unless there was a break-through in the negotiations we planned to leave after the next day's meeting. I was back in my hotel room.

Though the TV set was on and I was looking at the screen my mind was elsewhere. Realizing what was happening I turned the tube off and went to bed. Soon my mind was back at the conference room. My client with his zero contribution would be of no help so if I was to succeed I would have to dig deep into my bag of legal wiles. Think! think! think! Perhaps I could argue lack of intent, mistake or coercion. Tired of all this cerebral probing and unable to sleep I turned the TV back on and began watching an already in progress circa 1940s black and white movie. From what I gathered the husband had abruptly decided to go on a business trip and would be gone on the day he and his wife had been invited to their country club's social event of the year. "How," shouted the infuriated wife, "can you have so little consideration for my feelings and to the social damage our non-appearance will cause. No, you have absolutely no consideration for any of this, only your lousy, boring business matters to you."

Like in those cartoon pictures where a light bulb goes on above a character's head to indicate the sudden arrival of an idea, hundreds of these bulbs lighted above me and I pronounced the word "consideration" several times, the sound of which vaulted me back to my law school contracts class at Boston University. "All contracts other than those of gifts require consideration –something given in exchange- on both sides in order that there be a binding contract or for additional commitments to be validly made once the contract was in effect," I could hear Professor Gilbert saying. My mind fast forwarded. Assuming my client had in fact consented to the termination of his efforts for the company where was the consideration for him doing so? As far as I could tell there was none.

The following morning we were back at the company's offices. I opened the meeting by saying that if my client had agreed or had given his consent as was alleged, there is a fundamental rule of contract law which all of us lawyers learned in law school which requires that my client have been given some type of consideration for his consent. The company's lawyers were silent for a moment, talked among themselves and with a company officer. The *tet-a-tet* over, one of the lawyers looked me in the eye and with profound professional indignation said they did not need to be lectured on law school 101 material and that my point was way off the mark since the rule I mentioned was applicable only to the formation of contracts and not to situations that occur later. I was pretty sure they were wrong. I told them that in view of their position it appeared that the dispute would have to be settled in court. Meeting ended.

My client and I went to lunch. Upon our return to our hotel we found the anticipated message from a company representative. To my client's delight we settled the case for a healthy sum.

I never did find out the name of the 1940's black and white movie I saw that evening. It would have been a pleasure to see it again and to join the irate wife in saying to her husband that he had "no consideration" for her feelings.

****

His name was Yehan Numata. He was presented to me in my hotel room in Bangkok, Thailand. My indebtedness to him is great though we have never met nor does he know me.

I had forgotten to pack light reading material when I left for Bangkok. Here I was in a television-deprived Thai hotel room mentally tired from a full day of Management Committee meetings and desiring some relaxing reading. My briefcase yielded up memoranda, meeting notes and similar boring business papers. The Bible had not been opened by me for more years than I could recall and perhaps I could change all this if I opened the drawer of my night-table and found the Book, after all I was in an American managed hotel.

I got the drawer open several inches when it stopped yielding. Peering through the narrow opening into the semi-dark interior I could see that indeed it contained a book. Upset by the pig-headed stubbornness of the drawer in not opening completely I gave it a full-body yank and succeeded in pulling the drawer completely from the night-table and onto the floor. After cursing the hotel and the manufacturer of the furniture, I saw the book on the floor. I picked up the book and read its title "The Teaching of Buddha," under which were a series of Chinese ideograms obviously a translation. Not exactly what I was hoping to find yet it had nothing to do with legal matters and in that sense was welcome.

Settled comfortably in bed, I opened the book and as I did so a card fell out. It informed me I could take the book with me as a gift from the Buddhist Promoting Foundation of Japan and that I should feel free to write to it with my comments. The card went on to describe the origin of the Foundation and ended by inviting me to read the book and "Enjoy and Bathe in the Light of the Great Teacher".

Such a wish was enough to pique my curiosity so I browsed over the pages to get an overview of the book's contents. Up to this point my knowledge of

Buddhism was virtually inexistent beyond the fact the Buddha was a statue of a fat guy with a protruding belly which people touched for good luck. Best to start at the beginning I thought.

The introductory passage said that the book contained the essence of the Buddha's teachings recorded in over five thousand volumes preserved and handed down through more than 2500 years. The words of Buddha found in the book were said to have maintained their relevance to the present state of human life and mind.

With such enticing words floating in my mind, I entered Chapter One. Shuddhodana Guatama was the King of the Shakya clansmen who lived along foothills of the Himalayas in what is today Nepal. His residence was a huge majestic palace overlooking the land beyond from where it was said he, "ruled wisely to the acclaim of his people."

The King's wife Maya was the daughter of the King's uncle who was himself a king. Despite twenty years of marriage no children had been born of the union. One night, dreaming a strange dream in which she saw a white elephant enter her womb, Queen Maya became pregnant.

According to the custom of the time and place the Queen was required to return to her parents' home for the birth of her child. On her way she took a rest in the Lumbini Garden, a place suffused with beautiful spring sunshine.

> *All about her were Ashoka blossoms and in delight she reached out her right arm to pluck a branch and as she did so a prince was born.*

My skin tingled as I read this moving lyrical depiction of the birth of Buddha. As I was later to discover it was also the perfect form of birth with which to herald what was to become the life and teachings of the Buddha.

A hermit named Asita from far away noticed a radiance about the King's palace and interpreting it as a good omen came down to the palace and was shown the child, whereupon he predicted:

> *This Prince, if he remains in the palace will, when he grows up, become a great king. But if he forsakes the life of the royal court to embrace a religious life, he will become a Buddha, the Savior of the World.*

When he was seven years old the Prince had an experience which in a way was an early harbinger of what was to come. The King had taken his son on a day trip beyond the Palace walls. Along the way they stopped their carriage to watch a farmer plow his field. The Prince noticed a bird descend to the ground and carry off a small worm which the farmer's plough had unearthed. Moved by this the Prince sat in the shade of the tree and thought about what he had seen and whispered, "Alas! Do all living creatures kill each other?"

Concerned his son might be tempted to abandon his proscribed royal future, the King spared no effort to prevent him from again going beyond the confines of the Palace walls. But the Prince was equally intent upon seeing the outside world and managed to leave the Palace in disguise. What awaited him in the village were beggars, sickness, wrenching hunger, ravaged bodies and filth everywhere, the whole gamut of ills which characterized the de-humanizing condition of village life. Shaken and profoundly disturbed by all of this he returned to the Palace where it was said he underwent a long period of mental anguish. How to reconcile the polite life of plenitude within the Palace walls with the misery of the human condition he had witnessed outside.

In the end he decided to walk away from it all, from the comfort, privileges and luxury of Palace life, even from his parents, his wife and son, teachers and friends. One night after a brief farewell look at his sleeping wife and son he set out on his favorite horse accompanied by his faithful charioteer Channa into the wild forests. It was to be his last ride as a prince upon horseback. Reaching a secluded part of the forest, he dismounted, cut off the long tresses of his hair and, giving his princely garments to Channa, he donned the patched yellow robes which were the signs of homeless beggars. Taking a bowl in which to collect offered food, he told Channa to inform the King of what had happened.

The next forty years of his life were spent traveling, studying with the wisest teachers, achieving great meditative powers, living as a mendicant, spending years as an ascetic during which he underwent excruciating physical suffering and mortifications But he became disillusioned with asceticism for he felt it did nothing towards advancing his goal of achieving enlightenment. So he continued on and spent time with a master in meditation. It is said that in December 8 in the year of his thirtieth birthday he had found the path to enlightenment and the Prince became "Gotama the Buddha", spending the remainder of his life as the Great Teacher.

So fascinated with what I was reading I remained awake until 2:30 a.m. when my eyes refused to cooperate and the lids brought the day to closure.

I accepted the Foundation's offer and took the book with me. Over the intervening years I have read and re-read the book deriving much comfort, peace of mind and inspiration from Gotama's teachings. It has served as a springboard from where my interest in the wisdom of the East as manifested in many forms and disciplines. To this date the book can be found on the night-table next to my bed many thousands of miles from the night-table in which I found it years ago.

****

After a while I had to make heroic efforts to focus on what was being said around the circular table. The day before, seven year Dominic Jr. and I boarded a China Airways flight in San Francisco on our way to Taipei, Taiwan where I was to attend a Management Committee meeting. We arrived sleepy-eyed in Taipei this very morning at 7 a.m. after a twenty-plus hour flight and here I was at 10:30 a.m. attending the first session of our meetings.

We were in the Great China Hotel a structure of immense dimensions. Viewing it from the street level it loomed as an imposing imperial palace which I believe I was told it once was. The stairs leading up to the hotel entrance were wide enough to accommodate some 30 horses standing neck to neck and the stairs leading from the cavernous lobby were equally wide.

Upon our arrival at the hotel I took a shower, put on fresh clothes and headed for our conference room. Before leaving I suggested Dominic get some sleep, explained where I would be, told him how to order room service for food and gave him my conference room telephone number.

It was around 4 p.m. in the afternoon during our second meeting session that I received a call from the front desk advising me my son was not feeling well and that I should go to see him. Entering our room I saw him lying on the floor holding a face towel to his nose and still watching TV. Scattered on the floor around the room were towels and tissue paper red with blood. The sight shook me out of my jet-lag drowsiness as I hurried to him to find out what was wrong. He had a nose-bleed. When the room service delivery boy saw what was happening he brought ice to apply to the nose area. Dominic said the ice helped stop the bleeding for a while but later the bleeding began anew.

Concerned, I made two calls, the first to housekeeping for more towels and to have the blood soaked ones picked up and disposed of, the second to the front desk to have a doctor look at Dominic. The hotel had no in-house doctor but would arrange for one to come to us, although the hotel could not assure me of how long this would take. The nose continued to bleed but not alarmingly so. I requested more ice.

It was not until around eight o'clock and after numerous reminder calls to the front desk that there was a knock at our door. Standing there was a huge bushy moustache topped off by two equally bushy eyebrows, all three in cloud-white. "Hello, I'm doctor Milhap, I understand you have a youngster here who is not feeling well." He was taller than me, perhaps around 6'2", lanky and with surprisingly small hands, one of which he extended to me.

I stepped back gesturing for him to enter. As he did so a young oriental girl in a nurse's uniform carrying the doctor's black bag followed him into the room. Apparently she had been standing to the side out of my sight. After asking our names he turned to the nurse as if to indicate who he was talking about and said she was his nurse assistant.

Examining Dominic the doctor said there was no serious problem and proceeded to give us instructions on what to do – more ice, apply pressure at certain key points and a few pills which he furnished.

I asked him how much I owed him. "Don't worry the Hotel will put the charges on your bill, it won't be much on my part about $40, but the hotel may tack on an extra charge for its intermediary services."

"Just like a hotel to do that," I commented. "What's your connection with the hotel?"

"I'm with a service organization out of Hong Kong that provides medical and other services for hotel customers, the kind of services hotels are not in a position to furnish on their own or do not want the trouble or potential liability exposure. I hope I'm not too inquisitive if I ask where you are from."

"Not at all, we are from Colombia, South America, it is located…"

"No need to explain, I know where it is, as well as all the other Latin American countries, although I've never had the good fortune of visiting there.

We continued to talk as the doctor pulled up a chair. It was the beginning of a memorable evening with a master storyteller.

The doctor was 75 years old, a fact belied by his trim figure, un-aged skin and youthful air. Some twenty years earlier he had been a medical advisor to a special British Commission to India which had its permanent location in New Delhi, his introduction to Asia. At the present, the closest he had to a fixed home was in Bangkok since he spent most of the year traveling between Hong Kong, Bangkok and Taipei. He earned his traveling and living expenses by his medical services to hotels.

During this time his nurse sat on the floor occasionally rising to check on Dominic's temperature. To my offer of a chair she smiled while the doctor explained she preferred to sit on the floor as this was best for her posture and health.

"Do you have a nurse like this one – excuse me but I don't know her name – in all of the cities you visit," I asked.

"No, only Chin Lee "as he nodded to the nurse. "She travels with me wherever I go. She is a very special person. She carries an interesting story, would you like to hear it?"

"Why yes", I responded, "so long as she doesn't mind."

"No, she will not mind will you?" he asked as he turned to her.

She answered in Chinese though obviously she understood English. "She said she doesn't mind so long as I feel I want to," said the doctor. By this time we we're well into a room-service-delivered pot of coffee and I was wide awake and alert. By the way she understands English doesn't she. "Why shouldn't she," he said, "she's American." Expressing surprise I turned to her and sheepishly said "Hi" to which she answered with a smile.

Several years ago he was in New York City attending a medical convention when he met a representative of the City's Department of Social Services. Over lunch the representative, learning of the doctor's interest in the sociology of poverty, suggested the doctor take a tour some of the poorest areas in the city, like the Bronx. The doctor accepted.

Frank and John from Social Services and he walked the streets of the South Bronx. He was shown squatters occupying rotted buildings – a separate marginal society of indigents subsisting without heat, lights or water. Junkies who roamed the streets with dead men's belongings, garbage foragers, gatherers of cans and bottles, men who had arm-length lists of arrest warrants out on them.

"Look over there," pointed Frank, "see that girl, she can't be more than 12. Not much we can do since we don't have the manpower or resources to go tracking her or others like her down let alone help them." The doctor looked in that direction Frank was pointing and saw a young girl foraging through dilapidated trash cans. She was a lanky kid, quick and sure in her gestures. When Frank called out to her she darted down the street. The doctor suggested they try to get some information on the girl.

After talking to several people of the neighborhood they pieced together a profile. Her name was Roxanne. She lived in a nearby junkyard, sleeping in what remained of the body of a truck. The degenerate owner of the place lets her sleep there in exchange for certain favors. The girl was about 12 years old.

Though the day was winding down the three men went to look at the junkyard. There they found cannibalized vehicles, rusted refrigerators and stoves, a junk world of smashed wheel-less, roof-less, corroded, metal bodies with rats living in exposed trunks. A pantheon to the spiritual wreckage that was the neighborhood. The doctor felt sick at the sign and at the thought that a 12 year kid could be living among this festering mess. As they were turning to leave Frank said, "Look there she is see behind that upside down car."

As they quietly approached her, the doctor noticed she had oriental features, probably Chinese but not undiluted. They agreed to approach her from three directions. As they closed the ring a guy who later proved to be the owner of the place yelled at them asking what they were doing. Hearing this the girl looked around, spotted the men and tried to get away in the only direction which remained open, over the upside down car. But in doing so she struck her leg on something and fell. Bleeding she tried fiercely but vainly to escape. They took her with them telling the hysterical owner that if he didn't shut up they would have him thrown in the clink.

The doctor attended to her wounds – which were painful but not serious – at the clinic in the Social Services Headquarters. Over a period of a month of bestowing tenderness, understanding and gentle persuasiveness, he gradually gained Roxanne's trust, ultimately convincing her to go back with him to Asia to start a new life. He obtained a passport and took her with him to Bangkok.

That was ten years ago. Over this time he had her learn Chinese, fragments of which she remembered from her mother. The doctor took personal control of her general education and taught her the basics of nursing. He changed her name to Chin Lee. Though this was not discussed, I got the feeling that along the way the doctor had not touched all the legal bases.

He moved his chair closer to mine apparently not wanting anyone else in the room to hear what he was about to say, changed his mind and asked Chin Lee to get some ice down the corridor. Once she had left he thanked me for not inquiring about her mother which he was sure was a question lurking in the back of my mind.

Her mother was a prostitute. She had no relatives or friends in the U.S. and was originally from Hong Kong. A few years earlier in Hong Kong she had met an American who was very kind to her and convinced her to go to America with him where they could get married after his parents met her. Though not in love but wanting a better life for herself and against her parents' advice she accepted. He took her to New York where instead of introducing her to his parents he turned her over to another man who forced her into what she ended up doing.

Under the intimidating advice of the house madam, she had her breasts augmented with what the women believed was silicone. It worked for a while until one evening a breast apparently ruptured sending a smelly white liquid across the face of her customer. Infuriated he began pounding her with his fists until others came into the room and pulled him away. Dazed and in pain she ran out into the street and was never again seen nor heard from. Ten year-old Roxanne was taken in by one of the hookers for a few weeks but was turned out when the hooker realized some of her clients seemed to be more interested in Roxanne than in her.

At that point Chin Lee returned with a bucket of ice. We talked about Colombia for a while and then after checking our watches decided to call it a night.

I told him how much I enjoyed our conversation and gave him my card. He said he had no card but thanked me for mine. Apologizing for, "talking my ears off" he shook my hand again bringing my attention to how relatively small his hands were. As she was about to walk out Chin Lee turned and directed her first words of the night to me saying in perfect non-Bronx English that I should take good care of my handsome son.

As the couple walked down the corridor to the elevator, I noticed that the doctor limped slightly. Chin Lee carried his black bag in one hand and placed her other arm under his in an act of support for what I now realized were his weakened legs. They stood waiting for the elevator speaking in low tones. Noticing that the corner of his shirt collar had bent inwards, Chin Lee reached up and straightened it out and then when the elevator arrived held her arm out to assure the door remained open for the doctor. She stepped into the elevator. The door closed and they were gone.

PART SEVEN

THE DAYS OF EL DORADO

As the plane approached Bogotá the Savanna, which serves as a natural green carpet-entry into the City, spread before me. Soon I was flying over it. What a beautiful feast for the eyes. Then the city itself lying comfortably at the foot of the eastern range of the Andes. A lovely visual welcome to what would be my home for the next eighteen years.

LAW PRACTICE

Upon arriving in Bogotá my first task was to locate office space. Rather than incurring the expense of renting a full-fledged office of my own when I had not a single client, I opted to rent a small corner of the offices of attorney Hernán Silva to whom we were introduced by a Colombian attorney who the Curtis Mallet firm occasionally used. My second step was to learn something about Colombian law and what better way to do so than by researching and then writing a book-size pamphlet on the laws for use by foreign investors which The Royal Bank of Canada agreed to sponsor. For this I needed a secretarial help, more precisely a bilingual secretary since the book was to be in English.

I called a former secretary with Curtis-Mallet, Colt & Mosle who was now living in Bogotá. She told me she could not work for me (I later learned her boyfriend was an attorney who would be one of my competitors), however, she thought her sister might know of someone who could fit the bill. A few hours later I got a call from a young lady saying she had been told about my need for a bilingual secretary and would like to be interviewed for the position.

She was young, petite and pretty. No previous secretarial experience of any consequence. She knew English having spent a year of elementary school study in New York while boarding with her aunt and uncle. I could hardly detect an accent, we spoke at all times in English.

She was twenty years old, though she appeared to be younger. After explaining what I was looking for, about our law firm and my mission in Colombia, she said she was definitely interested in the job.

However, there was a <u>caveat</u> I should be aware of, namely, that she would not be able to work later than six o'clock because her mother would not permit it. I sat back and pondered what I had just heard. She was 20 years old and she needed her mother's approval? This is not exactly what one would hear in New York. A moment of silence while I considered the situation. "Fine, come in tomorrow at 9 o'clock." Alicia Bustos came in at the appointed time.

After the interview my thoughts went back to the six-o'clock work-limit condition and I realized this kind of parental control was reminiscent of transplanted mores prevalent among the Beech Street Italian families back in the 1930s. If this was an example of the society I was about to enter then this would be my Back to the Future.

I thoroughly enjoyed the law practice for it proved to be precisely what I had longed for when working on Wall Street. I was able to get some major corporate clients and achieve significant legal triumphs. Along with cases involving traditional lawyering, we handled a few colorful and peculiar cases some with a touch of drama thrown in. Two in particular tug at my memory.

Where Are They?

His name was Carlo Bianchini and he was a dear friend. Born in Colombia of Italian parents who immigrated to Colombia around the time my parents immigrated to the U.S. On occasions we compared our growing-up years as offspring of immigrant Italian parents in two very diverse settings. In many ways Carlo reflected the more salient character traits of his Italian heritage, a tendency to eschew the commonplace, the standard, the worn path. He did things his way, unpredictably with verve and gusto. How many people would build their own twin-winged plane and then fly (he was a licensed pilot) it in dare-devil stunts. Rumors were that he, though not technically an undercover agent, regularly furnished information to the U.S. Embassy regarding certain illegal operations being conducted in Colombia.

My initial contact with Carlo was on a lawyer-client basis and from this relationship our personal friendship evolved. Without any doubt some of the most unusual and challenging cases I handled in Colombia were those Carlo brought to me. Perhaps because of his exuberant temperament he had a tendency to get himself into legally bizarre situations from which I was always able to extricate him while at the same time making money for him. These were cases that, though a knowledge of the law was indispensable, required the essential element of strategy and a dollop of imagination. I handled one of his posthumous cases which though not unusually complex did have a heightened amount of drama involved.

It was a typical rainy Bogotá Friday night when Carlo locked up his office, stepped outside and made a dash for his car. From a parked car a hail of gunfire and Carlo was dashed to the ground bleeding from multiple wounds. He died almost instantly. When I heard the news I was stupefied. How can this happen to such a good guy with such an élan for living. My heart was heavy with grief at the loss not of a client but of my dear Colombian-Italian friend.

A few days after the funeral I received a call from his live-in friend of many years Mercedes asking me to come to Carlo's place to discuss an important matter. When I arrived it was evident she was still in the state of mourning. During my past visits I usually found an apartment flooded with rhythmic music, this evening there was only silence interrupted by the sound of her cat's meow. We had a drink and talked about Carlo, of our fond memories and how he would be missed. Then she turned to the reason for wanting to talk to me.

Prior to his death Carlo told Mercedes she was to have all of the shares of his company – which I shall call "Aguila" – upon his death. However, she could find no last will and testament, and apparently he had made none. Mercedes had literally turned the house inside out looking for the stock certificates but found nothing. As Carlo's lawyer would I go to his office and look for the certificates. I agreed to do so.

I had known Carlo's secretary Olga for a number of years so it was no problem in enlisting her cooperation. She helped me go through files and desks in Carlo's office which could conceivably harbor the certificates. It proved to be a futile search. Olga had no recollection of having seen the shares. Before I left the office Olga handed me a large manila envelope which she said contained some of Carlo's personal belongings and asked me to deliver them to Mercedes.

That evening I returned to Mercedes' apartment to report on my fruitless effort to find the certificates. She was in a funk when I arrived for she had received a call from Patti, Carlo's daughter from his first marriage, angrily warning Mercedes that Aguila belonged to her and that her father had told her so. She warned Mercedes not to try any chicanery to get the company for herself. She demanded that Mercedes turn over the company shares or face a criminal action for theft.

This added a new wrinkle to this case. Apparently, Patti didn't have the shares as I for a moment suspected she might. Who had them? Carlo had no safe deposit box at home, in the office or with any bank in Bogotá. We thought and thought but came up with no answers.

I was about to leave when I remembered the manila envelope and handed it to Mercedes. She opened it. Among the miscellaneous contents were several bank statements from Miami Beach banks. It seemed Carlo had checking accounts with all three but only one of which appeared to be active. We made lightly of the contents and I left.

That evening it occurred to me that it was possible that Carlo had a safe deposit box in any one of the banks in which he might have placed important documents such as the shares of Aguila or perhaps even a will. As I pondered this possibility I became increasingly convinced that this should be looked into. The next day I asked Mercedes to come to my office where I told her about my theory and strongly urged that we both go to Miami to check this out. Why didn't I go alone she asked. I told her access to any box would restricted to those persons authorized by the box's owners. Did she remember Carlo having a safety deposit box in any bank in Miami. She didn't remember. Had she signed any bank papers involving a Miami bank. Again, she didn't remember for he often gave her papers to sign without explaining their nature which she really didn't mind since she didn't want to get involved in his financial and business matters. I told her Patti may very well have retained an attorney to whom my idea may also occur. She agreed to go to Miami.

I had looked up the addresses of the three banks in which Carlo had bank accounts and decided we should first visit the one nearest us. We decided to walk to the bank since it was within a couple of blocks of Carlo's apartment. As we were about to enter the bank Mercedes asked what we should do if there was a box, if we were allowed to open it and found Carlo's last will and testament leaving everything to his daughter. I told her not to speculate or worry and that we should take things a step at a time.

Upon arriving at the bank I asked to have access to the safety deposit boxes. We were taken to a young lady behind a desk. She asked for Carlo's full name and after fingering through a file pulled out a card. She read it then asked for Mercedes' full name.

She handed Mercedes another card and asked her to sign her name on it and then proceeded to compare the two cards.

"Fine" said the young lady, "bring your key with you and I'll take you to the box." Mercedes looked at me with a "what do I do look in her eyes now?" I calmly asked Mercedes whether Carlo had given her a key. No he had not.

I'm sorry, without your key you won't be able to access the box. As is customary the box requires two keys, one is held by the customer and the other by the bank."

Feigning irritation I interrupted to say we wanted to speak to the manager for we had come a long way and had to resolve this situation. I knew the bank had a duplicate of the customer's key. We were taken to his office. No sooner had we taken two steps into his office when the manager stood up from his desk and extending his hand said "Mrs. Bianchini, how nice to see you again." Noticing that Mercedes seemed surprised by his greeting he went on to explain that they had met last year at a Chamber of Commerce dinner that she and Carlo had attended.

The safe-deposit-box young lady explained the situation. The manager looked at the signature cards. "Is Mr. Bianchini with you? he asked.

"No," I answered "he's in Bogotá."

"Sorry for the inconvenience" he apologized to Mercedes then asked the young lady to open the Bianchini safe deposit box for Mercedes. "Give my best regards to Carlo," he said as we were leaving the office.

We thanked him and were led to the security room where we watched the young lady open the safe deposit box. Mercedes was asked to remove whatever was inside. The only content was a metal box. We were then led to a private room and left alone. Mercedes placed the box on a table. We remained looking at it for a few moments. "Well," I said, "let's find out what's inside." But she said she wanted to first say a prayer. I waited for her to finish, in the meantime the tension in that little room made me feel as of everything in it was vibrating. Standing over the box Mercedes lifted the lid and pulled out the only content, a large manila envelope. Mercedes gave it to me saying she was too nervous and that I should open it. She closed her eyes. Opening it I found five stock certificates covering all of the shares of Aguila. I removed them, turned one after the other over to look at the back side. Then I gave out a loud spontaneous "Fantástico," as I embraced Mercedes. The certificates were all endorsed in blank by Carlo and by four nominee owners. My lawyer-mind took over and made an instant analysis. Whoever had physical possession of the certificates would by law be considered the owner provided legal delivery had been made to the possessor. The fact Mercedes had been officially given access to the box by Javier sufficed to qualify as "constructive delivery" of the shares. In short, Mercedes was now the owner of Aguila.

On my first day back in the office I received a call from Patti Bianchini's lawyer. He was fuming. I assumed he and Patti had gone to the same Miami Beach bank that Mercedes and I had gone to but did so after we did for how would he have otherwise known that I had the stock certificates. He threatened a law suit for having taken the company shares. He never carried out his threat.

The Wink

I looked up from my seat in the private plane flying somewhere between Rioacha, Guajira, Colombia and Barranquilla. Across from me sat two serious looking guys brandishing semi-automatic weapons. On the back of their shirts were the letters D.A.S. standing for Departamento Administrativo de Seguridad - Colombia's version of the U.S. Federal Bureau of Investigation. Next to me sat a silent disheveled redhead of an American in his late forties or early fifties wearing an expensive but unclean and wrinkled suit.

"Will you stay with me until I depart," he asked.

"Of course I will, you can count on it," I answered.

Again silence took over broken only by the sound of the plane's motor as it pierced its way through late afternoon sky. How, I asked myself, did I ever get involved in this case. My thoughts drifted back to a few days earlier in my office in Bogotá:

My secretary told me I had a call from the United States, a Mr. Samuels.

"Hello, this is Dominic Perenzin speaking."

"My name is Amery Samuels, I am an attorney with the a major U.S. law firm of Bar, Law and Pleading. Your name has been given to us by the American Embassy in Bogotá, which we followed up on by checking your firm through different sources. We would like to retain your services. By you I mean you personally."

"If I'm able I would be pleased to do so. What's involved?"

"At this very moment there is a gentleman in a jail in a place called Rioacha, Guajira, Colombia. He is an important figure and a respected board member of a client of ours, a large national bank. His name is Frederick Fuller. We believe he has wrongfully been arrested for allegedly trafficking in drugs."

I explained that our office did not handle criminal cases, though we confidently could refer him to an excellent criminal lawyer.

"We understand that but this matter must be handled expeditiously and quietly for which we need an attorney who is absolutely trustworthy. He will not be required to provide criminal law services. Our information is that you are such an attorney. We already have a criminal law lawyer in Rioacha who is provisionally handling the case."

"What are the services you require?"

"The Rioacha lawyer's name is Raul Mane. He introduced himself to Mr. Fuller at the jail where he is incarcerated. The first thing we would want from you is to check this lawyer out for professional competence, reputation and honesty. Since his English is hardly understandable find out from him what Mr. Fuller's status is at this time."

I agreed to do so. A couple of telephone calls and I learned that Mane was a good lawyer but as to honesty he had about as much as one could expect from lawyers working in his area of law and in the Wild West region of the country where he practiced. Successful, he was.

I contacted Mane, introduced myself and asked for a status report. He told me Fuller had already retained his services but had no money with him to pay fees. I told him from what I could determine the matter of fees would not be a problem, though neither I nor my firm would assume any responsibility for their payment.

Mr. Fuller was being held in jail while a judicial inquiry was conducted to determine whether he should be officially charged for drug trafficking. Several nights ago pilot Fuller landed a private single engine plane on a clandestine airstrip outside of Rioacha. The police had been keeping the airstrip under surveillance so that no sooner had the plane taxied to a stop when it was surrounded by police cars with blinding spotlights trained on it.

Fuller was removed from the plane, placed in a police car and taken directly to jail. The filed report stated an inspection of the plane turned up several bundles of cocaine. Fuller said he had no idea about the cocaine and that it must have been planted in the plane by someone. He said he was on his way to Venezuela from Miami when it began getting dark and strong winds kicked up causing him to lose his bearings. When he landed in Colombia he thought he was in Venezuela.

Mane explained he had already spoken to officials about the case and believed he could get Fuller released. However, he, Mane, must receive in cash, no checks, US$300,000. He went on to explain that the money must be in his hands within three days because at the end of the period Fuller would be formally charged with drug trafficking, too late to handle the case "expeditiously" and his fees would increase.

I called Amery Samuels and gave him the information. He answered without any hesitation, "It's a deal, we will want you to personally deliver the money to Mane which will be in your office tomorrow. You are to use the services of a private plane and fly to Rioacha as soon as you have the money and will stay with Mr. Fuller until he leaves your country. Let me know the cost of the plane and other expenses and your fees and we'll send you that money also."

The next day a package of 3,000 one hundred dollar bills were delivered to my office. I immediately arranged to charter a plane and early the next morning I was sitting by myself on a single motor plane on a bumpy way to Rioacha.

Upon landing I got a cab and went to the address given to me by Mane. It turned out to be a private residence. I was told doctor Mane was not in and that he would return in about an hour. I asked if perhaps I could save time by going to his office.

"You are already there, it is in the next room," I was informed by the boy who had answered the door. But I could come in and wait for him if I wished.

Some forty minutes later in walked Mane's huge bulk. He invited me to enter his office where he proceeded to count the money. Mane reminded me of Sidney Greenstreet in the movie Casablanca, the resemblance was startling. I glanced around the office and I saw not a single law book.

Money counted, Mane turned to me and said everything was in order and that we had to make haste to the courtroom, though I doubted he could get much haste our of his bulging body.

We discussed Fuller's case on the way to the courthouse. Mane said that in his opinion he was probably guilty and that the story about believing he was in Venezuela sounded like "bullshit" given that Fuller was an experienced pilot. Even if it were true it would not exculpate him for having drugs aboard. I pointed out that Fuller claims the drugs had been planted in his plane by somebody. Could it not have been the police themselves, after all, they had whisked him off to jail before searching the plane. Mane said that was the knee-jerk defense of persons caught with drugs. While anything was possible it was unlikely in this case since it would mean the police had cocaine in their possession when Fuller landed there unannounced, which he had never heard of happening and, he assured me, he had heard these stories before.

Why would Fuller be bringing drugs into Colombia. It doesn't make any sense, isn't the drug trade supposed to go the other way? Do we know for sure the police in fact did find drugs in the plane? Have you seen what they claim to have found?

He said that under the Colombian judicial system it's not possible at this stage to view the evidence. "I don't understand," he continued "is it your intention to fight this case in court, which we could end up losing or do you want to get him out of here as fast as possible?" This he said not angrily but in a calm matter-of-fact manner as if it made no difference to him one way or the other.

Upset by the choices he had given me and conscious of my instructions, I told him to answer was in the money I had delivered to him for his services.

I waited outside in the hallway for about an hour while Mane went from one office to another sporting a very business-like demeanor. Finally, he emerged from the door nearest me saying, "Let's go to the jail, here are his release papers." He flashed a document in the air.

We picked up Fuller and two D.A.S. detectives and as I read the court document we headed for the airport and to the private plane on which I had flown here. Mane shook our hands, turned around and left as Fuller, the two gun-toting D.A.S. guys and I boarded the plane for Barranquilla.

And now here I was on my way to Barranquilla where Fuller was to board a private plane sent from the States and fly away from Colombia. The D.A.S. guys' orders were to stay with Fuller until he was on the plane.

Once in the airport terminal Fuller wanted to wash up a bit and left for the men's room accompanied by one of the D.A.S. guys, the other waited outside the door. This gave me the opportunity to check on the whereabouts of Fuller's plane. I was told it would arrive in about one hour.

Fuller looked a little fresher. "What I want right now is a big scotch and soda and a huge steak," was Fuller's next request. The D.A.S. guys, still brandishing their weapons, said no to the scotch. But I convinced them to let him have his drink explaining all he had been through during the time he was behind bars.

As we made our way to the restaurant it seemed that the eyes of everyone in sight were on us as they looked from the semi-automatic weapons the D.A.S. guys kept in conspicuous view to Fuller and me. For a moment I vacillated between feeling like royalty or like a prisoner walking the gauntlet as people stepped aside to let us pass.

Fuller got precisely what he desired, a huge, thick steak lightly cooked, heaping French fries and hot bread rolls. After finishing diner – which he consumed without uttering a word – he became talkative about a single theme, his experience in the jail. When he entered the jail he had a bit of over $4,000 in bills which were taken from him together with all his identification papers. Anything he asked for he was charged outrageous amounts which were debited to his $4,000. For one American cigarette $3.00, for toilet paper $10, soap a modest $8, overseas telephone calls to his lawyers $1,500.

On one occasion the guards led him to another part of the jail where he was told to enter a room. Upon doing the door was immediately closed behind him. Standing in the center of the room was a woman wearing the scantiest mini-skirt imaginable. Against the wall a bed. Without even a slight suggestion of formality and without uttering a word she went to him and began caressing the back of his neck, then took his arm and gently urged him in the direction of the bed.   She was wearing a perfume which reminded him of toilet disinfectant.

Realizing what was happening he instinctively pulled his arm away saying, "No, No, No thank you," as he headed towards the closed door which he proceeded to bang on. The young lady stood there beckoning him to come to her. Once out of the room he was told this would cost him $800. No amount of explaining that nothing had happened in the room dissuaded his captors from debiting his account.

"By the way" said Fuller, "I don't think I'll again eat chicken."

"Bad experience?" I asked.

From the very first day he knew that if he had to eat the slop he was served for his first meal he would surely and quickly die from some kind of digestive catastrophe. The guard who brought the food, realizing Fuller's abhorrence, told him in fractured English – which he had picked up from other American prisoners – that his mamá could prepare meals for him. She would deliver them through the bars of his window. For each meal Fuller was to pay $15 to the mother and $15 to the guard. In the absence of a menu, he agreed.

And so it was chicken soup for breakfast and chicken, rice and beans or boiled plantains for lunch and dinner every day. When Fuller complained the guard promised to take care of it. But the chicken continued to be passed through the bars. When Fuller complained to the mother by pointing to the chicken and gesturing a "no" followed by a "moo-moo si," her face lit up as she smiled. But it was chicken again for the next meal. "The old hag must have been stealing her neighbor's chickens," grinned Fuller.

A young man came to our table to inform us that Fuller's plane had arrived and was ready for boarding. As we left the restaurant I noticed one of the D.A.S. guys picked up a bread roll Fuller had left and put it in his pocket. At the gate we shook hands as he thanked me for my help then turned to the two D.A.S. guys and gestured good-bye. Turning his attention back to me he winked, turned around and nonchalantly headed for the plane whose revving motors suggested urgency of departure. That wink troubled me for days. What did he mean by it? Had I been duped? Or was he expressing his delight on being free? Who was Frederick Fuller and what was the real truth about this allegedly respectable banker? As often occurred in Colombia the real stories

216

behind drug trafficking incidences were enigmas wrapped in mystery and thickly coated with intrigue.

****

TAXICAB

During the early years of the office Alicia played a major role. Her secretarial and managerial abilities were impressive as was her dedication to the office. The office was small so naturally we worked closely together resulting in a gradual and inexorable bonding between us. At first it was strictly a professional dependence on her, but as time passed and contact became a daily fact I discovered a new feeling arising not exactly related to business. I was seeing her now also as a person and a woman, and I liked what I saw. I found myself anxious to get to the office and reluctant to leave, largely because Alicia was there. Soon we started having lunch together and got to know more about our private selves.

We had worked late one day – the mother's six o'clock rule having become more flexible by this time – and since I didn't have my car with me I suggested we take a taxi. She agreed. In the taxi we chattered about office matters for a while. When I looked at her the passing lights from the street shown across her face highlighting her features. At times it was her forehead, eyes, her mouth or the silhouette of her nose. She was beautiful. The months of unexpressed and perhaps repressed feelings began to surface. She must have felt something was happening as she stopped talking and turned to look at me. Then it happened, one of those rare but wonderful moments in life when a number of pre-existing situations merge to produce an irrepressible and overwhelming impulse to express one's feelings. I moved closer to her, placed my hand gently under her chin and kissed her. She appeared surprised in a rehearsed sort of way.

218

She said nothing. As the cab drove up in front of her house I saw her mother ever vigilant waiting at the window where she could be counted on to be whenever Alicia was out. Alicia stepped out of the cab walked over to her front door, turned to look at me for a moment then continued into her house. The brief look she gave me spoke volumes. That night we both had trouble falling asleep but weren't concerned for something had happened that had relegated sleep to the status of dispensability. From that kiss on our romance took flight.

Two years after the taxi kiss we were married in a private ceremony at the home of one of my clients, Sam Stark.

****

At some point during the two years I met Alicia's family. As I observed the comings and goings of the members I felt overtones of the world of my Beech Street existence and of the close familial bonds that characterized it, awakening in me the slumbering memories of my youth years. As I was to learn, in no small way my Italian upbringing had prepared me well to appreciate and value the life that was about to open up to me.

In the Bustos family Alicia's mother Stella had a central role not so much as to the ostensible making of decisions but as a behind the scenes manipulator who functions through an intuitive awareness of what is happening in her immediate world that could affect her family. The father Jorge being more abstract and detached seemed less connected or aware. This became evident the evening I went to the Bustos house to comply with the local custom of asking for a daughter's hand in marriage. It was obvious clairvoyant Stella had anticipated the reason for my visit that evening while Jorge expressed surprise at what was happening. But more about that later.

Of Alicia's siblings the one that most impressed me on first encounter was Maria Victoria. There was a wholesomeness, up-front spontaneity and amiability about her. As time passed and I got to know her better I realized she had the ability to look out into the world with the delight and simplicity of a child, a genuine the-glass-is-half-full person. She was and remains the avatar of the adage long eschewed by politicians that says, "if you can't say something nice about someone don't say anything." As time went on I had an opportunity to know good-natured, musically talented, ad-hominem joke meister Arturo with whom I felt initially closest. Of the younger of the Bustos children Adriana (more affectionately known as "Cuca") I seldom saw for she was usually either absent when I visited the Bustos home or was inconspicuous. It was only after Alicia and I were married and had children that she became very close to us, as she proved to be a warm and caring aunt to our kids. As in Arturo's case I got to know Sergio only after my marriage and found him to have been cut from the same block as his father Jorge, restive, forever devising stratagems for new business deals. From early age he was single-minded about becoming a pilot. Maria Stella the eldest of the group was more of a motherly type, friendly but more constrained than Maria. All of the brothers and sisters were to weave in and out of our future marriage and in so doing maintained the close-knittedness of the family.

Returning to that evening when I asked for Alicia's hand, she and I met at a restaurant for cocktails. We knew there would be no rejection by the parents, after all this quaint practice was merely a relic from the past with no real consequences. Yet, I was curious and oddly excited as to what was about to occur.

Stella had been forewarned I was coming but not as to the reason for the visit but by native prescience she knew. We sat in the living room while Jorge was upstairs engaged in his favorite leisure time activity of watching television. Stella called him down. He seemed and clueless as what was about to unfold. After an exchange of innocent pleasantries I announced the reason for my visit. Alicia sat at my side and we held hands. I said we had known each other for a number of years, were in love and desired to marry. As if reciting from a primer on what to say on such occasions, I said I would do my best to make Alicia happy. Yes, there was a wide difference in our ages but we were convinced not only that this would not be a negative but that in many ways a positive.

With little hesitation Jorge gave us his approval accompanied by a short welcoming speech and we all embraced. Arturo, was called down from upstairs and told. Again embraces. I felt pleased by the warmth with which our announcement had been received. Alicia was radiant. The tone for our future relations was now firmly set.

During the courtship I was presented with what turned out to be the most unique couple I would meet in Colombia, Alicia's maternal grandparents Alejandro Botero and Alicia Restrepo de Botero affectionately called "Papapa" and "Mamama." It was a sort of a family social review where the grandparents had their first look at me – a sort of gracious passage of inspection. It went off well with courtesy, politeness and political correctness.

I was to revisit the grandparents' apartment many times in the years to follow, often on late Saturday afternoons to hear mass, something I had not done for many years. Normally, these masses were attended by members of various branches of the extended family, aunts, uncles, cousins. In addition to the religious aspect of these Saturday reunions, there was the social aspect of relatives visiting, exchanging news and stories.

The grandparents – a unique couple in anybody's universe – had for years been the heart of the Botero clan, the glue that kept things united. Alicia Restrepo de Botero bore a dignified air, schooled as she was in the art of fine etiquette and decorum. Soft-spoken but authoritarian she was the grand preceptor to her daughters as to the social graces of dignified speech, behavior, table manners, and all of the other accoutrements of graceful upper-class status. She was serious in demeanor and parsimonious in laughter.

Alejandro Botero in many ways contrasted his wife. An engineer by profession and apparently product of a less elevated social class he was able to laugh, joke, tell stories and be less rigid in his demeanor. While not contradicting his wife as to the primacy of discipline, he was able to show great affection for his five daughters – Dolores, Stella, Elizabeth, Gisela and Alicia – clearly a poster-perfect doting father.

Religion occupied a central place in the Botero family. Papapa's speech was often sprinkled with religious references. One of his favorites was to say that "Above God there resides no one" From this deep-seated religiosity sprang the couple's interest in helping the less fortunate. Through a non-profit foundation organized by them they had simple but adequate houses built on land which I believe was either owned by them or by the foundation which the couple then gifted to needy families. This was the *Perpetuo Socorro* (Perpetual Aid) housing project. Mamama would regularly go there to personally to distribute food and clothing which she actively obtained through donations. This was my first contact with an enterprise of this nature, a true paragon of altruistic, civic-minded compassion.

Papapa and Mamama were much in love, particularly palpable in Papapa who indulged his spouse in her every wish and desire. This profound caring endured to the very night Papapa passed away. At some point during that final night he asked Mamama whether she was all right. Assured that she was he peacefully closed his eyes and passed away. The final poetic expression of his life-long concern and love for his Alicia and ultimate reaffirmation of the place she occupied in his heart.

****

BUILDING A FAMILY

Alicia and I had been married a full year and were yearning to have our first child. I was no youngster and if I was to enjoy a family time would soon become my adversary.

December 1976. Alicia and I were in Massachusetts visiting my mother, brother and sister. Leno was living in Gardner with a lovely lady named Millie. It was New Years Eve and the four of us went to a dance party at a local private club. We danced, danced, drank and danced some more. Everyone was friendly as so often happens in small country towns. This was our second New Years Eve together, the first having been spent in Mexico during our honeymoon. We were relaxed yet quietly excited about the promise our nascent marriage held out for us.

At around 2 a.m. we left the club to go to Millie's house where we were to stay overnight and were pleasantly surprised to discover that while we were enjoying ourselves inside over a foot of snow had fallen. The drive to Millie's house was a ride through a real winter wonderland, a true Hallmark moment. Alicia snuggled close. All that was missing was a horse–drawn sleigh.

Millie lived in a large two-story house on Sutton Street. Our assigned bedroom was on the second floor which came complete with a huge king-size bed and loads of home woven blankets.

Through the windows we could see snow falling and brushing against the panes as we laid in bed. We were warm, content and much in love and feeling that all was right with the world. Nine months later our first child was born, Dominic Jr.

The next morning with a chill in the air we were awakened by the bustle of activities downstairs and by the delicious odors wafting from the kitchen. Millie had gotten up early and was baking the most luscious apple pies ever. Freshly ground coffee was percolating on an old fashion wrought-iron stove. I've often thought of the early morning scene as a simple, unpretentious, country-kitchen celebration of a marvelously magical event. A paean to the wonder of creation.

We were so delighted with our first-born that we thought it might not be a bad idea to double, triple and quadruple our blessings by bringing new members into the fold. And so it was that our three beautiful girls were born. First there was Gina Paola, our dark eyed, dark haired lovely, followed by the golden haired Laura and pretty Alicia Dennise.

Dennise's birth in 1984 was a miracle of its own because it was in 1982 that I had a near fatal heart attack requiring triple by-pass surgery. Laura had arrived eleven days before my heart attack.

The child whose arrival gave me much joy was that of Gina, for we had a boy and now wanted to balance the gender equation. We didn't really have any preference for our first-born. Gina's case was different. Laura on the other hand was our fair-haired beauty, delicate and sweet. Lovely Italian features Dennise we were particularly partial to, after all she was our youngest.

Colombians have a proclivity for creating rituals or ceremonies around certain events. I became a fast learner of this art. Soon after learning Alicia was pregnant, I would invite the Bustos family including grandparents over to our home for dinner. No reason was ever given for these invitations, which was not unusual since we occasionally made such dinner invitations. At the end of the dinners I would produce a tray of glasses and a bottle of champagne into the dining room and after getting everyone's attention say Alicia and I had an important announcement to make. After several births so accustomed had the family gotten to this ritual that on non-announcement occasions when I offered champagne after dinner, eyebrows automatically rose in anticipation.

With the arrival of our kids we embarked upon that treasured but mercilessly short period of watching them grow and mature. We did a lot of traveling; skiing in Vermont where we had a house in the woods and where Dominic soared over the hills and valleys in a glider, motoring to delightful places in New England – sand dunes of Cape Cod, fish in Glouster, lobsters at roadside tables in Maine, baseball at Fenway Park, amusement parks in New Hampshire – white sands of Acapulco, Indian villages in Taos, soaring through the Grand Canyon, driving along the ocean highway between San Francisco and Los Angeles, the Rose Bowl and Macy Parades, Radio City Music Hall, Paris, Rome, Venice, Florence...

During all of this and while engaged in her parental role, Alicia, a perennial fountain of energy and ambition, found time to embark upon a new career. After working in the law office a few years and getting a pretty good feel for what lawyers were all about, she decided she wanted to go to law school. Following her graduation from the Externado de Colombia Law School, Alicia joined the office as an associate attorney. During the course of her studies Alicia managed to add two members to our family roster. In 1985, at the suggestion of our firm's Washington Office, Alicia attended the summer program of the Academy of American and International Law held at the Southern Methodist University Law School in Dallas, Texas. I remained home with our four kids. The program brought together lawyers from all parts of the world for an accelerated overview of U.S. legal institutions. About half way through the program Alicia called to tell me she had been elected Secretary of the Class of 1985, the highest position. So delighted I was that I flew to Dallas for her graduation taking with me four year old Gina and three year old Laura.

We enjoyed meeting many of her classmates and were particularly proud to hear Alicia deliver an address at the graduation ceremonies.

JOURNALISM

In 1983 I came to the conclusion that Bogotá needed an English language newspaper. What papers were available were from overseas. I knew there was a sizeable English-speaking community in Bogotá as well as a number of bi-lingual Colombians. Alicia and I talked at length about the venture and did some checking on how to organize such an enterprise i.e. who would do the printing, initial capital needed to cover at least the costs of operation, government approvals, distribution, not to mention the paper's format.

On September 1, 1983 the first edition of THE PAPER was published. To celebrate the event we held a cocktail party on a landlocked sailboat at which a distinguished group of people attended – the President of Xerox Colombia, the General Manager of Bank of America, Colombia, the President of the Colombo-American Chamber of Commerce, David Manzur, famous Colombian painter, the President of The Royal Bank of Canada (Colombia) and representatives from the American Embassy.

During its three years of existence THE PAPER published unique occasionally controversial, but never insipid articles. We conducted the best if not the only comparative study of Bogotá's top private schools. David Manzur, the well-known Colombian painter, granted us a personal interview in which the readers were afforded a peek into his personal and professional life. Then there was the interview with Geraldo Silva Valderrama, Minister of Mines and Petroleum. We published an article reporting on our survey of prices charged by several supermarkets for identical products. This got one of our reporters ejected from a supermarket that had finished at the bottom of one of our earlier surveys. Mamama's and Papapa's charitable Perpetuo Socorro was the subject of a lengthy article replete with pictures taken of them at the site.

We gathered together an interesting and, in some cases, non-mainstream contributors of articles:

Thomas Quinn: wrote about his experiences living among native Colombians. Tom later became Time magazine's man in Colombia.

Charles Nicholls: submitted in-depth reports on interesting off-beat locations in Colombia. He lived with wife and a brood of kids in a trailer in which he traveled around the country.

Betty Stewart: interviewed important personalities. She did a great interview of Consuelo de Montejo, the maverick owner of the newspaper El Espacio.

William Aycrigg: provided reviews of local entertainment and art events and did a fascinating interview of Enrique Pulecio, a leading figure in Colombia avant guard theater circles. Bill was also Editor-in-Chief of THE PAPER.

Angus C: the pen-name of our quintessential hippie contributor Angus McPhearson, furnished articles about the drug culture and the closeted other face of Colombia.

Sabina Shalom: our British import wrote one of The Paper's most popular features, the "Dear Sabby" column. She and I were interviewed on a local T.V. talk-show about THE PAPER.

Though the venture into journalism added little to the bottom line of our personal financial balance sheet it did give Alicia and me a sense of pride and accomplishment. All of the labor, tension and time involved in bringing forth a new edition was more than the compensated for by the excitement of waiting for the first copies of new editions to be delivered to us. The delight and pride of authorship we felt as we fingered through the pages of the fresh edition would remain *non-pareil*.

DILEMMA

How outlandish the thought would have seemed that night in Cuba when I tried marijuana that someday the weed I held between my fingers would be the cause, *albeit* indirect, for the uprooting of my family. But that is precisely what happened in September of 1989.

From the date of my marriage embellished as it was with the arrival of our children life in Colombia had taken on an idyllic quality, a stream of relaxing pleasantries – extended family reunions, country picnics, kids' birthday parties, vacations in Cartagena, weekend trips to visit friends in other picturesque towns, Sundays at local theme parks, entertaining visitors from overseas, first communions, watching and being part of our beautiful kids growing up, summer vacations in the States, Saturday morning food shopping at the colorful outdoor markets and those delicious cold rainy evenings sipping a hot cup of chocolate or smuggling underneath a friendly blanket. I had developed new roots.

Around 1987 the illicit drug situation – which prior to that year was low profile – now took on scary dimensions. The Colombian drug traffickers had forged a powerful cartel operating out of the city of Medellin. Its grasp reached into all corners and strata of Colombian life. Attempts by the government to quash the illicit trade and bring the criminals to justice provoked a bloodbath involving the murder of many judges and the bribing of politicians and law enforcement officers. When the United States requested that Colombia extradite the Cartel kingpins the response of the Cartel was to unleash an even more bloody and extensive campaign of violence hoping therewith to dissuade the Colombian government from acquiescing to the U.S. Government's requests.

Alicia and I became increasingly concerned about these developments and the potential risk they posed for all of us. This became a subject of numerous discussions as to whether we should remain in Colombia or pack our suitcases. In our search for an answer we sought guidance by seeking the views of other Colombian-American couples. Our children were brought into the mix when during one of our yearly skiing trips to Vermont we asked them to write down what they liked and what they didn't like about living in Colombia. They liked their schools, friends and the fun things we did there but were very afraid because so many people were being killed. These observations from those who meant so much to us were not taken lightly.

My law partners had been regularly kept apprised of the happenings in Colombia. On more than one occasion I was asked to seriously consider leaving the country and placing the office in the hands of our Colombian lawyers to which I gave my knee-jerk answer that it was too early to contemplate such an extreme step.

Yes! No! Maybe! had been our thinking regarding leaving Colombia. On a Friday evening in September 1989 I remained up late into the night reviewing the layers of pros-and-cons we had accumulated. Alicia was tired and decided to call it a day leaving me alone to think and consume cups of coffee. I don't know what tipped the scales for me, perhaps it was the reluctance to leave behind the unforgettable halcyon days I had spent in Colombia or perhaps it was something as momentary as the coziness I felt as the rain brushed the windows of my room, whatever it was I concluded we should not leave Colombia. I awoke Alicia to tell her how I felt, she was quick to concur.

We discussed our decision for a few minutes. Feeling decompressed from tensions of uncertainty, we fell into a relaxing sleep caressed by the warmth of our decision. Early the next morning the walls of our room shook violently as pictures fell off the walls. Jumping out of bed I ran to our kid's room and finding them safe but nervous brought them into our bedroom. By this time Alicia had turned on our bedside radio. There had been a bomb attack against offices of El Espectador newspaper located on the same street but quite a distance from our apartment. As the news poured in it was becoming clear that the attack had been made or underwritten by the Medellin Cartel. El Espectador had adopted a staunch uncompromising ant-Cartel position and had frequently published scathing attacks against it. Extradition to the United States was strongly advocated on its pages despite violent threats of reprisal.

The El Espectador building had, for all practical purposes, been demolished as were two buses and a few cars that had the unfortunate luck of passing in front of the building when the bomb or bombs were detonated. There were numerous fatalities.

The atmosphere in our apartment became electric. It could have been us in one of those annihilated cars for we often passed this building with our kids. When and where will the Cartel strike again? No lengthy discussion was needed, no further weighing of pros or cons, we were leaving as soon as we could. I went to my office and dashed off a telex to our managing partner in Bangkok, explained what had occurred and told him we wanted to leave the country. Within a few hours I got his response, "Leave, go to our Miami Office."

The next few days were of frenzy of activities aimed at leaving things in as much order and as quickly as possible. Not knowing whether our departure would be permanent, we decided to leave our apartment as it was. We would only take with our clothes and important personal documents leaving time and future developments to decide what to do with the rest of our things.

As our plane flew over Bogotá and its sumptuous savannah – a delightful scene I had enjoyed on many occasions – my heart was heavy with melancholy. Somehow I knew there was a certain finality to this flight. The panorama below would never again be seen by me from the same perspective. I looked over at my family and wondered what laid ahead for us. Dominic was 12, Gina 7, Laura 6 and Dennise 5.

PART EIGHT

MUSINGS

LATE NIGHT THOUGHTS

Some of the most pleasurable moments in my life have been those enjoyed during quiet evenings alone wrapped around a good book. No sounds except for occasional soothing background music. After a while of relaxed reading the seductiveness of the evening often eases me into a reflective mood and some late-night thoughts.

I had just finished reading the last page of Philip Roth's recent novel "The Human Stain," a riveting tale of the amazing life and experiences of its leading character Coleman Silk. A life odyssey full of surprising twists and turns, heights and troughs. I was particularly stirred by the stark yet tranquil word-portrait with which the book ended of a man set off against the sound and fury of his past and of the outside world:

> Only rarely, at the end of our century, does life offer a vision as pure and peaceful as this one; a solitary man on a bucket, fishing through eighteen inches of ice in a lake that's constantly turning over its water atop an Arcadian mountain in America.

After reading this passage and reflecting on its overtones my thoughts drifted back to my Beech Street years and a particular scene. When I was around ten or eleven years young three of my friends and I occasionally went into the woods adjacent to the granite quarry behind my house to do some open-air cooking. Frankfurters, buns and mustard – occasionally joined by potatoes. Each of us would, through the actual or assumed generosity of his mother, make a contribution to these provisions. Oh yes, since none of us had been boy scouts we also brought matches and paper along.

Finding a suitable spot we gathered up dry branches and twigs placed them over the paper and started our fire. As it took hold we threw increasingly larger pieces of wood into it until we had a strong sustainable combustion. If we had potatoes we would place them in the ashes at the bottom of the fire, occasionally turning them over to brown or sometimes blacken them evenly, producing the most delicious, natural-flavor potatoes known to humankind. Each of us would find his own green branch, not too thick and not too thin, and with our pocket knives whittle down one end into a sharp point with which to pierce his frankfurter.

We sat around the fire extending the frankfurters-soon-to-become hot-dogs, just the right distance above the flames, a distance determined not from a cookbook but empirically from trial and error. At first there was quiet conversation then gradually as bubbles formed on the hot dogs and drops of juices began hissing into the flames a peaceful quietness enveloped the scene, the only sound that of crackling firewood. While this was occurring the outside world was restless about an eminent war in Europe and suffering the ravages of the Depression.

Both of these scenes speak to me of what in the end and after all is said and done is the solitariness of the individual as he stands naked before the Cosmic Infinity. Not visible on the map of the earth as it spins around at a thousand miles per hour and circles the sun at a velocity of sixty-six thousand miles per hour, occurring in an unending void, nothing more than a globe of cooling gas, located among billions of stars in one galaxy out of countless other galaxies, sits a solitary man on a bucket fishing in ice eighteen inches thick atop an Arcadian mountain and four silent youngsters sit around a fire in the soundless woods of Fitchburg holding hot dogs over its flames each wrapped in his private world.

****

I have read two excellent books dealing with the subject of death which have come to mind during my late night musings. One was written by the great Russian writer Leo Tolstoy entitled "The Death of Ivan Ilyich", the story of a high court judge who had never given the inevitability of his death a passing thought until one day to his shocked surprise he is brought face to face with his own mortality. The second book is more modern having been on the New York Times Best Seller List for over a year. It is the much talked about true story "Tuesday with Morrie" by Mitch Albom. A college professor in his late years learns he is soon to die. After surviving the shock of the news he decides to create something of value to the world about the very process of dying and agrees with a former student, now a sports writer in Detroit, to meet each Tuesday to chronicle what Morrie will feel and think during the period of approaching death.

Unlike Morrie, Ilyich attempts to fight off death and much is made of the anguishing moments he spent in its contemplation. His initial reaction upon learning of the terminal nature of his illness was to begin three days of incessant screaming. It was not until he could feel the cold breath of death and awakening from a sleep he felt his son kissing his hand and his wife standing beside him with tears in her eyes that he surrendered to the inevitable calmness with compassion and understanding.

The message of the book is summarized in a painful thought that occurs to Illyich at the very end of his breathing days. Illych asks himself, "What if I've lived my life wrong?" What a rueful question to ask as death stands before one with arms outstretched, a reminder of Macbeth's immortal, desolate exclamation upon hearing of Lady Macbeth's death:

Out, Out brief Candle!
Life's but a walking shadow,
A poor player that struts
And frets his hour upon the
Stage and then is heard
No more. It is a tale
Told by an idiot, full
Of sound and fury,
Significantly nothing.

In "Tuesday With Morrie" we are presented with a gentler though hardly less poignant account of the final journey of a retired professor who, in character, expounds his thoughts as if addressing a classroom. In a sense it is a reflection on how one should live one's life so as not to have to ask as Ilyich did "What if I lived my life wrong?" Morrie's story is replete with insight and wisdom.

In the course of his dictations to his former student Morrie at times alludes to Eastern thoughts and Buddhist concepts and in that vain tells a simple but profoundly moving story of a little wave which reminded me of the story of a musical note.

A lovely note came from the strings of a violin and floated blithely in the air when it noticed that other notes ahead of it were weakening until eventually they disappeared.

"Oh my God," said the note, "I am going to disappear just like them."

A note from a cello floated up next to the first note and asked why it was so sad.

"I'll tell you why, because I can see you haven't noticed, we are all going to disappear and no longer be. Look and listen to the notes ahead of us."

"It's you who has not noticed," said the cello note. "We have all been heard and are now a beautiful part of peoples lives, we shall not die."

I once had a dream that the God of Life and Death had become annoyed by the fact humans were so fearful of death that they banished the word from use and had it deleted from all literature, books, magazines newspapers and banned from all other means of communication. People were severely punished for mentioning the word or depicting or alluding to the dreaded event. The God of Life and Death decided it was time to put an end to this absurd foolishness. And so it was that one day indelibly engraved on the forehead of every human being was the word "died" followed by the date each person was to die.

****

I had attended mass that Sunday morning. It was a lightly cool sunny day and I felt good as I walked into the church. I felt even better when I learned that my favorite priest would be celebrating the mass and would deliver the homily. He had a gift for enlivening the subject not by exhibitions of emotion, but by approaching it in a laid back story-telling manner during which he wove what seemed like random threads into a lovely spiritual tapestry. Later that evening, my thoughts became troubled by what the priest had said as it rekindled a conundrum that had been with me for years and, I suppose, with civilization for centuries.

He spoke of the Protestant Saint Paul's church located in New York City next to the World Trade Center Towers a church which George Washington is said to have attended. On the day following the disaster of September 11 while the Twin Towers of the Trade Center had been reduced to a smoldering mass of rubble and the immediate surrounding buildings had been with heavy damages, St. Paul's stood untouched and unaffected. The priest's conclusion was that God had saved the church so that it could stand there as a symbol, a beacon of God's power and the hope that resided in turning to Him.

I asked myself if the amazing non-event of the Saint Paul's church, that is to say, the fact no damage was inflicted on it, was the work of God then whose work was it that leveled the Twin Towers resulting in the death of thousands and leaving young widows and fatherless children in its wake? I was left unsatisfied by the standard explanations which came to mind such as that the Twin Towers tragedy was the work of evil men, that God works in mysterious ways that humans cannot understand and that one should rely on one's faith in God and so on.

A number of years ago I read a book entitled "When Bad Things Happen to Good People" written by Harold Kushner, a Jewish rabbi. The book is an exposition of what the rabbi went through when tragedy befell his son Aaron, his only son. When Aaron was only three years old he was diagnosed with a condition called progeria i.e. rapid aging. Aaron died at the age of 15.

The rabbi tells of his first angry reactions, his feeling of having been betrayed by God. His son was a good boy, obedient, studious and loving. Why would God do this to him. In the end and after much soul searching and reflection he concludes that God has limitations, that He is limited by the laws of nature and by the evolution of human nature and human moral freedom. The rabbi concludes that some misfortunes are the result of bad luck, some are caused by bad people while others are simply the inevitable consequence of our being human and mortal and living in a world of inflexible natural laws. This appears to provide a pragmatic answer to the above questions, yet, if God's power to alter the laws of nature is limited them how does one explain just such alterations in the name of miracles?

Not so incidentally, several months after hearing the priest's homily on the St. Paul's church I learned that a Greek Orthodox church located next to the Twin Towers had been totally destroyed. I find this to be an example of how some clergy and the faithful have the salad-bar talent for selecting certain events as evidence of received truths and learned beliefs while conveniently ignoring evidence to the contrary. When this happens credibility is lanced.

****

Not all late evening thoughts involve philosophic themes, there are some that bring on a smile and chuckle. One the evening one of my daughters asked me a homework question involving the human anatomy which I couldn't answer. Later that evening, curious about the answer I turned to an encyclopedia. Skimming over the pages I came across a discussion of men's testicles which brought to mind two incidences involving this part of the anatomy.

I must have been around 10 or 11 and still at the Clarendon Street grammar school. Miss Keating was irritable that day when she pointed a menacing finger at me and snarled, "Dominic, why are you and Alfred talking and disrupting this class?"

"Alfred just asked me a question that's all," I answered, as Alfred nodded in agreement.

"I presume it must have been a very important question having to do with what I'm teaching, right?" she said "and would you mind telling the class what the question was."

"No Miss Keating, it wasn't that important," said Alfred.

"Dominic, the question!"

"He wanted to know what the word testicles means, that's all."

There were snickers from different parts of the classroom. "I see," said Miss Keating suppressing alternating smiles and sternness, "and dare I ask what your answer was?"

"I told him I didn't know."

"The next time you, and this applies to all of you in this class, want to know what a word means try opening a book which has been around for many years and which you may have heard about, it's called a dictionary, do you understand?"

"Yes, Mrs. Keating"

A few minutes later Jasper catapulted a note to me as Miss Keating turned to the blackboard. The note read "The balls we guys have are testicles, you dumbhead." My face flushed and I reached over to punch Alfred on the arm and he, trying to avoid the blow, fell off his chair. We both ended up in the Principal's office.

Later I figured this was all well and good for it was information which I might very well stand to benefit in the future as I came into contact with educated people and their highfalutin words.

The second incident could be called a case of "oops." It occurred when I was a member of the Toastmasters Club in Cuba. I and two others were selected to address the next dinner meeting. This was to be a special affair since those who were married or had girl friends were welcome to have the ladies attend as guests. Up to that announcement I had progressed rather nicely in overcoming my public speaking nervousness, but now I was to have a new public, not the same faces I had gotten accustomed to seeing in the audience. Moreover, I was given a choice of topics from a list of five possibilities where in the past I was given complete freedom of choice.

The room was filled to capacity. So many guests showed up that it was necessary to set up an extra tables. I was to be the first speaker of the night. To appease my nerves I had two dry martinis before dinner.

Gentlemen and invited ladies our first speaker of the evening is Dominic Perenzin. I went to the lectern and began my talk. Surprisingly soon my nerves ceased being a problem. Occasionally, I looked down at my note cards to remind me what I was to say next. I got to a point in my talk when I wanted to express the idea of how a certain historical figure tried to control and conquer everything and everyone within his greedy reach. And so I began "John Doe motivated by his insatiable hunger for power, spread his long testicles over all the land in an effort to grasp and bring into his control…" Immediately people looked surprised and ill-at-ease as they whispered to each other. Some tried to cover their laughter with their napkins. I was totally confused and distraught. I didn't understand why people were behaving so uncivilly. Maybe my fly was open? It was not until I sat down and from what my table companion said that I realized I had said "testicles". I couldn't believe it. My notes read "tentacles". If it were possible I would have hidden under the table out of sight. As the evening progressed I was sure all the women present were staring at me and thinking what a depraved monster I was. Certainly I would be ejected from the Toastmakers. For some time after his incident I swore-off the use of either "tentacles" or "testicles" in my speech. Wasn't it Saint Matthew who said, "By thy words thou shall be condemned."

Every so often I get the urge to do a little housekeeping by reorganizing the bookshelves in my office only to find that once I get to the stage of deciding whether a certain book continues to be worth keeping, the same old book lover's quandary stares me in the face. Should I or shouldn't I? And so I make two stacks, one for books that are to be discarded and the second I consider the Book Purgatory Group i.e. those which await future decision on whether they go back on the shelf or are to be thrown out.

One evening as I sat down to begin reading I noticed the stack of books which were still awaiting final judgment. I saw that the book on the top of the stack was "The Greening of America," by Charles Reich. It had been many years since I had read that book. Curious, I took it back to my chair and began browsing through it.

It didn't take me long to recall what the book was all about. Back in the 1970's Charles Reich, a Yale law professor, wrote this book in which he heralded a non-violent revolution led by America's college-age generation. He said he wrote it as the result of school cafeteria conversations he had had with students. His contention was that American youth had evolved a new consciousness, less guilty and anxious, non-judgmental, non-competitive, non-materialistic, affectionate, honest, unconcerned with status and careers. The new consciousness was compared to flowers emerging through the pavement, it promised a more humane community, a new and liberated individual. "Its ultimate creation will be a new and enduring wholeness and beauty – a renewed relationship of man to himself, to other men, to society, to nature and to the land," predicted the author.

If my memory doesn't fail me the book made the Best-Seller List of the New York Times. Everyone was talking about it and how it presaged the Age of Aquarius. I had witnessed the 1960's and thanks to my guide Carol Silver had become familiar with much of the thinking and ethos of the generation Reich was writing about.

What a difference 20-30 years can make in the dream, belief and aspiration contents of American culture. Today its all about Gucci-wearing, condo-owning, gourmet-baby-feeding, SUV driving professionals, packed college business schools, instant young millionaires, careers and success, and greed-bred "where-the-money is" lifestyles.

Sad how idealism and deeper understanding of life have been held hostage by a culture of me-ism. Despite these woeful situations or perhaps because of them I placed the Greening of America back on the shelf with the hope that someday someone might pick it up and read its message of renewal of the human spirit which is in danger of becoming a museum piece, a fossil of a forgotten and, heaven forbid, an irretrievable opportunity.

LIVING EPIGRAMS

Over the centuries observations of the life experience have been encapsulated into insightful epigrams. Perhaps because of the unchanging nature of the situations observed some of these epigrams continue to retain their relevance today. The settings may change but the essence of the observations remain valid. Occasionally, when certain epigrams cross my attention I am reminded of personal encounters that confirm their insightfulness and continuing relevance.

As the husband is, the wife is,
Thou art mated with a clown
And the grossness of his nature
Will have weight to bring thee down.
Jonathan Swift

He was short in height, stocky of frame with the large scarred hands of a laborer which he kept busy scratching one part of his body or another, even those which civility requires not be touched, let alone scratched in public. If he ever combed his hair it must have been when I was not around. His face had a primitive man's bone structure with cavernous eye sockets. His manner of walking left the impression he took each stride not with his legs alone but with the whole side of his body as if he wanted to make certain his legs would not walk way from the rest of him.

Talking to him, which I seldom did but have overheard others do so, called for special effort. To begin with it was often necessary to repeat sentences which I was convinced was due not to any auditory dysfunction but to a weakness of comprehension. His usual response to the first go around was "Ah?" meaning, repeat that will you. When he did speak it was with guttural sounds of strung-together words. It was as if on its path to the vocal cords the message from his brain in some inexplicable way got tangled up in his throat. Hardly helpful was the dull look of absenteeism in his eyes. It was widely conjectured that sometime in his life he must have received a damaging blow to his head.

Meet Alberto Giuseppi Rengo a denizen of our Beech Street community, married to Maria Fiorina. When Alberto Giuseppi was not begetting babies he was beating up Maria Fiorina, beating her so severely that she often ended up with swollen black eyes and red welts on her face, leaving to conjecture what other bodily abuses were hidden beneath her clothing. The neighbors for the most part limited their interventions to consoling Maria Fiorina. Only rarely did the men attempt to talk even a dollop of civility into his head, perhaps because it was felt it would be an exercise in futility. In retrospect, my buddies and I were insensitive to Maria Fiorina's plight, due probably to the fact we got so used to seeing her bruised up and figured that is what happens in life. We did have a special name for Alberto though, we referred to him as the "ape."

As time went by Maria Fiorina began acting strangely and abusively. She could be heard screaming at the milkman, at the newspaper boy and other non-neighbors. Her contacts with neighbors became less frequent and uneasy as she began to vent her fractured emotions less discriminately.

Upon Alberto Giuseppi's un-mourned departure from this earth, whatever he left of Maria Fiorina was a mere penumbra of the woman who first moved to Beech Street.

****

Patience is the virtue of an ass
That trots beneath his burden
And is quiet.
                    George Granville

I've seen the hillside "Ranchos" around Caracas, and the "Tugurios" south of Bogotá, in Brazil they're called "Favelas". They are ubiquitous and can be found in the Andean countries as well as in Bangkok (which I have seen), in Manila, throughout Asia, not to speak of the whole continent of Africa. The homes of those who live there are strikingly similar in the starkness of what is conspicuously missing and what is heart-renderingly present such as ill-fed children. It is the women who predominantly bear the greatest burden and depravation and do so alone as their husbands and/or fathers of their kids often abandon them to their fate. I have recently read about a section of Bombay, India where women relieve themselves only before dawn and evenings since they have no toilets and the only place they can squat to do so is visible to passing trains and buses.

Meet the inhabitants of the world's shantytowns where the more fortunate are at least able to cling precariously to the fringes of their country's economic life. They are, except during the times of election campaigns, the forgotten masses crouching and crawling at the bottom of the subsistence level. When lucky they can look forward to long days of arduous work for pay that is just enough to ward off starvation. School-less progeny, fodder for the cycle of hopeless poverty.

Whenever I've seen one of these shantytowns or read about them I've asked myself why is it that these people have not revolted and swarmed in mass against the governing bodies, demanded a fair share of the country's national product, and threatened to bring havoc to the country's institutions unless they are allowed to have the means to live a decent life. After all they do constitute a multitude of human beings who share the same basic needs and suffer from the same deprivations. I realize that what is absent and prevents this from happening is some kind of organizational structure through which they can make the weight of their combined power felt. There have been occasional glimmers of hope and a surge of expectations as in the case of Colombia where charismatic political figures such as Jorge Eliecer Gaitan and Luis Carlos Galan emerged championing the need for change and the rights of the under-classes, only to be assassinated. With hopes of improvements dashed too often the shantytowners recede into their traditional apathy and submission, resigned to their fate of traveling through life quietly beneath their burdens.

****

Blessed the man (woman) who, having
Nothing to say, abstains from giving
Us wordy evidence of the fact.
George Eliot

She had been mentioned on several occasions but I paid scant attention. A relative of Alicia who, it was claimed, could non-stop talk interminably and say nothing that her listeners could remember. A regular talking machine programmed to spew forth an endless number of words so banal, so devoid of interest as to cast a sleepy drowsiness so gripping that it required Herculean efforts for listeners to maintain even marginal attention.

Alicia announced that this very same relative would be among our guests at the upcoming Christmas Eve party. Not convinced that any person could possibly have the conversational traits ascribed to her, I looked forward to our meeting. If what had been said about her proved accurate I would surely be able to de-rail her and to take control of the conversation. I looked forward to the challenge.

During the course of the party I found myself in her presence together with several other guests. Before I realized what was happening and could brace myself she had started her discourse. Though she looked at us she seemed not to be speaking to anyone in particular or to us as a group. It was as if she had enclosed herself in a separate world and was actually feeding off the flow of her own words. Remembering my boast about de-railing her conversation, I tried to find a fissure in the wall of words which would allow me to slip in and disrupt her. My efforts were in vain. Her monologue was seamless leaving no place for interruptions and casting a spell which so numbed my mind that I could no longer distinguish individual words, all I could hear was a low-keyed droning. She occasionally gestured with her hands or changed the expression on her face to emphasize parts of her talk but the gestures underscored statements so bland that the gestures overshadowed her words.

Soon a strange unfamiliar feeling swept over me. I felt uneasy, nervous and trapped. I had but one desire and that was to break away, for I was now experiencing physical effects, a queasiness and perspiration. Four days later I suffered my near fatal heart attack. It would be an exaggeration to say that that Christmas Eve experience had anything to do with the attack, yet, I have never been able to completely quell the suspicion that in some way it played a vague role of some type.

****

I feel like one who treads alone
Some banquet hall deserted, whose
Lights are fled, whose garlands
Dead, and all but departed.
                    Thomas Moore

Look for them for they can be seen in most shopping malls. For the most part they go unnoticed by the busy shoppers since nothing about them is calculated to attract attention, to the contrary, their attire seems to have been carefully selected to avoid having eyes turned to them. Meet the unregistered legion of the lonely. Mostly they occupy benches and observe people passing, only occasionally showing a glimmer of facial reaction to things occurring around them. They don't shop and seldom if ever are seen inside any of the stores. The only purchase they make may be a small soft drink bought at the food court which they then patiently nurse as they sit alone at a table.

These are the unnoticed men, solitary figures seeking to be near people not for the purpose of conversations – for that would be too much to hope for – but simply to experience the community of other people. Once in a while and mostly when both are Cuban have I seen two of these men conversing with a semblance of animation only to see them lapse into their normal taciturn character once they part company.

Who are these old men? Surely they must be retirees, perhaps widowers or married men escaping from the humdrumness of their depleted marriages or hoary bachelors whose past freedoms had become their jail keepers.

What better place to seek escape from aloneness than in the Grand Temple, the Mecca of America's secular religion called Consumerism to whom homage is paid through the ritual of shopping. People on the move, music, voices, laughter, children crying, others smiling as they look in the windows of toy stores. Reminders of yesteryears when the lonely were participants and not observers. Free opportunities to revive – albeit in a plastic way – that once happy but now bittersweet parade of holiday seasons like Christmas, Easter, Thanksgiving, Valentine's Day, all reflected in the colorful ambience of the malls.

Two particular scenes I've witnessed have left an impression on me. The first involves a departure from the rule that these men do not enter the mall stores let alone purchase their wares. A short curly gray haired man whom I had seen sitting on several benches entered a clothing store and ambled with self-conscious steps into the women's lingerie section where he strolled around looking at the articles on display, at times seeming to want to pick one up. Having completed his inspections, he left the store without stopping at any other department.

The second scene occurred one evening when I went to pick up Laura from her part-time job. Since I had arrived early I sat on a bench to wait for her quitting time. It was late and the mall was mainly deserted. An elderly man sitting on a bench in front of me picked up a much handled newspaper that someone had left behind. He could not have read more than the headlines of the first page when he noticed a cleaning lady approaching pushing a trash container. She sent him a tired smile and he nodded in acknowledgement at the same time handing her the newspaper which she proceeded to throw into the trash container. He was about to say something but she, not noticing, continued on her way, oblivious of the unspoken words on his lips. A few moments later he got up, went to the Toys R Us window, looked inside for a while expressionless then with hands in pockets made his way to the mall exit and walked out into the warm Miami night.

PART NINE

PINK FLAMINGOS

The firm's Miami office never took roots and a year after my arrival it was closed. I had no desire to move on to another of the firm's offices so I decided to retire as a partner of the firm. My kids were happily in good schools, we had made new friends, Alicia's siblings were moving to Miami in growing numbers and her parents had decided to join all of us. Some eleven years have elapsed since we arrived in Miami and with the exception of Maria Victoria all of Alicia's siblings now live in the Miami area as do five cousins and two aunts. Our life was now firmly centered.

Since our arrival in Miami a number of events have occurred some of family interest, others of huge personal importance for me. To begin with sister-in-law Adriana's marriage shipwrecked on the shoals of her husband's infidelities. During the period of her post-divorce adjustment and re-entry into the social scene a knight in bright shining armor astride a white horse and humming native Vallenato country melodies who too had just emerged from a failed marriage came riding into her life showering her with merited kindness and affection. Soon they were married and now Adriana and Eduardo have two lovely girls, Jessica and Stephanie. Adriana's deep longing for motherhood was now fulfilled and they are destined to live happily ever after.

In 1996 my father-in-law Jorge passed away at the age of 81. It had become apparent over the prior year or so that his health was waning. Medical examinations showed he had prostrate cancer and emphysema, both in terminal stages. The news was jarring for though the family suspected he was not well the gravity of his condition came as a shock. Those of us who were made aware of this fell into a repressed depression as we helplessly stood by watching his life sustaining energy abandon him.

There were two poignant scenes that occurred in connection with Jorge's battle for life. The first took place while he was in the Kendall Regional Hospital. For several days his health had taken a sharp downturn so much so that his doctor informed us he had only about 24 hours of life left. This was told to us on December 31 after we had already decided to spend New Year's Eve together with Jorge in his hospital room. All of the Bustos family managed to make it, including Maria Victoria who had come from Colombia to be with her father. Jorge was aware of our presence in the room and even managed to smile and converse.

At midnight we formed a semi-circle around Jorge's bed and held hands, including those of Jorge, each lost in his or her private supplications. I felt energy coming to me from the hands I was holding which suffused my body producing a sense of peace and a feeling that things would be alright. As I looked at the faces around me I detected the presence of what I suspected was a similar emotion.

Jorge did not die within twenty-four hours but he did go home and, to the bafflement of his doctor, lived some nine more months. Something happened in that hospital room at midnight, a powerful force produced by the channeling and merging of our energies. Most of those present felt what happened was God's response to the supplications. Whatever it was it transcended the purely material.

The second scene occurred the morning of Jorge's death. At around 6 a.m. his wife Stella went to check on Jorge only to discover he had died. An hour later Eduardo Medrano, Cuca Bustos's medical doctor husband, came to the house and proceeded to examine Jorge. With stethoscope to his ears he listened for a sign of life from Jorge's heart, tried to take his absent pulse and checked his vacant eyes. Realizing there was only silence he literally tore the stethoscope from his ears and flung it angrily on the chair in a gesture of anger and frustration over what I interpreted as the impotence of science and medicine when confronted by mortality's ultimate claim.

When Jorge passed away his daughter Adriana was expecting her second child, an example of nature's Yin/Yang balancing act. On one of my visits to see Jorge in the hospital, I found him in bad shape with the imminence of the end clearly readable on his face. Heading out of the hospital and preoccupied with what I had just seen, I took the wrong turn and found myself entering the maternity section. Driving out of the hospital's parking garage and onto Bird Road I looked over at the hospital thinking how it encased the birth/ death cycle of life.

It wasn't long after permanently settling down in Miami did my brother-in-law Sergio's long held dream of being a pilot for a major U.S. airline became a reality. Those of us who knew him were aware this dream. What no one suspected was that his wife Constanza had her own infatuation, one which, as in the case of Sergio, manifested itself ferociously once the couple settled down in Miami. An image there, a toy here, household articles there. Before long it was all over, in the kitchen, bathrooms, bedrooms and living room, on furniture, dangling from ceilings, hanging on walls in other words it was omnipresent. Walt Disney from his glacial resting place smiled with joy as he looked into the home of Constanza. For there looking at him from every nook and crook was his favorite mouse. Anyone who visits Constanza's house and notes a strange mumbling sound should not be alarmed for it will probably be Walt's spirit and Mickey chatting.

We were in the year 2000, the first year of a new millennium and the twenty-fifth year of my marriage. It was now Laura's turn to see her obsession realized. She had for some time been insisting on having a formal celebration on the occasion of our anniversary. Though we initially were cool to the idea, preferring to memorialize the event in a more private way, in the end we acquiesced. Plans were made for a formal reception and dinner to which we would invite our family and a few of our friends. It turned out to be a stellar affair. Alicia and our girls were stunningly beautiful. A renewal of marriage vows, a ceremony in which my original best-man and dear friend Sam Stark participated. Laura and Dominic addressed heart-touching remarks to us which dampened the eyes of some of our guests. Dennise carried our renewal wedding rings. The sounds of the anniversary waltz quieted all conversations as Alicia and I stepped onto the dance floor. Laura and Dominic cut in to dance with us. A champagne toast, a slice of the delicious commemorative cake and then dancing by everyone.

Strange how a brief moment can encapsulate a long period of one's life. It happened to me that evening. The final number of the evening was one I had selected in advance, Barry Manilow singing "Where Does the Time Go" to which Alicia and I danced alone. Yes, I asked myself where does the time go. Twenty- five years of it felt like an instant to me. They were twenty-five beautiful years with a warm and caring woman who gave me four lovely children. While I didn't know the answer to the question of where the time went, I did know that, as the last line of the song said and which I whispered in Alicia's ear, "Wherever time goes, I will meet you there."

****

In a conspicuous position next to our Florida room television set is a trophy case containing a collection of trophies won in tennis tournaments played around South Florida over a span of some three years. They belong to Alicia Dennise.

When we first arrived from Colombia, we rented an apartment in an apartment complex which had tennis courts. Gradually my interest in the sport awoke from the slumber it had been in since playing tennis in Colombia and I began hitting balls again. Though all of our kids occasionally joined me, it was Dominic and Dennise who showed the most interest and talent and soon were taking lessons from a resident tennis coach. Both became members of the United States Tennis Association and played in-state tournaments. Unlike Dominic, Dennise continued on to become a ranked player.

I devoted considerable time to Dennise's tennis, attending all her practice sessions picking up balls so that her coach could devote more time to her lesson and not be interrupted to pick up balls, accompanying her to all her tournaments, working with her at home on physical exercises. Though this personal hands-on involvement brought me a great deal of satisfaction and excitement, it also may have contributed to her decision to abandon tennis. I began taking tennis too seriously, unfeelingly pushing her on, sulking or getting upset when she made a bad shot or lost a match. In my mind tennis should have been everything to her as it had become for me. But Dennise was not ready or willing to commit herself to that extent.

Shining through all of this negativity were those wonderful tennis moments which I shall long remember. A particularly poignant one occurred during a United States Tennis Association tournament held at the Sans Souci Tennis Club in Miami Beach. As sometimes happens in tennis it was a metaphor of life's experiences on a broader scale. Dennise had won her two Saturday matches and now was about to play her final match. It was late Sunday afternoon when the match began. Because of tiredness or lack of focus she was now playing at the level of the day before. Her opponent needed one more point to win the match and to take home the trophy. An argument arose between the players as to whether a ball hit by the opponent was in or out, making it necessary to call the head tournament Pro to settle the matter. His decision was to play the point over. This should have been a piece of cake for Dennise's opponent since all she needed was one point to win the match, and even if she lost the point she was far ahead in number of games won. On the other hand, if Dennise lost the point the match would have been over. The pressure was all on Dennise.

The point was played and Dennise won it. Her opponent was angry and her parents fuming. This meant the match had to continue on. The Pro remained courtside sensing the high tension.

And so the match went on and on into the early evening. All of the other courts were now empty and in the dark as all the other matches had ended. The only lights in the club were those illuminating Dennise's court creating the feeling that the whole outside world had been shrouded in darkness out of deference to what was unfolding on her court. This feeling was audibly re-enforced by the fact that the only sounds to be heard were those of balls being hit and the voices of the players urging themselves on.

Dennise was clawing her way back escalating the tension on the court. The players' attention was focused narrowly and exclusively on the game. They had no history, no future, no tiredness, no family, friends, school or anything else, as their very existence and the playing of each point were not merged into one.

For the second time it was match point but this time in Dennise's favor. Deep breaths. The opponent served the ball which Dennise returned to the opponent's forehand at a corner of the baseline. The opponent returned the ball to Dennise's backhand, a fatal mistake since the backhand was Dennise's strength. Dennise drove the ball hard to the opposite corner of the baseline which her opponent tried in vain to reach. Dennise jumped in the air, the match was over and she had won. The Pro approached both players and congratulated them on a great match.

When I drove out of the tennis complex the lights over what had been Dennise's court had now been turned off and the darkness and silence of the night was now complete. I turned onto Biscayne Boulevard and into the world of traffic and neon signs. Next to me was Dennise, sweaty and exhausted with eyes closed, her racket leaning against the door and her hands around the tournament trophy resting on her lap. It was one of those precious moments in life that makes all the past struggles worthwhile.

****

It all started the day my daughter Laura told Alicia and me that a movie was being filmed in Miami and that extras were needed. The movie would star Italian-American Al Pacino of The Godfather fame. Realizing that my grand acting opportunity might be at hand and prodded by Laura's persistence I agreed to go with Laura and Alicia to apply.

It will be recalled that back in my New York days I also attended the shooting of a movie scene and almost made it into the Midnight Cowboy. Years before I had taken the stage in elementary school and later tried to form a theater group. I began to suspect there must have been an unfulfilled thesbian streak in me.

We were immediately accepted and subjected to some pretty intensive rehearsals. We went over and over our scene until we got it right. But how could I possibly mind for little Domenico who sat in the darkness of the Strand Theater back in Fitchburg would soon be seen across the country on the screens of thousands of Strand Theaters.

Several months later the movie was released. It never became a blockbuster but it was good and more importantly I had my big moment on the screen. There I was with Alicia and Laura in the Miami Orange Bowl, sitting somewhere in a crowd of 1,000 people cheering for coach Al Pacino's football team in the movie *Any Given Sunday*. Admittedly, I may not be easily distinguished in the crowd but I was definitely there. Anyone determined enough to find me in the crowd should first consider practicing the game of Finding Waldo, renting a video of the movie and then using the pause button on the VCR for long spells.

****

Two headline-category events occurred following our arrival in Miami one of mostly local interest and the other global in scope.

In 1992 a ruffian named Andrew came roaring into South Florida with winds of up to 170 miles per hour, the strongest hurricane ever to hit the area. The night of the hit we were sitting on the floor and huddled together in a cubbyhole closet space in my office. The immediate family was there as was my sister-in-law Adriana and our dog Max. We had closed the door of the office and placed a chair against the knob for re-enforcement.

From a battery operated radio we received reports on the path of Andrew as it made landfall around Key Biscayne and then pursued its course south towards us. We could hear the roar of the wind and the bone-chilling sound of objects whirling around and wall-shaking collisions. Plaster dust began falling from the ceiling over our heads. We looked at each other with expressions of fear. Would the ceiling cave in on top of us? Were the walls sturdy enough to remain in place? We huddled even closer together. Then the dust stopped falling and the wind ceased blowing, all was silence except for the unforgettable sound of an electric-like humming. We were now in the eye of the hurricane. The sound was no less frightening than the wind as it gave the ominous impression it contained ferocious power which if released would obliterate everything in its path. It was an unnerving experience which fortunately lasted a bare few minutes when it was replaced by the return of powerful winds and crashing objects.

It was early dawn when Dennise said she could wait no longer and had to go to the bathroom. Unable to convince her to hold on for a little while longer, I got up removed the chair from the door and looked into the Florida room. Shock!!! The glass sliding door to the pool area was lying on the floor in the form of a thousand pieces and water everywhere.

By 7 a.m. we were walking around the house assessing the damage and uttering "Oh my Gods". It was awful. The second glass sliding door located in our dining room had also been knocked out and everything in the room plus the connecting living room had been either broken, filled with mud or soaked. Broken glass was everywhere. Nothing was left where it was when last seen.

Outside, the pool screen lay in shreds with the supporting beams resting at the bottom of the pool and tiles from the roof scattered on the lawn. Trees were uprooted. Our backyard shed was now lying on its site in our neighbor's yard. We had no electricity nor trustworthy water.

On the day after Andrew, Laura and I went in search for something or other from any food store we could find open. The panorama was surreal, trees strewn across roads, traffic lights dangling helplessly, roads impassably flooded. Literally a wasteland, our own Heroshima landscape.

The second major event was the arrival of a new millennium, the year 2000. Unlike the case of Andrew this arrival was publicized well in advance. The huge concern was the fact that most of the computers were not programmed to handle the date 2000 and forward. There was talk about computers failing around the world. Airline line schedules, financial transactions, business government and defense operations all collapsing.

Midnight came and months passed but nothing of consequence happened the big scare was over, the world had survived.

****

It will be noticed that the Italian theme so prevalent during my early years faded away once I left for the Navy, occasionally resurfacing briefly at different times only to again recede. But all of this oscillating would change when a letter arrived in my Miami mailbox and set a motion a chain of events that led to my personal renaissance.

PART TEN

THE ORIGIN OF THE SPECIES

Sometimes when returning from my mailbox with a handful of mail, I think about the economic and psychic benefits that would result if this scourge of the American home known as junk mail were to be banished. Postmen's work would be lightened as it would for those in the postal system who have anything to do with this sub-specie of communications. There would be less paper to re-cycle, fewer half-truths and outright lies deposited in the mailboxes of American homes, fewer traps for the gullible and less time and energy spent in sorting out the trash mail for disposal.

Yet, if such banishment had been in effect in 1997 I would have missed out on one of the most pleasurable and meaningful experiences in my life. It occurred one afternoon while checking the postman's delivery for the day and, as usual, separating out to the wastepaper-basket mail telling me or some other family member –including our dead dog Max – that we had been pre-qualified to receive a credit card, announcing the imminent stock market collapse, offering dozens of CDs for $1.00, or requesting donations for unheard of philanthropic organizations. Among the junk mail of that day was a letter that offered to send me a book containing the genealogy of the Perenzins. I threw it in the basket with the rest of the junk mail. Later that day the idea of a genealogical study of my family began tickling my curiosity and I was soon rummaging through the basket.

Thirty-nine dollars and the Perenzin family book would be mine. Unable to overcome the attraction of the enticement, I ordered it. While more than half of the book I received dealt with general data on immigration into the United States, demographics of immigrants and so forth, it also had a long list of Perenzins set out by country, city and street address, but no indication of genealogical connections. Most of the persons listed were located in Italy, more precisely in the Province of Venetto, with others in the U.S. (my father's family), France, Switzerland, England and Australia.

Why not test the book's veracity and write to some of the Perenzins listed and if I got sufficient responses perhaps I could take a shot at preparing a family genealogical tree. Though I had been in Italy some 40 years earlier for my father's funeral, I didn't remember any of the names of the Perenzins I had met. My brother Leno who had visited our relatives in Venetto just a few years earlier was helpful in identifying some of the people mentioned in the book.

I had forgotten too much to attempt writing the letter in Italian so I prepared a form letter in English which I then had translated into Italian. A copy of the letter was sent to some thirty Perenzins making sure each country of residence mentioned in the book was represented.

The first to respond was Gabriella Perenzin from Padova, Italy. Her letter with enclosed photograph was in English and contained the names of her paternal father and grandfather and their places of birth. Then came other letters one from Allessandra Perenzin from London who said she was responding to a letter I had sent to her mother Caterina Perenzin in Venice. As the letters accumulated my interest in the subject intensified to where I figured it would be a great experience to meet some of the relatives. I discussed this idea with the family and got one of those rare family opinion-poll results, a unanimous "yes." And so Alicia, Gina, Laura, Dennise and I flew to Italy in the summer of 1998. Dominic Jr. had college commitments and could not join us.

We flew from Miami to Paris from where we caught a connecting flight to Rome where we stayed for three days. We visited the usual tourist sights, the Vatican, the Coliseum, Trevi Fountains, Spanish Steps, Via Venetto, etc... Though Alicia and I had been to Rome on another occasion, it was a pleasant experience to do it again with our kids. I remember the vicarious thrill I got when driving into Rome from the airport as suddenly Laura gave out an excited wide-eyed "Look, look it's the Coliseum, we're passing in the front of it, it's the Coliseum." This set the tone of our trip.

From Rome it was a train east to Padova, the home of one of the oldest universities in the Western World. There we planned to meet Gabriela Perenzin, the first Perenzin to answer my letters.

At the Rome railroad station in it proved to be quite an ordeal to get accurate information on the track number of the Padova train. When we finally got the information and were at the indicated track number 2, a backpack carrying English couple standing nearby darted off shouting back to us that the Padova track was now number 7. Though I had no idea about the source of their information but convinced of the uprightness of the British, off we went behind them lugging our five suitcases, camera and other miscellaneous items. This proved to be our first encounter with the lack of disciplined order in Italy but also proof that in some mysterious way things do get done.

I loved the train ride, particularly the few moments I had in the dining car (actually a counter dispending drinks, pastry and sandwiches) drinking coffee as I sat next to a window from where I could see the countryside gliding past. I felt a strange emotion as I feasted on the pastoral landscape, the houses and the fields of huge yellow sunflowers, and as the train slowed down before entering Padova, an old woman sitting on a stool in her backyard snipping off the ends of string beans. Something in me was touched, a feeling that though I had never before been in this place it was not unfamiliar to me, it produced the type of warmth felt when returning home after being away for an extended period of time.

Arriving in Padua at around 2 p.m. we began the task of getting all our suitcases off the train. I was standing on the platform when a hand touched my left shoulder. Turning to see whom it was I heard a woman voice ask, "Domenico Perenzin?"

I turned to look "I am Gabriela," She had been waiting for me with her daughter Erika at exactly the spot on the platform from where we got off the train. How did she know my time of arrival and, more amazing, which car we were in? Her explanation was that I had given her the date of our arrival, the rest she intuited. Then began a practice which would be repeated many times in Italy, the kissing on both cheeks a forgotten experience for me and a new experience for the rest of us and quasi-traumatic for Dennise who during her brief life had never, as far as I knew, kissed anyone except under the severest of duress.

Gabriella insisted we go to her house where she would put something together for us. What she put together was spaghetti, not any ordinary run-of-the-mill kind but by our unanimous consensus the best spaghetti we had ever tasted.

The dining room was at a slightly lower level than the rest of the rooms and separated from them, a special place accessible only though a narrow opening and down a few steps. This I found to be an important architectural feature for it underscored the importance in Italy of dining and the conviction that it should be enjoyed away from disturbances of any kind. Dining I was soon reminded is something Italians take seriously and love to do at a slow pace, with gusto and outside of any consideration of time, a truly gastronomical celebration of life.

After lunch Gabriela produced a small wooden box with an heirloom appearance from which she proceeded to pull out pictures and papers in an attempt to find a link between her and the Perenzin families from Venetto, something we were not able to do with any degree of assuredness. We agreed to continue to investigate.

There was one place I wanted the family to see and would definitely not leave the country until we had done so, Venice. Gabriela said she knew the city like the palm of her hand and offered to go with us. The next day we were back on a train this time headed for Venice, a mere forty minutes away.

Venice, the once great maritime republic whose trading commerce spread over all of the Eastern Mediterranean, the great broker of the staple commodities of the West for the luxuries of the East, lay a mere few miles ahead. The home and place of work of the great painters Bellini, Titian, Tintorello and Veronese; where Vivaldi had lived, composed and taught; the home of the Venice Film Festival where renown actors, directors and other cinema people from around the world gathered every other year; the scene of countless movies including "Summer Time" a charming flick featuring Katherine Hepburne. Awaiting us was the Piazza San Marcos, the maze of canals with colorful gondolas and gondoliers, lovely Venetian glass and its famous craftsmen, the site of the Winter Carnevale with its dazzling masks and customs and non-stop merriment, the marvelous churches dominated by the Basilica di San Marco.

Among the numerous notes I brought along on the trip was one I pulled from my pocket and read as the train approached Venice:

> *The careless interplay of sunlight and water on the delicate surfaces create ever-changing impressions of beauty – a city that is bewildering, bewitching, elusive and unreal, one of those mythically romantic destinations many people spend their lives dreaming about.*

I have no doubt but that the Venice of my notes exists but I also know it will be hard to find during the summer months unless one's powers of imagination are strong enough to cause the swarms of sandaled-camera-

264

carrying tourists to disappear. Nevertheless, for our girls it was a wonderful experience just to walk along the pedestrian streets, down quaint alleys and over ancient narrow bridges as gondolas passed underneath, and to ride the vaporettto down the Grand Canal.

I cling to the hope that some day I will revisit Venice during the off-season, perhaps during the winter when, as a visitor once commented, "Venice is especially romantic with shrouds of fog wafting down the alleyways and canals."

The following day we departed by rented car from Padova for Conegliano, the town of my father's birth and where we expected to meet most of the relatives to whom I had written. Specifically, we would go directly to the home of my cousin Eguido Perenzin who had been alerted of the date of our arrival. From Padova we drove Arriving in Conegliano we had no easy time locating the address we had been given. After driving around a while we knew we were in the right town as we passed a building with a large banner with the name Perenzin written across it. One of the girls commented that we were famous. A few minutes later we found the address we were looking for, it turned out to be the "Latteria Perenzin," literally "Perenzin Dairy" but actually a cheese factory. Waiting for us was Eguido, my cousin, his wife Ivana, his daughters Margarita and Emanuela and their husbands Jovani and Carlo.

The cheese factory was located behind a charming storefront that served as a retail outlet for Perenzin cheeses but also offered a delightful array of other products such as hams, procciuto, wines, olives, spices, sauces, and more, truly an optic delight and an oleofactory banquet.

Eguido had retired from the operation and management of the cheese business having turned it over to his university-trained daughter Emanuela and her husband Carlo. I was told this was a continuation of the cheese business which my grandfather had established many years earlier and for whom my father collected milk in the mornings.

After chatting amiably a while, in my halting Italian sentences, we were driven to the house where we would be staying. A 100-year old farm house owned by Eguido which in its first life had been used to house cows.

The house was quite commodious in a rustic way and gave small hint of its vintage. Rich tiles covered the dining room floor while all of the second level floors were in wood. The bathroom was spare but functional provided one had patience. The glassless shuttered windows failed to live up to the task of keeping the curious and numerous hornets out. During our first night and in an effort to calm down my jittery young ladies, I gave out some homespun advice, "The hornets won't sting, just ignore them." Fortunately, I was proven right. The next morning was to bring a redemption for he shutters. As I was returning from my shower I drew open the shutters of the hallway facing the back of the house, an area I had not seen on our arrival. I stood there gaping at what I saw. It was one of the most strikingly beautiful vistas I had ever seen. For a moment I would have sworn I was looking at a painting but then again if that were so the artist could not have been painting a real landscape. Unless this was Shangrila, where on earth would he have found such a spectacular place? The artist certainly would have had to fantasize this scene and in the process say to himself, "First I'll use lush shades of green just like nature loves to produce, soft undulating hills will be essential, here and there quaint country houses, vineyards, sinuous, languid country roads playfully dipping out of view and then reappearing, and in the distance reining regal-like over the scene below mountains just like the Dolomites."

Because of the planned briefness of our stay we were limited in the amount of activities we were able to enjoy but thanks to Eguido our time was economically and pleasantly spent. On the day of our arrival we had lunch at a Perenzin owned restaurant at which Eguido's family and other close relatives were present. The next day we toured the cheese factory. Late that afternoon we visited three cousins who lived together on a vineyard located outside the town, two men and one woman, brothers and sisters, none of whom had ever married. I recall that while sitting in a circle outside the house making an effort to start a sustained conversation one of the brothers asked a girl to "bring it out." She entered the house and a few minutes came out gingerly holding something in her hand. It was a faded marriage picture of my brother Leno and his wife Alice. I never understood how this got there but my cousins seemed quite proud to have it.

Equido hosted a dinner for us to which he invited some of my closest relatives. The dinner was held at a hilltop restaurant commanding a lovely view of the city of Conegliano below. It was a lively, congenial, evening of picture taking, conversations, speeches and good cheer aided by much wine. Alicia demonstrated how fast a learner she is, by doing a creditable job of speaking Italian. Gina and Laura also did well, both had studied Italian in high school, whereas Dennise, not having studied the languate, leaned on Gina for translations.

During the dinner I distributed copies of a booklet Alicia and I had hurriedly put together for our visit entitled "La Gran Famiglia Perenzin.

Direttorio Mondiale" (The Grand Perenzin Family World Directory). It consisted of a list of names and addresses of Perenzins taken from the book I had bought and which I set out by country of residence. Throughout dinner I saw people browsing through the booklet.

Dinner completed, invitations for us to visit the homes or businesses of my relatives having been extended and embraces and kisses given we started on our way home. As we descended the winding road down the hill there was a sudden outburst of fireworks so impressive that we stopped and stepped out of the car to enjoy the colorful display over the town of Conegliano. A marvelous final touch to a warm and memorable evening I thought as I put my arms around Alicia. The expression on her face told me she shared my emotion.

The following morning we were to travel further north some 25 miles to the small town of Sacile where Basilio Mauro Perenzin lived with his wife, daughter and son.

Before going to Sacile we stopped at the home of my cousin Giorgio Perenzin. Giorgio, the consummate entrepreneurial type, is the owner of three clothing companies one of which we visited. It turned out that the building on which the huge banner reading PERENZIN we saw upon entering Conegliano was one of Giorgio's manufacturing plants. Giorgio and his wife Olga – a Barbara Streissand look-alike – and their son Francesco were our guides over the half hour tour. Giorgio's companies, all privately owned, produced fine clothing under their own labels as well as for upscale stores in the U.S. and Europe as well as well-known designers.

Sacile was a small out-of-the-way town with no special features that stood out. We had lunch on the balcony of Basilio Mauro's apartment with Basilio, his wife Mara, their daughter Alessia and son Simone. We learned that Basilio Mauro was an agronomist and his daughter Alessia a student at the "University For The Preservation of Cultural Assets," located in Venice. Her interest in art was reflected in the large number of paintings throughout the apartment, one in particular that barely missed covering a whole wall. After lunch we all strolled leisurely around the town, went to see the town's main attraction, a pool formed by a small waterfall which, we were told, was so deep no one had yet determined its exact depth. After savoring delicious *gelatos* we were off for Conegliano.

On the flight back to Miami I reminisced over our experience, of how warm, cordial and congenial my relatives had been and how richly diverse were the types of activities they were engaged in – teachers, cheese makers, restaurant owners, wine makers, interior decorators, clothing manufacturers, a dancer with the renown Milan Opera House. My grandfather Domenico and grandmother Benedeta would have been justly proud of their grandchildren.

Two years later I again visited Italy, this time with Alicia, Laura and Dominic. I had a three-fold reason for returning. Dominic had missed the first trip and as the member of my family who would carry the Perenzin name into future generations it was important that he experience his family roots. I wanted to meet more of my relatives. I wanted to experience living in Italy not from a hotel nor as a guest in someone's home but by renting my own apartment or house, doing our own shopping and cooking, taking out the trash and doing all the little things people did there, a total emersion of sorts.

From my aunt Checa's brother-in-law we rented one of his houses located a few blocks outside of downtown Conegliano where I fully realized my desire to go native, a marvelous way to fully experience Italy.

Sentimental and emotional Laura left more in love with Italy than ever. I shall never forget her heart broken voice saying as we were driving away from Conegliano to Milan, "Oh Daddy, I don't want to leave, can we stay longer, look how beautiful," as she pointed to a charming town lying at the foot the Dolomite Mountains. During the flight back to Miami I looked over to Laura and whispered inaudibly "We will return, yes we will return God willing."

But in a real sense I had returned, returned to find the part of me I had left on Beech Street back in 1950 when my saxophone in hand I departed for the Navy. Italy felt like home not in any physical way but in the deeper sense of being a part of me, embraced as I was by the sound of that soft, musical, poetic language that Italian is, by the marvelous food, the lovely music and the warmth and closeness of the family relationships, the beauty of the landscapes and the charming character of the people. I felt reunited with a part of me that had its beginning on that drizzly January morning in Fitchburg.

If I needed an affirmation of the re-encounter with myself and my Italian heritage, I found it poignantly on the last day of my visit when cousin Eguido took me down into the cellar of his 100 year old farmhouse where I saw a familiar grinding machine and press with which he produces his own Wines of October.

EPILOGUE

Throughout the course of writing these memoirs I have attempted to adhere to a commitment made to myself before putting pencil to paper, namely, to refrain from preaching to any of you my children on how to live your lives. I have set out to tell my story of how my life was lived, of the world in which it has been lived, of some of the people who crossed my path as well as those who accompanied me along the way. At times a glimpse of how I have viewed the world and life may have shown through right, wrong, insightful or misguided as it may have been. But I have tried not to sermonize or pontificate for any personal world view I may have been tempted to urge upon you. Over the years we have been together I have endeavored by my conduct and hopefully with some success to convey what I consider certain basic values which have served me well in what can be an increasingly confusing and complex world. If at times my efforts were flawed it was only because I suffered the failings and weaknesses that go with being a less than perfect human being. As you surely have figured out by now fathers are not the do-it-all, know-it-all persons that inhabit a young child's fairytale world. But I am not concerned for I know my children well enough to take comfort in the fact they are deeply good, honest and compassionately caring persons, qualities which together with their intelligence will, in the end and in the only way that really matters, serve them well.

As to preaching I will make what will be my sole and only request to my children. The request has little to do with behavioral, moral or ethical values but rather with a sense of rootedness and identity. Perhaps the part of my life which I most deeply regretted began that day when my teachers made fun of the Italian sailor suit I wore to class. For years afterwards I avoided any association with things Italian, even to the extent that my very name Dominic caused me embarrassment. Fortunately, with the passage of time and encounters with beautiful people and things Italian my defensiveness crumbled. Today, as you all know, I wear my Italianness as a chevron of pride.

All of you my children carry within you the genes of those great people whose history stretches back to the Roman Empire and beyond. And what a history it has been. Perhaps some day one or more of you may wish to look more closely into some aspect of the rich history of Italians and their magnificent contributions to just about every aspect of Western Culture.

Burnished in the firmament of the world's greatest painters, sculptors, musicians, composers, singers, scientists, explorers, educators, not to mention saints, are names such as da Vinci, Vivaldi, Puccini, Galileo, Marconi, Fermi, Machiavelli, Saint Frances, Saint Thomas Aquinas, Caruso, Toscanini, Colombus, Petrarch, Boticelli, Stradivarious, Montessori.

Over the ages the Italian genius for producing beautiful works of all kinds has lost none of its brilliance. The phrase "Made in Italy" continues to bear the connotation of elegance, style and beauty be it in haute couture, footwear, men's wear, automobiles, glass, furniture accessories and on and on.

Unquestionably, music ranks among the highest expressions of the Italian artistic genius. "During the 1950s American popular music was all about rock and roll leading through a series of permutations to rap and hip-hop music with their messages of violence, social protest and eroticism. A few years ago during all of this a beautiful voice from the land of Luciano Pavarotti came flowing across the Atlantic to America singing of love and romance. Americans first heard this voice on a televised concert from a town in Tuscany performed among ancient Roman ruins, a beautiful reminder of the continuity through time of a beautiful voices and music of Italy.

Many of those who heard the voice paused, listened and found something long repressed stirring in them. At later concerts people could be seen rhapsodized by the voice, women with the heads resting on the shoulders of their companions, husbands, lovers and couples holding hands. It was the music, the soul product of an Italian, this time in the person of the blind Andrea Boccelli that caused the hectic world to slow down just a bit and people to become conscious of and friendly with their deeper selves.

In the United States from the genetic pools formed by Italian immigrants in their Little Italys emerged sons, daughters and grandchildren who would become important and at times towering figures on the American landscape in music, business, politics, law, cinema, banking, finance, literature and sports. Along the way they founded the Bank of America, rescued Chrysler from bankruptcy, got the Nobel Price in Physics, earned Academy Awards and made it into the baseball and football Halls of Fame, dominated popular music, produced classical movies, became head of the New York Stock Exchange, were appointed to the Supreme Court, became CEOs of major U.S. corporations or successfully built their own important businesses and were elected governors of New York and mayors of the city of New York.

Unfortunately, as you are all aware there is the popularized darker presence of Italians in a segment of organized crime a.k.a. the Mafia and Cosa Nostra. The media has done much to draw the public's attention to this situation and in the course of doing so has stereotyped all Italians into these criminal activities. The foregoing partial list of the achievements of Italian-American over the years clearly demonstrates how out of focus this perception is. It has been observed that if every one of the 5,000 or so known members of the organized crime in the U.S.A. were Italian, they would constitute less that a mere 0.0003% of the nearly 26 million of the Italian-American population.

How has the media succeeded in causing the public to associate Italian Americans with the criminal few. In a way, the inherent character of the Italian of being dramatic, charismatic, of acting things out with a flair, of having an innate charm and stylishness when combined with a public's fascination with the workings of the underworld and the clandestine has certainly played a big role capturing the attention and fascination of Americans. Add to this the lazy tendency to view the world in terms of categories and the explanation is irresistible.

There is a curious irony in all of this. The genius of director Francis Ford Coppola together with the brilliant acting performances of fellow Italian-Americans Al Pacino and Robert De Niro turned Mario Puzo's novel "The Godfather" into one of the greatest cinematographic works of all times.

I am pleased you have visited Italy and have met many of your relatives. This will help to fill in the blank spaces in the understanding of your heritage and has allowed you to see Italians in their home surroundings, and to understand why Italy is such a magnet to hoards of foreigners who flock there year after year, not only to visit the country's beautiful cities and see the sumptuous collections of artistic expressions but also to enjoy the laid-back, happy, carefree human ambience.

All of you carry within you the genes of your Italian ethnicity. While this is no guaranty that any one or more of you will take a place in the firmament of famous Italians it does mean that in one way or another you, your children or your children's children may some day notice a certain character trait, a feeling of being in honest harmony with the world, a desire to sing, a tendency to cry, to laugh with gusto, to be outrageously theatrical in behavior, to delight in the small and large expressions of artistic creation, to celebrate the unadorned, the simple, natural essence of things. When this happens – and I have already seen signs in some of you – I urge you to hold on to it, caress it, indulge yourselves in it, encourage its growth and embrace it as a special gift to you handed down through generations of your Italian forbearers.

It has been said that in his heart everyone, wherever born, whatever his or her education and tastes, there is one small corner which is Italian, that part which abhors rigid regimentation, is fascinated by larger-than-life personalities and heroes, loves performances and ordinary things done theatrically and with a touch of art and who in every field of human activity is the inveterate dreamer of the impossible.

If this be so of everyone, then how much more so in the hearts of my children, descendents of this proud Italian father.

About the Author

The author is an Italian-American native of Fitchburg, Massachusetts. His first professional work was as a big band musician.

He graduated from Boston University Law School with fellow classmate F. Lee Bailey. He taught law at the Institute of the Americas at Southern Methodist University and practiced law both on Wall Street and in Colombia.

He is a contributing author of a multi-volume work on U.S. Corporate law, and has written numerous articles for the Bureau of National Affairs, the Lawyer of the Americas and the Law Review of the Autonomous University of Mexico Law School.

Mr. Perenzin started and ran Colombia's only English language newspaper in which he had a regular column. He currently lives with his wife and children in Miami, Florida.